For Gilbe[...]
the latin A[...]
Institute —

— in appreciation for your
support & encouragement
at an important stage
in my work. — gracias
Steve Silverblatt

P9-DFE-927

MOON, SUN, AND WITCHES

MOON, SUN, AND WITCHES

Gender Ideologies and Class in
Inca and Colonial Peru

IRENE SILVERBLATT

PRINCETON UNIVERSITY PRESS
PRINCETON, NEW JERSEY

Copyright © 1987 by Princeton University Press
Published by Princeton University Press, 41 William Street,
Princeton, New Jersey 08540
In the United Kingdom: Princeton University Press, Guildford, Surrey

All Rights Reserved
Library of Congress Cataloging in Publication Data will be
found on the last printed page of this book

ISBN 0-691-07726-6 (cloth)
     0-691-02258-5 (pbk.)

This book has been composed in Linotron Sabon

Clothbound editions of Princeton University Press books
are printed on acid-free paper, and binding materials are
chosen for strength and durability. Paperbacks, although
satisfactory for personal collections, are not usually
suitable for library rebinding

Printed in the United States of America
by Princeton University Press
Princeton, New Jersey

For Hilda, Salvin, and Helene Silverblatt
—with deep love and admiration—
and for *mis compañeras*—for always keeping the faith

CONTENTS

CONTENTS

CONTENTS

FIGURES

ACKNOWLEDGMENTS

The signed, written word belies the collective effort behind its creation. I have been fortunate to have my teachers, friends, colleagues, family, and other intellectual and emotional inspirators. First thanks go to the people who introduced me to anthropology at Swarthmore College, Steven Piker and Victor Novick. I would like especially to thank three of my teachers at the University of Michigan. Michael Taussig, whom I will presumptuously claim as my lifetime advisor, directed the dissertation on which this book is based. He introduced me to the devil, among other things, and has taught me much by his joined intellectual creativity and political commitment. Susan Harding showed me that a woman's work is always undone, while Jeffrey Parsons opened up the depth of Peru's cultural history to me.

Rayna Rapp, Mona Etienne, Eleanor Leacock, Anna Rubbo, Pilar García, Constance Sutton, and Ana María Portugal showed me the unity of personal, political, and intellectual feminism. Christine Ward Gailey, certainly one of the most penetrating theoreticians of state formation and gender hierarchy, let me see the Andean world with new eyes. She has patiently and consistently helped me understand the significance of my work, when it was not always clear to me. Harriet Rosenberg's uncanny knack of pulling together centuries and continents without losing sight of the day-to-day details of life makes her an exceptional ethnohistorian. Both Christine and Harriet have showered me with their intellectual gifts and with the warmth of long standing friendships. Nan Elizabeth Woodruff introduced me to the South's lessons for understanding changing class relations as well as its lessons for living. Her committed scholarship has put Peruvian cultural transformations in an important comparative light, while her friendship and intellectual companionship have been joyous sources of nourishment.

Richard Lee and Terence Turner contributed excellent suggestions for revisions and helped, in immeasurable ways, to get the manuscript on to completion. I unabashedly called upon Tom Patterson, whose insights into pre-Columbian history and my own procrastinating personality proved invaluable.

I first walked on Andean soil with Anna, David, and Laura Holmberg. John Earls, who often kept me from falling, opened up the Andes to me; I will always value the work we did together. Henrique Urbano, in spite of himself, revealed the order of Andean thought and the role of Mama Guaco in it. Billie-Jean Isbell continues instructing me in what "la otra mitad" is all about. Helaine Silverman and Enrique Mayer, so often my family in Lima, provided me with much nourishment and support—intellectual and otherwise. Sabine Mac-Cormack opened my eyes to the complexity of early Peruvian historiography. Disagreements withstanding, Tom Zuidema shaped my vision of the Incas and I will always prize our coinciding research trips in Cuzco. Kitty Allen, Jeannette Sherbondy, Debbie Poole, Gary Urton, Bill Isbell, Liz Overgaard, Ann Wightman, Tito Flores, Lucho Millones, and Chinaco Sandoval taught me about Andean life in Peru and in the United States.

How can I thank the people and institutions of Peru for opening their minds, hearts, and doors to this *gringa*? I thank, most deeply, the *comuneros* of Sarhua and Misterkay, the archivists of the Archivo Arzobispal de Lima, the Biblioteca Nacional, the Archivo Departamental de Cuzco, the Archivo Departamental de Ayacucho, and the members of the Centro Bartolomé de las Casas. I also owe much to Guido Delran, Doris and Victor Laus, Salvador Palomino, and Mari Solari— friends who taught me the generosity of the Peruvian way of living.

During the course of writing this book, I have received financial assistance from several sources whose magnanimity I much appreciate. The Doherty Foundation, the Wenner-Gren

Foundation, and the Organization of American States funded various stages of my dissertation research (1975-1978). The Faculty Research and Development Committee of The College of Charleston awarded me a summer stipend to carry out major revisions, and the Provost's Office, through the College Foundation, provided me with funding for word processing.

The Latin American Institute, at the University of New Mexico, named me a Visiting Scholar, which enabled me to make use of the University's facilities. I want to thank the Institute as well as Gilbert Merkx, its director, for their backing.

My departmental co-workers at The College of Charleston have been uniformly encouraging. Moreover, they created an ambiance that let me transform the thesis into a book in spite of my new teaching responsibilities. In addition, the College's librarians have unflinchingly hunted down the most obscure references and tracked the most hard-to-place interlibrary loan material. I want to express, again, my appreciation to the College for its support.

This book has several unsung heroines whom I acknowledge with gratitude. Danielle Frenette typed the original thesis, and Jill Conway helped put the revised manuscript into the word processor. Dottie Donegan, the book's midwife, did most of the word processing, including entering the interminable revisions that word processing seems to encourage. Thank you all.

In several articles already published, I began to pull together some of the data and to work out some of the arguments that, in a revised and expanded form, I present here. I gratefully acknowledge those occasions. My first attempt—gracias a Rosalía de Matos—was "Principios de organización femenina en el Tawantinsuyu." "Andean Women in Inca Society" owes much to Rayna Rapp and Christine Gailey. " 'The Universe Has Turned Inside Out . . . There Is No Justice for Us Here': Andean Women under Spanish Rule" would never have been written if not for the prodding and suggestions of Mona Etienne and Eleanor Leacock. Finally, I would like to express thanks to Arthur Kleinman for encouraging publication of

ACKNOWLEDGMENTS

"The Evolution of Witchcraft and the Meaning of Healing in Colonial Andean Society."

Several people associated with Princeton University Press contributed in significant ways to the book's final outcome. Kay Warren, as a reader for the Press, offered especially valuable suggestions, criticisms, and insights. Sanford Thatcher, Princeton's editor for Latin American Studies, not only made on-the-mark suggestions regarding the book's content and form, but actually made the publishing process a humane experience. I was most fortunate that Charles B. Purrenhage was the book's copyeditor. More than an exacting and helpful editor, Charles is a knowledgeable Andeanist. All three helped make this a better (and, I should honestly say, different) book.

Words of thanks are redundant to a family so bound up together as mine. My parents have been constant reservoirs of strength, and their abiding sense of fairness and humanity, coupled with a sense of humor, have kept my feet firmly down to earth. I worked with my sister, a psychiatrist, during several field periods in Peru. While showing me that issues of healing are windows on social process, she has never let me lose sight of the individual in my search for cultural forms. Helene has always been with me, even if far away, and she has kept my mind and heart alive with her compassionate intellect, warmth, and generous spirit.

INTRODUCTION

> In certain temples in the outskirts of the city we found many life-sized statues and figures of gold and silver, all cast in the image of a woman.
>
> [Estete (1535) 1968:393]

> The grandeur of the [Temple of the Sun] was so incredible that I would not dare to describe it, if it were not for the fact that all the Spanish historians of Peru have already done so. But neither what they have said nor what I will say will ever be able to capture the significance of what it was. . . . The image of the Sun was so large it filled the front of the temple from wall to wall. . . . After drawing lots, the image fell to a noble conquistador, named Mancio Serra de Leguizamo, whom I knew, a big gambler, who . . . bet it and lost it in a single night.
>
> [Garcilaso (1609) 1959, I:263-64]

> It should be pointed out that there was one kind of sorcerer that the Inca kings permitted, and these are like witches, and they take any appearance they want, and they fly through the air . . . and they see what will happen; they speak with the devil, who responds to them by means of certain stones or other things they highly venerate . . . and they say that it is usually old women who perform this act.
>
> [Acosta (1590) 1954:172]

The Spanish confronted a similar yet strange, yielding yet defiant, sophisticated yet pagan world when they landed on Peru's shore in 1532. Their mission was to create a colony; and as they conquered the Incas, and then struggled to bend their prize to fit colonial demands, peninsulars recorded the history of their creation.They wrote of what startled and they wrote of the familiar, they unveiled their dreams and, under the shield of bravado, expressed their fears. Conquistadors, bureaucrats, and priests marveled in concert at the sumptuous cities they uncovered for Western view: the golden gardens, fabulous temples, luxurious palaces—the magnificence of it all transcending even their wildest hopes for treasures.[1]

The Incas provided Spaniards with clues into the nature of the society they dominated—clues found in imperial social relations and in the Andean landscape which men and women, living these relations, had transformed. The irrigation projects that changed the courses of rivers; the mountains converted into lush, terraced fields; the well-stocked storehouses; and the extensive, intricate highways told of a complex social order whose rulers' attention to planning and provisioning exceeded Spanish concerns. The seemingly imperious command of those that ruled, the fear with which they were held, the elaborate rituals that celebrated gulfs of class, along with the privileges that conspicuously marked them, told of a people at least as stratified and as conscious of social hierarchy as the European newcomers.

The European experience helped Spaniards understand that the highly ritualized class divisions of the Inca drove the production of much of the wealth they beheld: they were aware that the visible riches of the Andes were anchored in the Incas' control over the labor of others. Spaniards could revel in the material goods their eyes devoured, knowing that as the Incas' supplanters, they also had within their grasp the empire's true source of wealth.

The Incas, then, appeared highly sophisticated to Spanish eyes; after all, the social hierarchy and social surplus they commanded were marks of civilization. Yet they could hardly be civilized, for the Incas were ignorant of the true faith, or per-

[1] All the archival material and most of the published accounts which I consulted for this book were written in Spanish. Any translations, unless otherwise specified, are my own.

haps, even worse, were practicing heretics and reprobates. Most Spanish arbiters of religious orthodoxy believed the devil had already visited the Andes. How else to explain the heresies the Indians committed in the name of religion? The Incas did not know Christ, but worshipped the Sun as father and their dead kings as ancestor-heroes. Even more startling, and perhaps even more damning, women worshipped the Moon as mother while venerating Inca queens, her closest daughters, as founders of female dynasties. Confirmed! The devil must be at work. And, of course, as the Spanish expected, he had to work through the most wretched and vulnerable of society, poor women who joined his ranks as witches.

Moon, Sun, witches—these gender ideologies shaped and were shaped by the experiences of Andean women and men whose social universe was fractured by class.[2] This book examines the complexities of interplay between political hierarchy and gender, as first the Incas and then the Spanish consolidated their rule. It explores how empire building transformed gender ideologies as the Incas, followed by their Iberian conquerors, strove to dominate the Andes. It unravels how ruling groups manipulated the ambivalence of gender images to buttress their political control while native peasantries, also playing on gender's ironies, challenged and resisted imperial authority. Thus, this book holds that the problem of power and its insinuation into cultural forms is central to historical process. Accordingly, gender systems—metaphors as well as conduits for the expression of power—stand out as pivotal to the creation of, and challenge to, social class.

The Spanish conquest of the Andes merged the destiny of

[2] This book follows a Marxist tradition in its use of the term "class." Class, broadly speaking, is seen as a social relation, defined in terms of relationship to means of production: class divisions, then, center on those who, through their control over the means of production, can extract surplus products or labor from those who do not. In keeping with this tradition, the process of class formation is seen as an inherently political process. For the creation of class entails the institutionalization of the means to facilitate, ensure, and regulate the appropriation of surplus—in other words, the process of state formation itself.

Iberia and Europe with the destiny of the Incas. Conquest intertwined their futures, and twentieth-century hindsight
should have intertwined their histories. But mainstream social
science has ignored much of our shared trajectories. While it
has recognized the heroic encounter of Inca kings and Spanish
conquistadors, it forgot that the clash of social forces thus set
in motion has continuously shaped the lives of Andean peoples
(as well as our own). Academic wisdom, colluding with Western "common sense," rendered Quechua peoples, to use
Wolf's phrase (1982), a "people without history."[3]

Ethnohistory challenges conventional anthropological por-
traits of the world's peoples.[4] By calling into question the supposed immutability of such peoples—for example, Andean
peasantries who participated in the turmoil of state formation
for centuries before contact with the West—ethnohistory has
laid bare the anthropological biases that sanction assumptions
of timelessness. The following pages, I hope, contribute to this
critical tradition in anthropology which, while sensitive to the
past of peoples whose history convention has denied, brings a
self-critical spirit to the examination of its own.[5]

[3] This section is indebted to Wolf's critique of that brand of anthropological
theory and method which canonizes the "timelessness" of non-Western peoples. It also draws extensively from his digest of the history of anthropology
and the social sciences (1982:3-23). Other influential works of self-criticism
that have attacked anthropology's conventional ignorance of the colonial
process include Asad (1973), Hymes (1969), Diamond (1974), Gough (1968),
and Worsley (1957, 1984).

[4] Ethnohistory, as an anthropological subfield, had its origins in the study
of North American Indians. In the mid-1960s, ethnohistorians incorporated
themselves as a society whose objective was to study the cultural history of the
world's peoples.

[5] Much contemporary anthropology bears the legacy of theoretical orien-
tations that have played down social conflict and history in cultural process.
Functionalism, inspired by models of social life that favored synchrony and
order, has tended to deny that people had a past before colonialism as well as
to ignore the trajectory of conflict that colonialism precipitated. Peasant communities are studied as if they were "traditional" bounded enclaves existing
independently of the class structures that formed them. Or they become func-
tional reflexes of dominant economic and political structures. Social change is

History making (which includes history denying) is a cultural invention;[6] and in stratified, class-ridden societies, versions of the organization of the past, like other ideological constructions, are brewed in political cauldrons. As social relations are politicized, history tends to be "made" by those who dominate—by chiefs, noblemen, and kings (Diamond 1974:1-48). For the prerogatives of power enjoyed by reigning

---

trivialized—reduced either to "modern" elements that penetrate traditional boundaries or to structures that serve the needs of impinging state institutions. Critiques of functionalism are extensive and growing (see fn. 2).

Structuralism, searching for human universals and for constants of form, also casts a homogenizing, timeless shadow on cultural constructions. It diminishes both the conflicting social relations that inform cultural meanings and the historical process that produces them. While structuralists have favored "cold," or timeless, peoples as their subjects, recently they have turned to the study of complex societies experiencing profound change (see Sahlins 1981, 1985; Todorov 1984). For critiques of structuralism centered on its inability to wrestle with issues of history and change, see Wolf (1982:16-19), Anderson (1984:384-89), Diamond (1974:292-331), and Thompson (1978), among others. Several historians have expressed concern at their colleagues' use of structuralism to bolster historical method. Weighing history's attraction to anthropology since the 1960s, E.P. Thompson (1977) and Fox-Genovese and Genovese (1976) have spoken out against an uncritical alliance between the two disciplines. Thompson argues that history is mismatched with a social science perspective that presumes invariance in the structures which underlie social processes and that divorces features of human life from their social contexts (1977:256-59). Sharing Thompson's concerns, Fox-Genovese and Genovese are suspicious of structuralist tendencies in historical analysis that play down historical process in general and then proceed to minimize human agency and political dimensions of change (1976:209). Ethnohistorians have pointed to the problems of tying structuralist method to their discipline. Christine Ward Gailey has written an excellent critique (1983a) of Sahlins' historical writings.

Todorov (1984), using structuralist/semiologist methods for analyzing cultural forms as systems of meaning, has even analyzed the Spanish conquest of Mexico as a conflict between competing communications systems. While he has interesting things to say about the relation between forms of communication systems and different societal responses to external threat, his work minimizes the relations and forces of power that must be taken into account in any analysis of colonization.

[6] Sahlins (1985) has contributed insights into how structures of meaning organized the historical experience of contact.

groups facilitate not only the realization of their intentions, but the celebration of their heroes in authoritative renditions of the past. They can insist on universalizing their history, in an attempt to conceal the fact that commoners, as they shape and set limits to governing forces, challenge ruling heroes. Claims of universality belie the struggle that sanctioned history wages against other versions not so privileged in record or in power.

Heroic versions dominate histories recorded in European journals, court records, and official reports. However, as Hobsbawm (1984) reminds us, these histories should not be confused with popular sentiments and beliefs. If we forget Hobsbawm's warning, if we ignore the political antagonisms that color historical ideologies, we run the risk of colluding with "chiefs" and canonizing their partisan stance. We should not take chiefs at their word.

Nor should we take the Spanish at theirs. The Spanish could understand the world they conquered only through the categories and perceptions that their culture provided.[7] The chroniclers' prejudices, however, were more pervasive than the justifications they presented in support of Spanish rule or Catholic evangelism. Basic assumptions of how the universe worked, of the nature of humanity and society, along with deeply rooted senses of personhood, responsibility, social hierarchy, social justice, and history,[8] were trapped in Spanish

[7] Sabine MacCormack is studying the historiography of early Peru. Her important research (1985) traces intellectual influences on the writings of the early chroniclers.

[8] These included conceptions of history, cast in the European heroic mode, in which the past was structured by dynasties of kings. The Spanish converted myths of origin dominated by hero-kings into Western-style histories of dynastic succession. R.T. Zuidema (1964), attentive to discrepancies in chronicler accounts, challenged the interpretive nature and biases of early Spanish histories of the Incas. Pointing to some of the glaring misconceptions which the Spanish presented as "fact," Zuidema began to chip away at the uncritical acceptance of chronicler accounts which marred many contemporary studies of Inca culture (also see Urbano 1981, 1982).

Zuidema made Inca history truly heroic. He showed that what the Spanish

accounts of the Inca world. This Hispanification of Inca history, mirroring the dynamics of colonial politics, was bound in the colonization process itself.

The names cited throughout the body of this work—Cieza, Murúa, Molina, Sarmiento, Arriaga, Guaman Poma, Acosta, Polo, Pachacuti Yamqui—provide us with the major corpus of information we have about Inca and much of early colonial society. Most of these writers are Spanish; some grew up spanning both worlds. The Spanish writers were far from a homogeneous lot: some wrote official histories for the Crown; others wrote official histories for the Church; still others were adventurers who set down remembrances for themselves. Some traversed the Andean countryside, providing rich commentary on local customs; others focused on the center of imperial power, Cuzco, listening to its deposed sovereigns. Some of the accounts were composed within three decades of the Conquest, others after a hundred years of Spanish rule (see A Note on Sources). Chroniclers wrote for different sponsors, out of different interests, and at different times; their stories of Inca life reflect these divergencies.

Neither did the "indigenous chroniclers" speak in one voice, nor were their perceptions of the pre-Columbian past separable from their experiences in a colonial world. Titu Cusi Yupanqui (1973), Pachacuti Yamqui (1950), Guaman Poma (1936, 1956), and the Huarochirí manuscript compiled by Ávila (1966) constitute these "native" sources (see Salomon 1982).[9] The first three were privileged men from the ranks of the conquered. Titu Cusi was the next-to-the-last sovereign to

and subsequent generations of Inca scholars presumed to have been flesh-and-blood kings, succeeding themselves one by one in Western dynastic fashion, were rather the stuff from which legends are made—mythic representations that embodied Andean conceptions of how hierarchy and history should be structured (Zuidema 1964, 1982; Duviols 1979).

[9] Structuralist method, by abstracting myths from their sociopolitical context, loses important dimensions of power and history which inform them. For example, Zuidema minimized tremendous differences between Huarochirí and Inca tradition by focusing exclusively on their structural isomorphism.

lead the Inca resistance against Spanish rule; and Pachacuti Yamqui, writing more than forty years after Titu, was from the middle-ranking non-Inca nobility outside Cuzco. Guaman Poma was also of privileged birth, but from a family living in the Province of Ayacucho.

Guaman Poma's compelling, thousand-page letter to the Crown—in which he protests the degrading conditions of colonial society, drawing comparisons to Andean life before the arrival of the Spanish—is rich, intriguing, contradictory, and the object of much new and exciting scholarly inquiry (Adorno 1978, 1982; Ossio 1973, 1976-77; Murra 1980; López-Baralt 1980). Critical studies of Guaman Poma's writings make clear the hazards of presupposing that native colonial writers present untainted indigenous perspectives on the pre-Columbian experience (Duviols 1980). Yet for its poignancy, for its suggestive content, and for the detail with which the previous ages of the pre-Columbian past and the shocking conditions of the colonial present are described, Guaman Poma's chronicle is a major contribution to our understanding of both epochs in Peruvian history. His work, like those of the other native chroniclers, must be interpreted with care. He, too, had his own reasons for writing; he, too, bore the pressures of political exigencies and ecclesiastical eyes; and he, too, straddled and was part of the conflicting worlds that produced him.

Among indigenous chronicles, the Huarochirí manuscript is unique for conserving, in Quechua, a regional mythology of heroes. These heroes—battling and making allegiances with other lords and Inca kings—contour, through legend, the destiny of local communities. The manuscript is linked with Francisco de Ávila, a priest who, while attacking native religion as heresy, may well have played a role (albeit an unclear one) in the compilation of this wonderful text (Salomon 1982:24-31). Yet even though the Huarochirí manuscript may take us closest to regionalized understandings of the nature of social and cosmological order, its exposition is shaped by—and in confrontation with—the colonial enterprise.

Whatever the chronicle, indigenous authors wrote in a

highly politicized, contradictory milieu which saturated their work. They too have often been idealized, presumed to speak of and for a "pure" Inca past. Mirroring the anthropological mainstream, which sees its objects of study as timeless peoples, Andeanists (myself included; see Silverblatt 1976, 1978) in search of a pristine Inca culture have fallen into the trap of abstracting native chroniclers from the colonial world.

The Incas, on the other hand, appreciated the politicization of the social conditions in which subject peoples lived and reproduced their lives under imperial rule. They also discerned the dynamics of power that infused the creation of history (Collapiña et al. 1974; Cieza 1959:187-88). Savvy to the ideological might of historical reconstructions, the lords of Cuzco tried to imprint a particular vision of the past onto those whom they conquered—a vision in which the Incas emerged as the venerated kinsmen of all.

Dimensions of power diffuse Inca history both as it was recorded by the chroniclers and as it was related by the Incas. The Cuzqueñan rendition of history, forged in the context of empire building, was painted in colors of Inca legitimacy. The history of the Andes, then, is more than the heroic history which the Incas presented of themselves, and which they struggled to impose. Like most popular history, that of the Inca-controlled Andes scarcely speaks in the written sources left us. But we hear it emerging in the Huarochirí manuscript and other indigenous chronicles, in some reports by priests about communities they were surveying, in inquisitorial-like proceedings brought against native idolators, and in chronicler descriptions of the Andean countryside. We also hear it around the edges of the Inca ideology that tried to absorb it. We should not take the Incas at their word.[10]

The same intellectual tradition that refused colonial peoples a place in history denied women theirs. In Peru this legacy had

[10] Their accounts have been called "chronicles of the impossible" (Salomon 1982:9) because they attempted to construct a narrative history of the past from Andean materials that were antithetical to European concepts of time.

its roots in the colonial enterprise itself. Spanish chroniclers of Inca life looked at Indians (a preeminently colonial creation) and women in much the same light: both were dependent, childlike, incapable of autonomous, responsible action. Spanish expectations regarding the nature of civilization—some of which were shared by colonized indigenous chroniclers—assigned peculiar characteristics to women that presupposed their inherent impurity and their inferiority to men.

During the last twenty-five years, mainstream social science has been challenged by those whom dominant theory excluded as marginal and whom Western society defined as "other"— blacks, the Third World, ethnic minorities, laboring people. Criticisms levied against the omission of women from conventional analyses of culture are part of this onslaught.[11] Challenges have broadened inquiries. While women's displacement from social and historical process has been questioned, our understanding of gender has swelled. Gender systems legitimize what it means to be male or female, and we now are aware that gender ideologies overflow male and female identities to infuse the fabric of social life; they permeate much of human experience, extending to our perception of the natural world, the social order, and structures of prestige and power.

New scholarship, while agreeing that woman's voice had to be heard, disagrees about the nature of that voice and why it was muffled. Theoretical divisions within academic disciplines are resurrected in feminist critiques. In anthropology, debates

[11] Inspiring works in this trend include Reiter (1975), Rosaldo and Lamphere (1974), Ardener (1977), Atkinson (1982), Sanday (1981), Quinn (1977), Rogers (1978), and Ortner and Whitehead (1981). See Gailey (1976, 1981, 1985) as well as Rapp (1977) for the most insightful theoretical developments in the analysis of relations between class formation and gender hierarchy. Also see Gailey (1983b, 1985) for an analysis of the effect of class formation on kin-based communities. Among the growing number of works that discuss the role of women in contemporary Andean societies are Isbell (1976), Bourque and Warren (1979), Harris (1978), Deere (1976, 1977), and Deere and Leal (1983). Lyon (1979) analyzes the status of female supernaturals in the pre-Columbian past, while Burkett (1977) examines the position of women in coastal Peru during the colonial period.

rage over the transculturality of women's subordination.[12] For many, this proposed universality is a projection of specifically Western gender configurations onto colonized peoples, another example of how Western expectations regarding the nature of social life are misrepresented as authoritative descriptions of "reality." These critics contend, moreover, that claims of global inferiority overlook the transforming experience of colonization itself on the lifeways of women and men (see Leacock 1983).

This critical stance, inspired by Marxist thought, compels us to see gender as a highly complex social construction. Firmly planted in historical process, the study of gender would not only encompass reproduced and transforming definitions of masculinity and femininity (and their ramifications throughout social experience), but would embrace a critical awareness of the emergence of gender as a category of social analysis. Engels, in *The Origin of the Family, Private Property, and the State*, insisted that changes in the position of women are inseparable from the profound transformations in political economy spurred by the formation of social class. Contemporary Marxist tradition also privileges the articulation of gender relations and power. While Engels' analysis must be refined in light of the wealth of new scholarship recent decades have produced, his insight into the dynamics of gender hierarchy and political relations still rings true. My book is Engels' child.

Women are being "added to" anthropology as they are being added to history (Fox-Genovese 1982). But to continue Fox-Genovese's penetrating concerns, the object of our inquiries is not merely to increase the information we have about women in other societies, just as it is not, to continue Wolf's concerns, solely to increase the information we have about the lifeways of colonized peoples. If all it makes of the outcry of "others" is a residual category in a marginalized anthropol-

[12] For seminal work outlining the debate, see Rosaldo and Lamphere (1974), Etienne and Leacock (1980), Ortner and Whitehead (1981), and Leacock (1981, 1983).

ogy, then the science of humankind is in danger of diverting the genuine challenge that women's studies and ethnohistory have provoked.

Our foray into the dynamics of power and gender ideology begins by examining how the Inca construction of class relations altered, in disproportionate ways, the material conditions of life for peasant as well as elite women and men. It goes on to ask how interpretations of gender changed as the Incas dominated not only Andean politicoeconomic relations, but cultural systems of meaning. Gender could be a metaphor for both complementarity and hierarchy in the Andes. Not surprisingly, the Incas picked gender ideologies both to mask their control over others and to create relations of domination.

Andean peoples interpreted the workings of nature through an ideology of gender complementarity. Male and female interdependent forces were also ancestor-heroes and ancestor-heroines of the mortals whose gender they shared. Constructing the supernatural with familiar materials, Andean women perceived kinship and descent to follow lines of women, just as, in parallel, men saw themselves as descending from and creating lines of men.

The Incas claimed to be children of the god and goddess whom they had made the most powerful in the Andes. Touching the divine in a familiar form, they used the frames through which Andean peoples interpreted the world to justify their political dominion. The Incas manipulated popular structures of gender complementarity and parallelism to coax the underprivileged into acquiescing in their loss of autonomy. Encrusting traditional gender values and institutions onto the ropes that tied Cuzco to conquered women and men, the Incas tried to cloak imperial demands in accustomed phrases and practice. The degree to which the peasantry internalized imperial gender definitions as part of the complex of meanings, values, and feelings through which they understood and acted on their social reality would be a test of Cuzco's success.

Gender ideologies were also ideologies of hierarchy. They expressed rank and ordered internal community divisions.

Not surprisingly, the Incas took this frame of gender to construct imperial relations. They used it to design and then to forge the ties which both bound the conquered to them and marked the asymmetry of that bond. As political relations supplanted kinship, gender became the trope through which power was expressed and articulated. Now more than metaphor, emerging imperial institutions fused the control over women with the control over humankind; gender became a form through which class relations were actualized. The formation of class transformed gender distinctions into gender hierarchy.

Even as the Spanish marveled at the world the Incas dominated, they were party to one of the most profound social battles ever to mark the Andean countryside—the transformation of the Andes into a colony of Spain. The economic, political, and religious institutions through which Spain created colonial Peru were alien to Andean peoples. The Incas might have exploited their countrywomen and men, but at least they shared basic understandings of the limits within which power could be wielded as well as how the universe was supposed to work. No such common understandings linked the Spanish conquerors to the colonized. Spanish gender ideologies, as foreign to Andean peoples as peninsular economics and Catholicism, were implanted in Peruvian soil. They, too, were intrinsic to the formation of colonial Peru.

Spaniards were as conscious of differences in status as the Incas they conquered, and peninsulars bestowed different economic rights to indigenous peoples according to the rank they held in the political hierarchy of the Inca empire. Women of the Inca nobility, privileged by the Spanish, could take advantage of the new property relations of colonial Peru. Mocking their peasant countrywomen, some parlayed their advantages into security and wealth. But all native women witnessed the erosion of the deeply rooted traditions that had ensured them autonomous access to their society's material resources. Peasant women, at the bottom of the colonial hierarchy, suffered this loss the most.

Men were considered innately more suitable to public life by the Spanish. Their values, imposed on the colonies, favored men as society's representatives, administrators, and power brokers. Spanish political models guiding colonial policy prohibited and prejudiced women from participating in legitimate structures of indigenous government. The few women who held public office were the exceptions who proved that strictures of class took precedence over norms of gender in colonial politics. They were also sad reminders of an Andean past when structures of gender parallelism allowed women control over their own political and religious institutions. This book will unravel how the colonial regime, which tended to recognize men as the legitimate representatives of polities, and patrilineal modes as the principal means of succession, undermined customary Andean gender chains of dual authority.

Native women saw themselves being cut off from their communities' legitimate institutions of government. Coupled with political disfranchisement, they were harassed economically and abused sexually. The double burden of class and gender was particularly severe for women of the colonial peasantry. Andean women fought back, and their position in the colonial world shaped the form their resistance to that world would take. This book concludes by exploring their struggle, which became manifest in the emergence of Andean "witchcraft."

Spanish clerics unearthed witchcraft in Peru, claiming that the most dangerous of all witches were poor, native women. No doubt Spanish priests and administrators were predisposed to finding poor women witches, for they came to Peru fresh from the European witchhunts which damned women (particularly the indigent) for heresy and susceptibility to diabolic influence. This stereotype, transported to the colonies, molded the Andean witchhunts—the seventeenth-century campaigns to extirpate idolatry.

Catholicism was the ideological arm of colonial rule. By maintaining idolatrous and heretical beliefs, by practicing witchcraft (much the same thing to Spanish authorities), indigenous peoples were subverting colonial power. While Spanish gender norms may have rendered women invisible, they also transformed them into witches. The Spanish provided native women an ideology of rebellion.

The dialectic between Spanish policies and the native social experience transformed the lives of women in the colonial *ayllu*. By exploring this dialectic, we can grasp how women tried to shape their futures and thereby marked the histories of the Andean native peoples. As active participants in an underground of resistance to peninsular rule, Andean women—defending themselves as colonized women—played a crucial role in the defense of their culture.

CHRONOLOGY

Late Intermediate Period (regional political and cultural development prior to Inca expansion)	c.800-c.1450
Inca Empire	c.1450-1532
Period of Spanish Conquest	1532-1572
Pizarro seizes power	1532
Rebellion of Manco Inca and formation of Neo-Inca state in Vilcabamba	1536-1572
Taqui Ongoy, native millenarian movement	1565
Classic Colonial Period	1572-1826
Francisco Toledo conquers Neo-Inca state	1572
Implantation of Toledo's reforms, including *reducciones*	1572-1582
Campaign to extirpate idolatry	1610-1660
Rebellion of Tupac Amaru II	1780
Wars of Independence	1818-1826

MOON, SUN, AND WITCHES

CHAPTER I

Producing Andean Existence

> The women have their spindles and skeins of
> spun cotton, the men their *tacllas* or hoes to
> work the fields, or the weapons they used in
> war.
>
> [Arriaga (1621) 1968:27-28]

As Inca empire building profoundly altered the Andean landscape, as once autonomous communities became enclaves in
an imperial vise, gender ideologies gave form to emergent relations of power. Gender ideologies were a powerful tool in ce-
menting Inca dominion over the Andes. Their force was rooted
in and meshed with gender systems that pervasively shaped the
social experience of Andean women and men.

The experience of growing up female or male in Andean society is inseparable from the practical activities by which men
and women reproduced their lives. And these activities, in
turn, are indebted to the cultural meanings through which Andean peoples constructed identities of gender—constructed
Andean women and Andean men. We need first explore the
practical activities of men and women and the traditional
meanings of gender that were wedded to them. Then we can
explore how the construction of an empire dominated by the
lords of Cuzco affected the traditional meanings imputed to
gender as well as the companion activities by which men and
women reproduced their world.

At the time of the Inca conquest, the Andean region was a
cultural mosaic. Peoples speaking different languages, worshipping different gods, and venerating different founders
were tied together through conflict or through bonds of coop-
eration and trade.[1] While their political organization may have

[1] For descriptions and analyses of some of the different peoples and cultures

varied in complexity, for the most part these diverse peoples shared the experience of living in communities in which all were kin.

These communities, which we can gloss with the Quechua term *ayllu* (see Appendix), provided their members with the means to create and re-create their lives. As an *ayllu* member, one was born with rights and obligations that could be expected of, and were owed to, those whom the Andean world defined as obligable relatives. These rights and debts in turn framed claims to land and other crucial resources that formed the basis of Andean subsistence. The *ayllu* embodied this intricate interplay of social responsibility and kin expectations, and in so doing guaranteed every Andean man and woman access to community lands, herds, and other material resources needed to reproduce their existence (Murra 1956:53, 56; Spalding 1984, 1967:63, 68). As an autonomous community, the *ayllu* held ultimate control over how its members produced and reproduced their lives.

KINSHIP, RESOURCES, AND
EVERYDAY LIFE UNDER THE INCAS

As the matrix of social relations through which claims on the material bases of life could be made, the *ayllu* forged its members' identities as gendered human beings who were obliged to and responsible for others. Cultural meanings imparted to gender shaped the creation of Andean kinswomen and kinsmen. And kinship marked potential channels of access to community land, herds, and water, just as it dictated those whom one might oblige or be obliged to, how, and to what degree.

Kinship ties and kinship ideology framed the practical activities and consciousness of Andean women and men. At the

that inhabited the Andes, see Silverblatt and Earls (1977a), Duviols (1973), Huertas (1969), Lavallée (1973), Murra (1964, 1967, 1968), Rowe (1948), Rostworowski (1977, 1978), Salomon (1980), Spalding (1984), and Stern (1982).

time of the Inca conquest, the dominant kin mode found throughout much of the Andean highlands was one of parallel lines of descent. Women conceived of themselves as the descendants, through their mothers, of a line of women; men, in parallel fashion, saw themselves as descending from their fathers in a line of men (Zuidema 1977a:240-55; Lounsbury 1964). This organization of gender relations and kin ties through parallel descent was inherent to the ways Andean women and men created and re-created their social existence. The values and tone of gender parallelism were continuously reinforced in the practical activities through which they constructed and experienced their lives. (See Figure 1.)

Men and women could base their claim to *ayllu* resources on several sets of systems governing access to community wealth. Although parallel transmission was not the only means through which rights to land and herds were acquired in the Andean *ayllu*, it was an extremely important one. Women, through their mothers, enjoyed access to community land, water, herds, and other necessities of life (Duviols 1971:373, 383; Murúa 1946:427; Zuidema 1967a, 1977a:240-56; ADC; AHU:Leg. IV, V, VIII; Spalding 1967:126). Accordingly, women perceived that it was through relations with women that they could make use of their environment's riches.[2] We cannot estimate what portion of the *ayllu*'s resources were in the hands of women, but we can note that parallel transmission rights ensured that women, independently of their kinsmen, enjoyed access to society's means of subsistence.

The Incas extracted tribute from the conquered peasantry in ways that did not impinge on women's traditional rights to their *ayllu*'s resources. After conquering a new territory, the Incas created imperial fictions, declaring major sources of productive wealth to be under the state's jurisdiction. Lands and herds were set aside to support the state's political and reli-

[2] Any discussion of Inca economic relations owes a tremendous debt to the pioneering work of John Murra (1956, 1975, 1978).

FIG. 1. Pérez Bocanegra's Diagram of Andean Kinship (Reproduced, by permission of The American Anthropological Association, from The American Anthropological Association Special Publication no. 7, 1977, p. 249. Not for further reproduction.)

gious structures. In exchange for working the lands and tending the herds that supported the Cuzqueñan nobility, the imperial bureaucracy, and the state religion, the Incas allowed the peasantry they created to retain some of the rights over their *ayllu*'s bounty which they had enjoyed as autonomous peoples. The Incas wanted to appear like kin, like generous chiefs. Of course, they were neither kin nor generous. They were rulers who demanded the labor of those they had conquered. Nevertheless, Inca rule was prudently indirect; it made use of traditional religious, political, and economic practices (Spalding 1967:178). So long as state needs were met, the Incas did not intervene in the ways in which the peasantry went about making their lives. The Inca conquest, then, did not drastically alter the traditional control that peasant women exerted over their society's means of subsistence (Silverblatt 1978).

The Pan-Andean tradition of parallel descent also shaped the demands that women of the Inca nobility could make on the empire's wealth. As with their commoner counterparts, noblewomen's relations to kinswomen allowed them to claim Andean resources. Rights to rich fields in the Cuzco region were passed down from noblewoman to noblewoman (Zuidema 1967a). Unlike their sisters of the peasantry, however, they also enjoyed the prerogatives of class. Noblewomen, like the goddesses and priestesses of the empire, were designated shares of the tribute that the peasantry rendered to the empire (Villanueva 1970:21, 35-39; Murúa 1946:85, 87, 90, 94; Guaman Poma 1956, I:253, 264, III:132; Polo 1917a:56, 96, 1917c:50; Cieza 1959:247; Estete 1968:393).

This structure of social relations that shaped the lives of Andean peoples divided the experienced universe into two interdependent, sexually linked spheres. Andean peoples, whether of the Inca nobility or of the vanquished peasantry, perceived their social world as divided along gender lines. This perception made sense of Andean patterns of inheritance, and was confirmed in the social relations embodying obligations, claims, and coercion which marked out rights to the critical resources of the imperial Andes.[3]

Andean men and women experienced their lives in gender-specific worlds, yet these worlds were also interdependent. Perhaps no Andean ritual more clearly expressed the interdependence and complementarity of male and female spheres than marriage—the rite of passage into Andean adulthood and the rite that joined together parallel descent lines. Rituals surrounding marriage shouted an ideology of gender equality. Whether that ideology was true to the substance of gender relations is another question.

Marriage rites, whether binding together peasants or the Inca elite, celebrated the formation of a new unity made up of equals. Accordingly, wives and husbands saw themselves as contributing in complementary but commensurate ways to the formation of the household. In the ceremonies that attended the wedding of the Inca king and queen, formal speechmaking and the ritual exchange of clothing expressed their equality. Similar kinds of exchanges, on a less sumptuous scale, characterized the wedding of commoners. The chronicler Bernabé Cobo recounts:

> [The bridegroom] in testimony that he received her as his wife, placed a woolen slipper on her right foot . . . and upon arriving at his house the bride took out, from under her belt, a shirt made from fine wool . . . and gave it to her husband . . . and [the kinsmen of the bride and groom] gave each other presents, in accord with what each one had [Cobo 1964, II:248].

Ritualized gift giving between social peers marks equality in the Andes. The celebrated trade of gifts between bride and husband and between their respective families affirmed a balance between kin groups and between man and wife (Cobo 1964,

[3] Another rule that underlay pre-Columbian inheritance was that of cross-transmission. According to this rule, the significant relations were between father's sister and mother's daughter and between mother's brother and sister's son (Zuidema 1973:253).

II:248-49; Murúa 1946:235, 240, 244; Molina 1943:68; AAL:Leg. 5, Exp. XIII).

The balance that was struck in marriage between woman and man in Andean society encapsulated the different contributions that each made to the reproduction of the *ayllu*. Within the *ayllu*, the organization of work turned around a division of labor based on age and gender. Andean norms defined certain tasks as appropriate to men and others to women. But in any case, the division of labor was never so strict as to prohibit one sex from doing the other's task if the need arose (Murra 1956:123). Andean gender ideologies recognized that women's work and men's work complemented each other. Their interplay was essential for Andean life to continue.

Women were the weavers of Andean society. Never idle, women were always spinning—on walks, during conversations with family, while watching over children (Cobo 1964, II:258; Garcilaso 1961:138; Murúa 1946:233). Women made sure that their family was clothed. Once they became subjects of Cuzco, the obligation to weave cloth for the state fell primarily on their shoulders (Murra 1956:128; Murúa 1946:33; Díez de San Miguel 1964:75).

Although Andean gender norms might designate weaving as the quintessential female activity, women's contributions to production were manifold. Cooking, brewing *chicha*, preparing fields for cultivation, planting seeds, child rearing, harvesting, weeding, hoeing, herding, and carrying water also filled a woman's day (Arriaga 1968:33-35; Cobo 1964, II:25, 253; Garcilaso 1961:138; Díez de San Miguel 1964:100; Guaman Poma 1956, I:36, III:277, 285, 291, 298; AAL:Leg. 6, Exp. X, Leg. 6, Exp. XI). Women's work in the *ayllu*—from weaving, cooking, and sowing to child care—was never considered a private service for husbands.[4] These were the contributions

[4] On the importance of not imposing norms derived from Western experience onto evaluations of what we call "domestic activities," see Edholm, Harris, and Young (1977:104).

women made toward the continuance of their household and their community. (See Figures 2-4.)

Giving birth and rearing children did not impede Andean women from playing an active role in community life (Garcilaso 1961:137). The Spanish chroniclers of the Andean world, however, interpreted women's vigor as a sign of enslavement:

> . . . and among these people, women were so subjected and worked so in the service of their husbands. . . . [T]hey did not just perform domestic tasks, but also [labored] in the fields, in the cultivation of their lands, in building houses, and carrying burdens when their husbands were going away, in peace or war; and more than once I heard that while women were carrying these burdens, they would feel labor pains, and giving birth, they would go to a place where there was water and they would wash the baby and themselves, and putting the baby on top of the load they were carrying, they would continue walking as before they gave birth. In sum, there was nothing their husbands did, where their wives did not help [Cobo 1964, II:247].

Father Cobo's opinion that Andean women lived a life of drudgery is rooted in a Spanish association of physical labor with inferior status. Men and women living in Andean culture could not have disagreed with him more. The Inca himself began the planting season by ritually sowing sacred fields in Cuzco. Native peoples harbored their own opinions about the Spanish. The part-Indian chronicler Guaman Poma was disgusted by the decadence of Spanish aristocratic ideals. He condemned all Spanish women and men as lazy and immoral, precisely because they would not work even when they were physically capable of doing so (Guaman Poma 1956, II:154). In his chronicle–letter-of-protest to the Spanish Crown, Guaman Poma pleaded that indigenous women be protected from the abuses of Spaniards, arguing that their labor in conjunction with that of men was necessary for the maintenance of Andean life (1956, III:66, 130, 136, 294). In the eyes of Andean men and women, their complementary activities were essential to the reproduction of Andean society.

FIG. 2. Andean Women and Men Plowing (Guaman Poma 1936: f. 1153)

FIG. 3. Andean Women and Men Sowing (Guaman Poma 1936: f. 1165).

FIG. 4. Andean Women and Men Harvesting (Guaman Poma 1936: f. 1144)

When they devised their tributary system, the Incas stuck to this conception of interdependent male and female activities as the keystone of the labor process. The household, and not the individual, was the minimal entity liable for labor service to the state. Only upon marriage was a man recorded in the state's census rolls and considered responsible for corvée labor obligations. Although the male head of the household wore the "public face" as its representative to imperial administration, the Incas defined the effective labor unit subject to tribute demands as having a male and a female component (Murra 1956:164). The complementarity in labor of men and women was culturally recognized in Andean society. Work, by *ayllu* and Inca definition, required the mutual interaction of woman and man.

If weaving and spinning were considered the epitome of "feminine" activity, plowing and combat were the tasks that represented Andean malehood (Arriaga 1968:27; Guaman Poma 1956, I:137; Murúa 1946:324; Murra 1956:177). Of course, men did much more than that: they weeded, helped in the harvest, carried firewood, built houses, herded llamas and alpacas, and even spun and wove when necessary. Nevertheless placing the foot plow in the earth and bearing arms were the domain of men.

Andean gender ideologies, then, associated women and men with certain tasks. Even though there was very little that either sex could not or would not do, the pairing of women with the making of cloth and men with plowing and bearing arms was a critical part of the construction of Andean personhood. Women and men carried the tools of their sex with them to their graves: "The women have their spindles and skeins of spun cotton, the men their *tacllas* or hoes to work the fields, or the weapons they used in war" (Arriaga 1968:27-28).

From Gender Distinction to Gender Hierarchy

The Incas made use of these community definitions of gender when constructing their census. They were concerned with knowing not only how many people were under their domain, but what their productive capacities were. Census rolls, therefore, were constructed around a tenfold classification of men and women based on their ability to work. From the attributes of manhood that they could have picked to mark the mature male liable for tribute duties, the Incas chose just one: the ability to bear arms. "Soldier" (*aucacamayoq*) was the title given to commoner men when, as married adults, they were inscribed in imperial census rolls (Guaman Poma 1956, I:137; Murúa 1946:324). The equivalent category for women was "soldier's wife" (Cobo 1964, II:112).

Remember, only married men were subject to labor duties for the state; the Incas implicitly recognized male and female labor as forming a unity necessary for the reproduction of social existence—a unity that was made up of equals, at least as far as marriage rites were concerned. Still, men and not women represented the household to the imperial administration. And the men who now became public figures for state purposes were characterized as arms bearers with wives. In building their empire, the Incas froze certain attributes of gender—attributes that had been part of the construction of maleness and femaleness—to facilitate imperial governance. What they chose to highlight, however, had profound implications for what men and women could become. The Incas, by using gender distinctions to frame relations through which the conquered were ordered and controlled, had begun converting gender differences into gender hierarchies.

As the Incas tightened their grip over others, the imperial ideal of Andean malehood increasingly became the norm. Not only imposing or re-enforcing this definition with every married man's inscription on the tribute rolls, the Incas also asserted it as new positions in government emerged. The association of men with conquest and arms helps explain why the Incas appointed men to the new positions of power which developed with the expansion of the empire. Noblemen were the empire's judges, magistrates, captains of war, overseers, and governors. They were the census takers, controllers of state-

15

built storehouses, imperial architects, and counselors (Cieza 1959:162, 165-67; Cobo 1964, II:126, 148; Guaman Poma 1956, I:266-72; Murúa 1946:206, 209, 212, 217). In keeping with royal gender norms, the Incas, who governed through a system of indirect rule, tended to confirm headmen as links between conquered *ayllus* and the bureaucracy of Cuzco (Murúa 1946:47, 166, 169, 228; Ortiz de Zúñiga 1967, I:46, 66, 69; Hernández Príncipe 1923:52 et passim; Cieza 1959:148, 157). The power brokers of the empire were male.

Pre-Inca communities had demonstrated considerable diversity in their sociopolitical organization, and within some *ayllus* a higher-ranked group known as *curacas* ("headmen," local ethnic leaders) enjoyed certain privileges in relation to their fellow *ayllu* members. The principal advantages that *curacas* enjoyed lay in their ability to make a greater claim on the *ayllu*'s wealth and labor. However, as part of a society whose relations of production were governed by kin-based norms of reciprocity, their activities were constrained by the framework of mutual obligations and responsibilities that shaped the community's economic activities.

The degree of social stratification within the *ayllus*, and thus the power and activities of the *curacas* prior to the Inca expansion, are not well known. Although a tendency for the position of *curaca* to become hereditary was emerging in some ethnic groups (Spalding 1967:136), in others no permanent headman status existed before the community was incorporated into the Inca empire (Ortiz de Zúñiga 1972, II:66). Where this position was not hereditary, leaders were selected as needed, and they resumed their customary *ayllu* status after their designated task had been completed (Murúa 1946:47). It is most likely that where a hereditary tendency was developing, the position itself was embedded in the emergence of more powerful descent groups within the ethnic community as a whole (Spalding 1967:195; Hernández Príncipe 1923:50-55; Ávila 1966).

While it is difficult to specify the position of *curacas* prior to the Inca conquest, the role and activities of women within this higher-ranked group is even more problematic. Although the chroniclers would seem to imply that local leaders were men (they rarely mention women in this role), there is some evidence that female leaders of ethnic groups held important positions in the governing of their communities. The most intriguing evidence of the ability of women to wield power as *ayllu* leaders comes from a document published by Oberem (1968:82, 83). This is a fragment of a will left by an Ecuadorian headman and headwoman, husband and wife, who lived to see the Spanish conquest. Each was independently "crowned" by the Inca in an elaborate ceremony confirming their positions. Part of the coronation ceremony entailed the ritual granting of separate and independent areas of jurisdiction and control to the *cacique* and *cacica*. The *cacica*, whose rights to political office were inherited from her mother, was also granted control over an ethnic group of central Peru which was relocated in her territory. She states in her will:

> . . . I declare that when I left the burial rite [part of the Inca ceremony legitimizing her position] at Malaleji, all things that could be seen from that mountaintop, on all sides, were given me as possessions. I also declare that I acquired, in my name, the Angaraes Indians, promising them land for their subsistence, and . . . they fled . . . and I went in person to Hambato in order to catch up with them and I brought them back from Hambato and resettled them according to my wishes, and thus I gave them my lands in the orchards of Mulinlibi [Oberem 1968:83].

Some analysts of Andean society have denied that women of higher rank within *ayllus* actually exercised political control, asserting that they were entitled only to economic privileges (Espinosa 1978:334). Doña Francisca Sinagigchi's testimony, which was confirmed by her husband's, certainly casts doubt on the affirmation that local political power was exclusively in male hands.

The exploits of other female leaders of provincial groups have also been recorded by choniclers. While it is difficult to

17

evaluate the historical veracity of this event, Sarmiento de Gamboa writes that during the Chanca attack on Cuzco, a *cacica* named Chanan Curycoca, head of the *ayllu* Chocoso-chona (located in what is now the Cuzqueñan parish of Santiago) bravely defended this quarter against the Chanca invaders (Sarmiento 1960:233). During Manco II's siege of the newly installed Spanish regime at Lima, the Spanish found an ally in Contarguacho, the *cacica* of Hatun Jauja. She led troops from her *ayllu* in Peru's central highlands in order to assist the defeat of the Cuzco-led revolt against Spanish rule (Espinosa 1978:338).

While the feats of these headwomen loom as exceptions in the documentary record, the rights of women of the upper ranks to a greater claim on the wealth and labor within the *ayllu* is well supported. Women, as members of higher-ranking descent groups, did enjoy, as did their male counterparts, a privileged access to the material resources and labor of their communities (Díez de San Miguel 1964:100, 107; Guaman Poma 1956, II:69, 92, III:104, 146).

Within the structure of reciprocal obligations that under-scored and justified the *curaca*'s access to land and labor, the headman's privileged position was legitimated by virtue of his function as administrator, war leader, arbiter of justice, and emblem of the moral order of his community. If women also obtained economic privileges in the ethnic community, was their privilege solely by dint of membership in a ranked descent group? Would they not have been expected to recipro-cate appropriately; that is, to exercise similar functions, hold similar roles, as headmen?

Although the documentary evidence paints an almost over-whelming picture of male predominance in higher-ranking positions within local ethnic political structures, the few examples mentioned above at least indicate that local headwomen could and did exercise the kinds of roles that would legitimize their economic privileges in terms of Andean politicoeconomic equations. It is difficult to know whether we are confronting regional variations—if the Incas, in systematizing relations with conquered groups, tended to designate male *curacas* as representatives of *ayllus*; or if the Spanish, who primarily dealt with male *curacas* as intermediaries under the colonial regime, were blind to the realities of pre-Columbian structures of authority in which women might assume positions of rank and power. Unfortunately, the scope of headwomen's activities in the *ayllu* remains largely a mystery.

Women did retain independent access to economic resources in the Inca Andes. The scant documented exceptions to male leadership bear witness to how women could manipulate the privileges with which structures of parallel descent endowed them (Oberem 1968:82-83). Yet the Andean norm attaching masculinity to political power and conquest skewed the balance of gender relations as the empire expanded, as men filled positions of authority in the Inca administration and military which were denied to women of an equivalent social status.

Further, men who held these positions were rewarded by the Incas. They were lavished with gifts (rewards in land, produce, even women) that women could not receive (Murra 1956:71-77; Cobo 1964, II:122; Polo 1917a:72). In so doing, the Incas were creating, in embryo, conditions that would allow men to enjoy a privileged access to the bounty of the Andes in ways unknown before.

Inca empire building generated contradictions in the economy that were directly tied to the meanings and interpretations Andean peoples gave to gender. Using gender ideologies that gave shape to what Andean men and women were supposed to be, the Incas were setting new limits on what they could become. Imperial construction was changing the material conditions of life of once autonomous Andean peoples, just as it was transforming the material conditions of life of women and men. The control of one portion of Andean humanity over another was wed to privileges of one sex over the other. Pulling at distinctions between the sexes, class formation in the Andes left gender hierarchy in its wake.

CHAPTER II

Gender Parallelism in Local Communities

> She declared that there were two idols in her
> village, one was called Auquilibiac, whose
> owner was Antonio Tapaojo, and the other was
> named Mamaraiguay, and [she] is the inheritor
> of this idol, because her mother had left it to
> her.
>
> [AAL:Leg. 3, Exp. XIII, f. 5]

CONSTRUING THE UNIVERSE

The social relations into which Andean women and men
were born highlighted gender as a frame to organize life.
Chains of women paralleled by chains of men formed the kinship channels along which flowed rights to the use of community resources. The material well-being of Andean men and
women was attained through bonds with same-sex kin.
Women and men acted in, grasped, and interpreted the world
around them as if it were divided into two interdependent
spheres of gender. Armed with this understanding of the workings of the world, and of the role of humankind in it, Andean
mortals structured their cosmos with goddesses and gods
whose disposition reflected these conditions of life.

Women and men conceptualized the functioning of the universe and society in terms of complex relations between sacred
beings, grouped into sexually distinct domains, and between
sacred beings and humankind. The majority contrasted the
powers of the earth with powers embodied in the skies and
mountains. Andean peoples populated their heavens with deities who took on a masculine cast when counterposed to the
female images of earthly regeneration contained in the Pacha-

20

mama (Earth Mother)[1] and her sacred "daughters" (Arriaga 1968:11, 23; Avendaño 1904:380; Cobo 1964, II:205; Duviols 1971:377). Resembling her human counterparts, Pachamama embodied procreative forces, while the gods represented political ones. It was agreed that their interaction—the dialectic between female and male forces—was essential for the reproduction of social existence.

Norms of reciprocity that governed interpersonal relations also shaped ties between Andean peoples and the supernatural. The gods bestowed life, and ultimately ensured the reproduction of the Andean world; Andean mortals owed this divine generosity products of labor as well as appropriate worship. Many (though not all) of the religious cults organized to honor the Andean divinities were divided along gender lines: women and men sponsored their own religious organizations dedicated to the appropriately gendered divine beings of the cosmos. Moreover, these organizations controlled rights to land and its produce which, following Andean custom, met the gods' due.

STRUCTURING THE COSMOS

The god of thunder and lightning, Illapa (or Rayo) dominated the heavens of many non-Inca Andean communities. Andean gender ideologies, encrusted in cosmology, knit two strands to tie this male deity to the goddess of the earth: as provider of rain and as god of conquest. Illapa could manufacture hail, clouds, lightning, and terrible storms in addition to much-needed rain. Polo describes him as a cosmological force:

> . . . they called him by the three names Chuquiilla, Catuilla, Intiillapa; pretending that he is a man who is in the sky with a slingshot and pitcher, and that in his hand lies the power

---

[1] Although the domains of these divinities were viewed as interdependent and mutually defining, the nature of the relationship between them was always contextually determined. Andean dialectical logic would not accept the attribution of intrinsic or absolute qualities to perceived constituents of the social, natural, or supernatural universe.

21

to cause rain, hail, thunder, and everything else that belongs to the region of the sky where clouds are formed. This *huaca* is worshipped by all Indians, and they offer him diverse sacrifices [Polo 1916:6].

Cobo elaborates:

. . . they thought he was a man who was in the sky, formed by stars. . . . [T]hey commonly held the opinion that the second cause of water which falls from the sky was due to Thunder, and that he was responsible for providing it when it seemed appropriate. They also said that a very large river crossed the middle of the sky . . . [which we call] the Milky Way. . . . They believed that from this river he took the water which was spilled over the earth. Since they attributed Thunder with the power to cause rain and hail and all the rest which refers to clouds and the celestial regions where all these imperfect mixtures were fabricated, under the name of Thunder . . . they adored the lightning, the rainbow, the rains, hail, and even storms and whirlwinds [Cobo 1964, II:161].

The Pachamama, who embodied the generative forces of the earth, needed a male celestial complement to realize her procreative powers. So Andean thought paired her to the god of thunder as bestower of rain. Similarly, the Andean way of seeing the world would consider Illapa's rain-causing powers meaningless if not tied to his capacity to generate fertility in the earth (Albornoz 1967:19; Polo 1917b:189). This was one dimension of the dynamics of Andean thought which bound the god of heavens to the goddess of the earth.

Thunder was also a conqueror. And as the emblem of powers that allowed one portion of humankind to control others, Illapa was set off against forces of natural fertility and bounty. Many Andean peoples conceived of Illapa as the ancestor-father of heroic founders of descent groups whom myth had proclaimed as the conquerors of other native kindreds. These mythic victories made sense of the internal ranking of descent groups which together formed an *ayllu*, or community (Her-nández Príncipe 1923; Zuidema 1973).[2] They also help ex-plain why this divinity, as well as the descent groups claiming his direct ancestry, could stand for all the social descent groups which formed a political unit.

Rodrigo Hernández Príncipe, a priest who was sent to the northern highlands to root out idolatry, was seized by the "pa-gan" displays of worship surrounding the god Thunder. He has left us the most detailed portrait of how Illapa and his de-scendants were venerated. Each family would establish a shrine to Thunder, on a mountaintop outside the village cen-ter, which was attended by male heads of household. As rep-resentatives of their families to Thunder, these men were named *churikuna* (in Quechua, *churi* is the way a father calls his son). In this manner, household heads were transformed into the descendants of Illapa. Each perceived himself as a knot on a genealogical thread which ultimately emanated from this god. Note that the knots on this thread were male; for the links connecting the deity of conquest to his mortal children were made through men.[3]

[2] Zuidema's pioneering work in deciphering Andean social structure is ex-emplified by his insightful analysis (1973) of Hernández Príncipe's document.

[3] It might be helpful to make a comparison with one of the manifestations of ancestor worship found today in Andean communities (see Earls 1971; Quispe 1969). The mountain gods of Peru's south-central sierra, known as Wamanis, are the contemporary analogues of the thunder god described by Hernández Príncipe and others for the *ayllus* of Ancash and the Lima high-lands. Fernando Fuenzalida (1968), who analyzed cults to the divinities of the mountains in Huancavelica, demonstrated that their origin could be traced to the pre-Hispanic adoration of Illapa. While the association between the moun-tain gods and rain is not clearly articulated in communities in the Departments of Ayacucho and Cuzco, mountains are considered to have control over the water derived from mountain springs and glacial melts, which are said to fer-tilize the earth. The dominion of the Wamani also extends over the herds pas-tured on his slopes, as well as over the pasture land itself. Moreover, the Wa-mani is an ancestral god. When a new *estancia*, or pastoral territory, is claimed, a Wamani-ancestor must be designated as the founder of the lineage or kindred which asserts its right to pasture in that area (Earls 1971). During the biannual or yearly celebrations to the mountain gods in these communi-

Andean gender norms might have conceived men to be the sons of heroic conquerors, but the Pachamama had a special place in her heart for women. This is not to say that men were not devoted to the goddess of fertility. Spanish colonizers frequently commented upon the reverence in which Andean peoples, regardless of gender, held her (Cobo 1964, II:161, 167; Murúa 1946:278; Polo 1917b:191-93). She was, after all, the embodiment of the earth's regenerative powers. Women and men alike needed to honor her and be mindful of her; the Pachamama would allow only those who worshipped her properly to receive the benefits of the earth's fertility. Thus:

> All adored the earth, which they called Pachamama, which means Earth Mother; and it was common for them to place a long stone, like an altar or statue, in the middle of their fields, in honor of this goddess, in order, in that spot, to offer her prayers and invoke her, asking her to watch over and fertilize their fields; and when certain plots of land were found to be more fertile, so much greater was their respect for her [Cobo 1964, II:161].

> It was a common thing among the Indians to adore the fertile earth . . . which they called Pachamama, offering her *chicha* by spilling it on the ground, as well as coca and other things so that she would provide for them; to mark this, they placed a long stone in the midst of their fields in order to invoke the virtues of the earth from that point, so that she would protect their fields; and at harvest time, if Indians saw potatoes that had a different form from the rest, or ears of maize or other crops with a different shape from the others, they had the custom of adoring them and making many cer-

---

ties, a man always represents his kin group when offerings are made in the Wamani's honor. Nowadays, men and women concur that the sacred shrines to the Wamani, where he is given *chicha*, coca, and other ritual items, are dangerous places for women to be. A woman might become deathly ill, or be swallowed into the mountain's interior, if she should approach one of these shrines. Thus, only a man can go to represent the household to its mountain ancestor.

emonies to venerate them, drinking and dancing, viewing these as signs of good fortune. . . . [A]nd thus, for the same effect, when it was time to plow, turn over the earth, sow and harvest corn, potatoes, *quinoa*, and other vegetables and fruits of the earth, they would offer her, in similar fashion, fat, coca, *cuy* [guinea pig], and other things, and all the time drinking and dancing [Murúa 1946:278].

The Pachamama disclosed other signs of her reproductive powers to the Andean universe: her daughters were emblems of the specifics of highland bounty—maize (Saramama), potatoes (Axomama), coca (Cocamama), even metals (Coyamama) and clay (Sañumama). Saramama and Axomama, sacred beings that Murúa describes in the above passage, reveal themselves through the "extraordinary" forms in which they appear. Possessing an outstanding quality or unusual characteristic, such plants housed divine powers to engender themselves in abundance. Polo de Ondegardo, who wrote one of the earliest chronicles of Andean life, provides us with this description:

> May is the month when the corn is brought in from the fields. This festival is celebrated while the corn is carried in, during which they sing certain songs, praying that the corn lasts for a long time, and each one makes a *huaca* [shrine] from the corn in their house; and this Saramama, made from the maize from their fields which stands out the most because of its quantity, is put in a small bin they call *pirhua*, with special ceremonies, and they worship it for three days. . . . [A]nd this maize is placed in the finest shawls that each one has, and after covering and adorning it, they adore this *pirhua*, and they hold it in great esteem and they say it is the Mother of Corn of their fields and that by virtue of her, corn is given and preserved [1916:20].

Seventy years later, an extirpator of idolatry extracted this testimony from Hacas Poma, the *curaca* of Otuco, who described his *ayllu*'s idolatrous practice of worshipping the Mother of Corn:

... and when they harvest the best ears of corn from their fields, those of five to a stalk, or if the corn is what is called *misasara* which has rows of kernels that are brown, violet, white, and other colors, or other cobs that are called *airiguasara* which are half white and half brown, these ears of corn are placed in the middle of the field, and they are covered with corn silk, and they are burned in offering to the same field so that it be strong and provide a good crop for the coming year; and when they found this corn called *airiguasara* and *misasara* they made *chicha* out of the corn from the section of the field where it was harvested, and they drank it with much dancing and joy, and part of the *chicha* was offered to the idols. . . . [A]nd when corn stalks that were imbued with the fertility of the earth were found in their fields . . . they collected them and kept them in storage bins which were reserved for their idols and ancestors, where the corn was adored and reverenced because it was said that they were Saramamas, mothers and creators of maize; and when they made sacrifices to and reverenced their ancestors, some of these Saramamas were burned and sacrificed to the idols and a portion was sown in their fields in order to increase their production [AAL:Leg. 6, Exp. XI, f. 12v].

Some of the corn that was imbued with the fertility of the earth was returned to it: that which was fertile would make for more agricultural fertility. Yet a portion of this sacred corn was given to the gods who embodied generative powers. Offerings were made to the earth. Offerings were also made to the ancestors, to Hacas Poma's forefathers who were Illapa's sons. Arriaga tells us (1968:30) that after these holy stalks with many ears of corn were honored, danced to, and danced with, sacrifices were made to Lliviac—a name by which the god of thunder and lightning was also known—to ensure a good harvest. Although celebrations of Saramama accentuated female powers, the interdependent dualities of the Andean cosmos, metaphorized as male and female forces, were expressed and realized in carrying out this ritual of fertility.

Our most complete descriptions of the Pachamama's many manifestations are of Saramamas. However, Saramamas were but one emblem of the Pachamama's attributes. Just as "special" ears of maize were venerated as Mothers of Corn, so were unusual (in the Andean meaning of the word) potatoes, coca leaves, *quinoa* plants, and other crops essential to Andean life (Arriaga 1968:21, 30, 31, 156; AAL:Leg. 2, Exp. XXVII). But the Pachamama's generative powers were not limited to the creation of abundant harvests. Products of the earth herself also supported existence in the Andes and were reverenced for their contribution to social life. An *ayllu* of potters in Ancash worshipped the Sañumama, the Mother of Clay, for providing them with the means to create their pitchers, bowls, and pots (Arriaga 1968:82; Hernández Príncipe 1923:34). The metals of the earth which the Pachamama produced, molded into beautiful adornments and representations of gods, were also sacred manifestations of the Earth Mother's forces. Corn and clay, potatoes and gold were linked together as emblems of female powers of creation:

> They chose the most beautiful fruit and kept it, and in its likeness they made others of different stones or of gold or silver, like an ear of corn or a potato, and these were named Mamasara and Mamapapa; and they did the same with the rest of their fruits and vegetables, and in like manner with all minerals, gold, silver, and mercury, which they discovered many, many years ago. They selected the most beautiful stones composed of these metals and they kept them and they still keep them and they reverence them, calling them the Mothers of these minerals. And before going to work [in the mines], on the day they are to work, they reverence and drink to that stone, calling it the Mother of that mineral on which they will labor [Albornoz 1967:18].

If priests who hunted Andean idolatries in the seventeenth century did not uncover Pachamamas, they did find goddesses

27

of like kind. The story of one of these heroines, Mamarayiguana, was related in the testimony of Hacas Poma, the *curaca* of Otuco in the highlands of Cajatambo. Mother Rayiguana had the *conopas* of all the fruits and vegetables that formed the basis of Andean subsistence in her power. *Conopas* were miniatures or models that could generate the items they represented. Some Saramamas and Axomamas, for example, were discovered in the form of *conopas* (Arriaga 1968:82; AAL:Leg. 2, Exp. XXVII); the stone or metal images of corn and potatoes that Albornoz speaks of were called *conopas* by their Indian owners. These were in the possession of Mamarayiguana; and, not surprisingly, it was a male divinity of the sky, the bird Yucyuc, who was instrumental in catalyzing her procreative powers. Hacas Poma recounts:

> . . . when the fields were plowed in preparation for seeding . . . the bird [Yucyuc] was taken out in procession through the streets by the *pallas* [princesses] who played little drums, singing to him, "O Lord Bird Yucyuc . . . because you brought us the *conopas* of food and stole them from Mamarayiguana . . ." For their ancestors held the tradition and belief that the bird Yucyuc implored the tiny bird Sacracha to carry a fistful of fleas and throw them in the eyes of Mamarayiguana, who was in the village of Caina, so that as she scratched the bites, she would let loose her child *conopa* which she carried in her arms, and then the bird Yucyuc would steal it . . . and Mamarayiguana begged him not to take her little child, that she would distribute all the foods; and thus she gave potatoes, *ocas*, *ollucos* [*ullucos*], *masuas*, [and] *quinoa* to the highland Indians, and corn, manioc, yams, and beans to the lowland Indians; and for that reason they adore Mamarayiguana as a goddess and creator of foods, and they worship the bird Yucyuc as an instrumental cause and because of whom Mamarayiguana distributed all of the foods [AAL:Leg. 6, Exp. XI, f. 21v, 22].

The same logic that shaped the relationship between the Pachamama, her *conopa* manifestations, and the god of thunder is at the root of this legend. While Mother Rayiguana contains the sources of fertility and creation, food production can be carried out only if a male celestial deity intercedes. Each is incomplete without the other. Gender symbols, structured by a logic of mutuality, gave form to the ways in which Andean peoples construed their universe.[4]

Andean peoples paired gender symbols with cosmological forces as they interpreted the world around them. The sacred beings of the Andes reached out, however, to the human beings of their own sex. Mother Earth, like Mother Rayiguana, smiled favorably on women. The goddess of fertility was close to them, just as they, in turn, held the Pachamama in special reverence. Native men and women both gave offerings to the Pachamama, but only women forged a sacred tie with her. The Andean division of labor had women put seeds in the earth as men broke the soil with their foot plows (Arriaga 1968:22, 27; Duviols 1971:370, 377; Albornoz 1967:18; Guaman Poma 1936:f. 1153, f. 1165). Like anyone who was going to meet the gods, women had to purify themselves before sowing (AAL:Leg. 6, Exp. XI, f. 22). They experienced this act as a holy one, the time to consecrate their bond with the Pachamama. Talking to her, invoking her, reverencing her, women placed seeds in the earth (Arriaga 1968:22).

The Pachamama also embraced midwives, who parlayed the sacred forces of fertility into human reproduction. Their special role in community religious life has been hidden by the prejudices of the Spanish chroniclers. The chroniclers saw nothing special in midwives, whom they lumped together with other herbal curers and "doctors" of traditional medicine. Imposing norms of a righteous Catholicism, the Spaniards condemned all of these practitioners as sorcerers (Murúa 1946:228, 295, 321; Polo 1916:35). In spite of themselves, however, chroniclers let slip that those native to the Andes

---

[4] The origin myth of the Cañari tribe of Ecuador also relates the creation of food and seeds to two goddesses whose gifts of food are mediated through men (Molina 1943:15; Cobo 1964, II:151-52).

viewed midwives in a special light. Garcilaso de la Vega, who defended traditional herbalists from the witchcraft charges levied against them by most of the Spanish establishment, was adamant that "women who served in this function [midwives] were more like witches than anything else" (1961:137). Perhaps they were "like witches" because, as several observers pointed out, women had to celebrate special rituals before being able to practice midwifery (Murúa 1946:321; Polo 1916:35):

. . . There were also women midwives, some of whom said that in their dreams they had been given this office, and others dedicated themselves to this office when they had two babies at one birth; in which [i.e. in order to become midwives] they had to perform many ceremonies, fasts, and sacrifices [Cobo 1964, II:228].

Midwives, then, recognized their calling in dreams or by giving birth to children who were somehow special and unusual. "Extraordinary births" were signs of the Earth Mother; they were manifestations in human beings analogous to the many-eared corn stalk or the double potato, which marked the forces of fertility that blessed Mother Corn and Mother Potato. Dreams revealed a religious vocation in the Andes. Like others who were "called" into the service of Andean gods, midwives too were made aware of their mission in dreams. As representatives of the Pachamama, these women had to attend rituals that prepared them to commune with the sacred.

Guaman Poma de Ayala, who was raised in a colonial Indian community, gives us other clues to the specialness of Andean midwives. Like other chroniclers of the Andes, Guaman Poma talks about midwives as part of his general discussion of traditional curers and herbalists. Nevertheless, he does distinguish them from other native healers. Only midwives are called *comadres* (godmothers) and *beatas* (blessed, devout); no other Andean curer is so named (1956, I:137, III:72, 135). Guaman Poma chooses the terms by which he designates midwives with care. *Comadre*, a Spanish word, points to a special relation between the sponsor, the godmother, and divine beings. Women who have helped others give birth were "blessed" in Andean eyes because they were standing for and facilitating sacred powers of fertility. Today, midwives are called *pachacomadres* (godmothers of the earth) in the village of Hualcán (Stein 1961:154). As midwives, they become the godmothers of the children they deliver, an aspect of the hallowed bond they forge between the Earth Mother and human reproduction. The *beatacomadres*, the blessed sponsors of birth, represented households to the deity who embodied powers of procreation, thus tying human genesis to the goddess of fertility.

DUAL RELIGIOUS ORGANIZATIONS

The gods of the Andes seemed to favor mortals of like sex. Some of them even desired to be worshipped through religious cults whose members were exclusively of the appropriate gender. Or so many Andean peoples believed. It is not hard to see why. They were conceived into a culture that accented gender as a structure for the social relations of life. Men and women of the Andes attained material well-being through ties with family of the same sex. Kinship, the bedrock of *ayllu* organization, was conceptualized as parallel chains of men and women. The organization of religious life into two gendered worlds was a dimension of the Andean social experience segregating women from men. Andean mortals, then, populated their cosmos with gods whose predilections mirrored the conditions of human life.

Although men and women throughout the Andes worshipped Corn Mother, Saramama, for her powers to make corn grow bountifully, women felt especially tied to this daughter of the Pachamama (Arriaga 1968:22, 30, 31; Murúa 1946:278, 347; Guaman Poma 1956, I:171; Cobo 1964, II:215; Polo 1916:20; Molina 1943:67). Saramamas held an exceptional place in the life of women from the village of Pimachi. There women built a cult around them. Fields were set

31

aside, and their produce was earmarked for the festivities which celebrated two *ayllu*'s Saramamas. Twice a year, at *pocoy mita* (time of the first rains) and *cargua mita* (time when corn turns yellow prior to the harvest), women hosted celebrations in their honor. In the early-seventeenth century, Bernardo de Noboa, who had been sent by his Limeñan archbishop to uncover Pimachi's idols, found out that María Chaupis Tanta watched over the Corn Mothers' ceremonial clothing and silver offerings. Following Andean norms of cosmic gender relations, the Saramamas were sisters of Pimachi's two dominant gods (Duviols 1971:369).

Carrying out his mission to root out pagan and idolatrous traditions, Noboa levied charges against several women. The ecclesiastical tribunal convicted them for being "confessors, dogmatists, witches, and leaders of [idolatrous] ceremonies" (Duviols 1971:385). Noboa's condemnations disclose that these "witches" and "female dogmatists" led a female constituency. Isabel Yalpay, Francisca Quispe Tanta, Francisca Quillay Tanta, María Chaupis Tanta (minister of the Saramama cult), and Francisca Nauim Carhua were sentenced for being the confessors of women: leading and instructing women in idolatrous practices, teaching them the traditions of their ancestors, insisting that they maintain the adoration of their native deities in defiance of colonial civil and ecclesiastic regimes. Noboa passed sentence:

> Be attentive to the charges and merits of this suit, because of the crime committed by the aforementioned women, whom I should condemn and do condemn—the aforesaid Isabel Yalpay . . . to go out with her hair shorn . . . and to be whipped one hundred times astride a colored llama through the public streets of this village, as the voice of the town crier makes known her crime, and to serve four years in the church in the town of Acas and to be for a period of ten years at the disposition of its priest . . . and because of our mercifulness we did not make her serve double the time in the Hospital of Charity in Los Reyes [Lima]; and Francisca

Quispe Tanta for the same reason, for being a witch confessor who teaches rites and ceremonies to all the Indian women [receives the same sentence] . . . and María Chaupis Tanta for the same reason, for having been a witch confessor and for having exhorted all Indian women not to adore Christ our Savior, but the idols and *guacas* [*huacas*], I condemn her to be shorn and to go out in the manner of a penitent with a rope around her throat . . . and with a cross in her hands . . . and to be given one hundred lashings through the public streets astride a llama as the crier denounces her crime, and to serve in the church of Acas for ten years at the disposition of its priest, and if she breaks sentence, she will be punished by serving twice the amount of time in the aforementioned Hospital of Charity . . . and Francisca Nauim Carhua for the same reason, for being the leader of [idolatrous] ceremonies and confessor, preacher of idolatry who commanded them no longer to adore Christ our Savior, but to return to the idols, *guacas*, and other rites and ceremonies of their pagan ways [receives the same sentence]. . . . And in addition to the sentences imposed on all the aforementioned women, [I order] that they never meet together in public or in private, nor when they pray with the boys and girls, and that they be isolated . . . and this is my definitive sentence, having acted with due kindness, piety, and mercy [Duviols 1971:385].

Other ecclesiastical suits brought against those who remained faithful to their pre-Hispanic religious traditions document the communal yet female-dominated devotion shown toward Saramamas. In several communities of the north-central sierra (see AAL:Leg. 4, Exp. XVIII, Leg. 6, Exp. X), Corn Mother was the central figure of cults presided over by women "witches and dogmatists." Saramamas were either the wives or, as in Pimachi, sisters of the principal gods of these *ayllus*. As in Pimachi, Saramamas were bestowed with fields and herds to maintain the cults devoted to their service. Followers

CHAPTER II

showered them with sacramental objects and fine garments in
deference to their powers to ensure bountiful harvests.

Andean women felt close to the goddesses of the cosmos for
the ability they shared to reproduce life. Some even expressed
this affinity as kinship, claiming the goddesses as their ancestors. Priests rooting out idolators in the village of Coscaya (Department of Arequipa) uncovered this relationship between
women and Corn Mothers, or Mamayutas. The inquisitors, in
the proceedings of ecclesiastical trials, described rites celebrating Mamayutas' generative powers. During one of the central
rites, women presented Mamayutas with offerings of aborted
fetuses and of children who died soon after birth. Hernández
Príncipe witnessed a comparable ceremony in the north-central sierra; he was horrified upon discovering that the shrines
constructed by male household heads, *churikuna*, to the thunder god contained similar kinds of offerings (1923:27). These
symbolized the kinship felt between men and Illapa and were
a sign of the reverence with which they held the celestial
founders of their descent groups. Similar offerings made by
women to Mamayutas suggest analogous structures.

Coscayan women looked to Mamayutas as their ancestors,
as the founders of a female line of which they were the living
descendants. Daughters of Mamayutas were also the inheritors of her powers. A witness, Juan Carama testified

> how Catalina Marmita had told this witness how in the
> heights of this village she guarded and cared for some
> earthen jars which were named Mamayutas, that one had
> breasts and the other was a man, and she kept them inside a
> trough, and for this purpose she had placed inside [the
> trough] coca, plumes of birds, and ears of corn and balls of
> colored wool; and these Mayutas were kept there in that
> trough as the Mother of the corn of their fields and of other
> things which they take to be in their [Mamayutas'] name.
> . . . [A]nd in like fashion, next to this trough they have an-
> other, and inside of it women place their newly born chil-
> dren who had died, whom they take there to offer to the Ma-

34

yutas in order that they consume them; dead guinea pigs wrapped up in bits of cloth are also in the trough, all as offerings to the Mamayutas [BN:B1715, f. 21v].

Two men, familiar with these rites, declared:

> . . . and Don Diego Ogsa and Don Pedro Cayo were directed [in these rites], in times long past, by Catalina Marmita, now dead, an old woman and very elderly. . . . [I]n the heights of the village [there were] two troughs in which two figures of clay, like half-pitchers, one with breasts which they called Mamayuta, and the other the husband of this Mamayuta, were kept . . . and in [this trough] there were dead guinea pigs wrapped in bits of cloth and feathers . . . and two degrained ears of corn . . . and the aforementioned corn was sent by the Inca of Cuzco to be adored. . . . [A]nd these two [Don Diego and Don Pedro Caya] were accomplices, and . . . the old woman instructed all the Indian men and women of this village in this adoration [BN:B1715, f. 23v].

Like the thunder god, Mamayutas were worshipped by both men and women. Nevertheless, Andean kinship placed Illapa at the head of a chain of sons and grandsons, while Mamayutas narrowed their kin to daughters and granddaughters. Andean gender ideologies had Thunder, the god of conquest, share his powers of domination with men who, as heads of household, were formal representatives of household politics. At the same time, Mamayuta, goddess of fertility, was transmitting powers of procreation to women.

True to Andean "dialectical" tradition, Mamayuta had a masculine aspect as well as a feminine one, but clearly the latter predominated. For an elderly woman presided over her cult: Catalina Marmita, the priestess who instructed both men and women in the rites celebrating Mamayuta's divine powers, and who guarded the offerings presented by women's hands.[5]

[5] The Andean perception of the universe was relativistic; in other words, the distinctive units in any equation of oppositions were reciprocally defined and

Spaniards did not expect to find women presiding over their own religious organizations. Self-fulfilling prophesies saw to it that descriptions of cults to female ancestors or to goddesses are very scarce. This makes it hard to flesh out the structures of these cults—to learn which women joined them, who became leaders. It seems that women attained positions in these ritual organizations by several means. Some might have rotated through a series of ranked offices in a way similar to the *varayoq* systems or civil-religious hierarchies in contemporary communities (see Guaman Poma 1956, II:66, 69, 92, III:22-24; Duviols 1971:370; Hernández Príncipe 1923:28, 32, 39; Zuidema 1973; Isbell 1973:81; Belote and Belote 1973; Silverblatt 1981:212-17). Some probably succeeded their mothers in office.

Murúa (1946:427) tells us a legend about an elderly woman who was the proud possessor of a staff that had originally belonged to a female deity. Staffs are symbols of office in the Andes, and we can presume that this one was passed down through a line of women. Women were the inheritors of ritual staffs, an expression of the transmission from mother to daughter of posts in a religious organization.

---

contextually determined. Within a context defined by the parameters of the forces from "above" (the past) versus those from "below" (the future), the symbolic referents associated with them are male in opposition to female. However, if we examine the constituent entities within the frame or category marked by "the above," we can find male/female oppositions structuring its internal relations (see Earls and Silverblatt 1976b), just as we find the female/male Mamayutas in the category "below." Returning to Hernández Príncipe's document, we discover that the worship of ancestors, perceived as an agnatically phrased descent group, was an important element of the religious life of these communities. The *ministros* (male ministers) responsible for this facet of ritual organization, those who were in charge of the maintenance of ancestral cults, seemed to have inherited their positions. Son succeeded father, and the office was delegated to he who stood in a direct line of descent from the group's progenitor (Hernández Príncipe 1923:26, 30, 34, 37, 46).

I do not want to give the impression that all *ayllu* religious activity was structured by the model of gender parallelism. The parallel structure of the politico-religious organization in the *ayllu* was only one of several principles that shaped ritual life.

Several testimonies recorded in the suits brought against heretics describe how rights to office in native religious structures were determined by parallel transmission. In the village of Caxamarquilla, for example, the renowned priestess Guacayllano, passed down her position and authority to her daughter, Catalina Mayhuay (AAL:Leg. 4, Exp. XVIII, f. 5). The celebrated creator of food, known as Mamaraiguay in the town of San Antonio de Lancha (Province of Cajatambo), was under the guardianship of María Catalina. This elderly woman inherited her ritual duties, obligations, and knowledge from her mother, María Cocha. She stated in her declaration:

> ... asked why it was prohibited to eat meat or chili pepper [*ají*], or why married men could not sleep with their wives when yams were sown in her village ... [she] answered that this was a custom that their elders had transmitted to them; and that she was taught this by her mother, María Cocha. ... [S]he declared that there were two idols in her village: one was called Auquilibiac, whose owner was Antonio Tapaojo, and the other was named Mamaraiguay, and [she] is the inheritor of this idol, because her mother had left it to her [AAL:Leg. 3, Exp. XIII, f. 5].

Parallel transmission bestowed María Catalina with her mother's authority in a religious organization that extolled a female sacred being, the fertility goddess, Mamaraiguay. Called Mamarayiguana in a neighboring village, she was heroine of the myth that explained how humankind received their subsistence. We discover in this testimony that Mamaraiguay was the divine object of a religious cult in which women held the preeminent ritual positions. Moreover, at least in Lancha, Mamaraiguay was cosmologically paired with Auquilibiac, whose name alone reveals his association with the thunder god. The cult to Auquilibiac, as María Catalina testified, was led by a man, Antonio Tapaojo. In Lancha, Andean gender ideologies grasped Mamaraiguay and Auquilibiac as the interdependent female and male forces of all creation. Favoring the mortals of their respective genders, this god and goddess chose to be celebrated in cults that mirrored the sexual division of the cosmos.

Gender parallelism was strikingly apparent in Andean ritual. During the ceremonies of *Oncoy llocsitti*, the two sex-specific worlds of the Andean community stood out. This festival was celebrated in Huamantanga, a village of the Lima highlands, when potatoes were prepared for processing into *chuño* (a kind of freeze-dried potato). During moonlit nights, men and women would make offerings to their shrines and ancestors, thanking them for allowing the potatoes to mature. The women and men of Huamantanga performed these rites in lines: ". . . and the women all in one procession on one side, and the men together on the other" (AAL:Leg. 2, Exp. XI).

Another telling ceremony was *Vecochina*, which was solemnized by descent groups from the village of Otuco. During this rite, they joined together to worship common ancestors and divinities. Everyone left their homes to honor their shrines and progenitors, singing and dancing through all the village streets. This procession was led by the ministers of the gods, who were counterposed by the "old women" who sang the songs of their gods' histories.

> The *Vecochina* . . . meant that everyone from all the *ayllus* . . . left their houses, led by the priests and ministers of the idols and by the old women who accompanied them with their small drums, playing them through all the streets, chanting songs in their native language following their ancient custom, referring to the histories and ancient deeds of their ancestors and gods [AAL:Leg. 6, Exp. XI, f. 10].

Whether women officiants were entrusted with the devotion of female deities or not, ties articulating women often prevailed, as women priests tended to be confessors of those whose gender they shared. Leonor Nabin Carhua, who devoted her life to the care of several of the principal divinities of Otuco (both male and female), nevertheless heard the confessions of the other women of her *ayllu*. When, in a dream, ancestors told Otuco's *curaca* that Leonor should be ordered into the service of its gods, they specified that her responsibilities included the confession of women. She testified:

> . . . when her husband died, Hacas Poma told her not to marry because the *huacas* and ancestors told him that it was indispensable for her to become a minister, to make *chicha* for the offerings to the idols and ancestors, and that likewise, she had to become a confessor, in order to hear the confessions of the Indian women of her *ayllu* [AAL:Leg. 6, Exp. XI, f. 57].

Women and men in the Andean *ayllu* apprehended a world crisscrossed by bonds of gender. It remains to see how the Incas made use of this dimension of Andean experience as *ayllus* were entrapped in an imperial web.

CHAPTER III

Gender Parallelism in the Imperial Order

> The reason why Indian men do not take women
> very much into account when they record their
> histories is an old tradition. Not even the Inca
> paid much attention to the worship of the
> Moon, since women were in charge of the cult
> to her, as was the case regarding [the cult to]
> Mama Huaco, the sister of Manco Capac,
> [which was established] because she sowed the
> first corn there was.
>
> [Hernández Príncipe (1621) 1923:53]

LEGITIMIZING POWER

Like other Andean peoples, the Incas perceived their social
universe as divided into gender-linked spheres. Like other Andean peoples they interpreted the world around them, and
their experiences of that world, through symbols of gender.
Like other Andean peoples, the Inca imaged kinship relations
as parallel chains of women and men. But apparent similarities
are deceptive. For the Incas orchestrated gender ideologies
with new meanings as they dominated the Andean countryside. By manipulating modes of thought and ways of perceiving the world that were anchored in common structures of social life, the Incas transformed symbols of gender parallelism
to fit new relations of power and economy.

As the Incas dominated Andean politics, so did they dominate cultural systems of meanings through which gender was
interpreted. While they used structures of gender parallelism
to bind *ayllus* into their dominion, the Incas strove to impose
their interpretations of gender on tributed *ayllus* under their
rule. The Incas' struggle to do just that—measured by the de-

gree to which conquered peoples shared in the Inca version of gender parallelism—was a test of their ability to maintain a hold on Andean peoples they vanquished.

The Incas structured their cosmos in ways that other Andean peoples would understand. Their gender-divided universe was inhabited by some of the same gods and goddesses that non-Cuzqueñans placed in their heavens. Unlike others, however, the Incas chose the Sun to preside over and represent the conquering empire, while the Moon held sway over all that was female.

The Incas unequivocally presented their view of the cosmos and of the order of natural, supernatural, and social relations in the interior design of Coricancha, the empire's principal Temple of the Sun. Thanks to Pachacuti Yamqui, a native commentator on Inca society, we have a diagram of Cuzco's central shrine (Pachacuti Yamqui 1950:226; Zuidema and Quispe 1968) (See Figures 5 and 6).[1]

The Incas structured their universe by parallel hierarchies of gender which ranked gods and categories of humans in the language of descent. At the top of the cosmological order was the androgynous divinity, Viracocha. Pachacuti Yamqui leaves no doubt as to Viracocha's sexual duality, for above his/her image are the inscribed words "whether it be male, whether it be female" (Pachacuti Yamqui 1950:226; La Fone 1950:306).[2] Viracocha incorporates the opposing forces that each gender represents: "the sun, the moon, day, night, summer, winter" (Pachacuti Yamqui 1950:220). Heading a hierarchy of descent, Viracocha is the founder of parallel chains of gods and

[1] R. T. Zuidema was one of the first analysts of Inca cosmological systems to underscore the importance of the paradigm of sexual parallelism and its conscious manifestation in Pachacuti Yamqui's diagram of the Temple of the Sun (Zuidema 1972:197; Zuidema and Quispe 1968).

[2] For a different interpretation of Viracocha, see Urbano (1979a, 1979b, 1981). Urbano analyzed several Inca origin myths in which "Viracochas" are named. They are analyzed as "culture heroes" representing various "functions" of Inca society.

41

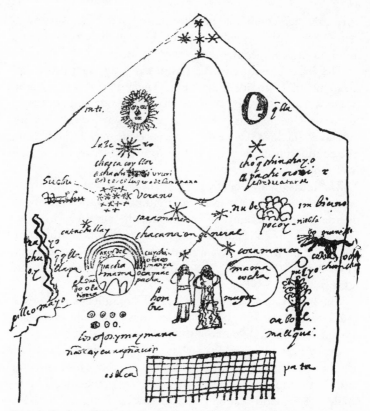

FIG. 5. Pachacuti Yamqui's Diagram of Inca Cosmology (Pachacuti Yamqui 1950:226)

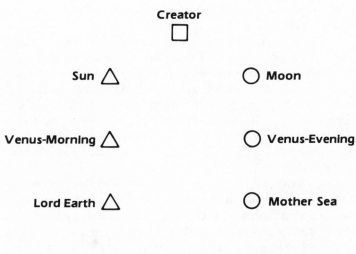

Creator
□

Sun △   ○ Moon

Venus-Morning △   ○ Venus-Evening

Lord Earth △   ○ Mother Sea

Man △   ○ Woman

▦
Storehouse-Terrace

FIG. 6. Schematic Version of Pachacuti Yamqui's Diagram

goddesses who engender men and women as lowest-ranking descendants.[3] Looking at the masculine generational hierarchy, we find the Sun to be Viracocha's first descendant, followed by the planet Venus in its morning apparition, the Lord Earth, and man. The female chain is headed by the Moon, followed by Venus of the Evening, Mother Sea, and woman. (Other chroniclers who refer to this cosmological structure include Cieza 1959:183; Cobo 1964, II:70; Guaman Poma 1956, I:303; Garcilaso 1961:393; Molina 1943:34; Murúa 1946:71; Polo 1916:3.)

Inca ideology joined human labor with cosmological order: the culturally elaborated means by which men and women materially created their existence were symbolized by the *collca pata* (storehouses and agricultural terraces) at the bottom of Pachacuti Yamqui's drawing (Figures 5 and 6). Women and men working together appropriated the bounty of nature. Andean morality, seconded by the Incas, required that human beings re-create the balance which labor disturbed, by offering products of the interaction of women and men to the deities who sustained society's life (see Earls 1971; Earls and Silverblatt 1976a, 1976b).[4]

[3] The concept of an androgynous originator is an old one in the Andes. The Tello obelisk (Lathrap 1971) and Rowe's "smiling god" (1967:103), both of the Chavin Period in Andean prehistory, contain hermaphroditic elements. Other hermaphroditic deities were often described as *huacas* with a male figure and a female figure carved on either side. The *iscay* (two) *guaris*, which were discovered by the extirpators of idolatry in local communities, are good examples.

[4] As with the model of parallelism which structured the perception of the universe in other Andean cultures, the Inca variant was anchored in the concept of a necessary interdependence and mutual definition of opposing forces. Similarly, these forces were distinguished by means of symbols embodying gender associations: Sun, Venus of the morning, Lord Earth, and man constituted one line of masculine emblems defining and being defined by a hierarchy of the Moon, Venus of the Evening, Mother Sea, and woman. Each level is thus conceived of as a dynamic unit comprising intrinsically linked male and female entities. The forces derived from the reciprocal interplay between "the masculine" and "the feminine" were conceptualized as creating the driving ener-

The interior of Coricancha formalized the perception of the order of things held by the rulers of the Andes. It was a cosmological image pregnant with politics. In what must be one of the most obvious ideological ploys to justify power, the Incas claimed to be children of the gods, direct descendants of the Sun and Moon (Garcilaso 1961:43-45, 47, 49). The Moon might be the mother of all womankind, and the Sun the father of all mankind, but some humans were closer kin to the gods than others. The Inca called himself the son of the Sun, and he made no bones of the fact that having the Sun as father enabled him to be victorious over other Andean peoples. The queen declared similar privilege (Cobo 1964, II:70).

Official ideology also accounted for the new power brokers in imperial politics. The Incas established a system of indirect rule in which headmen of kin-based communities served as intermediaries between the Cuzco rulers and the peoples brought under Inca domination. Local chiefs were tied into Cuzco government as middlemen, and their political role was encoded into Inca cosmology. The Inca as the Sun's son shared Venus's position, and local chiefs (or headmen) claimed Venus as their divine father (AAL:Leg. 6, Exp. XI, f. 14). Inca logic, then, turned the Inca into the father of chiefs. These genealogical transformations continue. Chiefs, by virtue of their struc-

---

gies of the universe (see Zuidema 1972; Earls and Silverblatt 1976a, 1976b; Isbell 1976, 1978). This cosmological paradigm also expressed a relativistic concept of the nature of the universe (see Earls 1973; Earls and Silverblatt 1976a, 1976b). The actual positioning of the model's component symbols, as well as the character of the relation which they exemplified, was always determined by context. Although most pictorial representations of this structure place the masculine emblem on the right, the feminine symbol would occupy that position when the paradigm was employed in a context in which women's activities, interests, or associations predominated. Similarly, the nature of the relation between "male" and "female" elements could be specified only through context. In terms of Pachacuti Yamqui's diagram, for example, given a general frame of reference, the relation of the units on any one horizontal level suggest parity or equivalence: the relation between the Sun and the Moon, or between the two Venuses, is a case in point. However, in a more restricted context, in which other parameters are specified, the emblems of the right-hand position predominate.

45

tural equivalency to "Lord Earth"—echoed in popular beliefs wherein local leaders were transformed into divine ancestors (Hernández Príncipe 1923)—became the "fathers" of commoners.

The Inca restructuring of genealogical history was a model of social hierarchy that neatly legitimized class relations. It also hid them. The rights and power of chiefs vis-à-vis their *ayllus* in no way matched the Incas' control over conquered peoples (chiefs included). Expressing politics in terms of sacred genealogies masked inequities of power and economic exploitation. It trivialized differences in power relations while hiding them behind the skirts of consecration. Some conquered peoples accepted Inca claims to sacred origins, thus bolstering Cuzco's control over them:

> His name [Mayta Capac, the "fourth" Inca monarch] instilled fear throughout all the land because of the fact that he persuaded the people . . . from other tribes and nations . . . that the god Sun and the goddess Moon communicated with the Incas, who were their children [Cobo 1964, II:70].

The Inca reconstruction of the ancestral relations of subordinated *ayllus* (to fit into the Cuzqueñan scheme of things) constituted an ideological battle. As such, it formed part of the larger struggle to create and maintain an empire. The Incas' hold on many provinces was fragile; continual rebellions of encapsulated, tribute-paying kin groups tell of the empire's weakness (Mena 1968; Trujillo 1968; P. Pizarro 1968; Sancho de la Hoz 1968). As in other precapitalist states, the Incas used kin—kin terms, kin idioms, kin expectations—to cloak the political and economic nature of their dominion. Inca remaking of the past, which lies behind the remaking of genealogies, was a means of camouflaging the politicization of kin ties and the coercion of tribute which class formation is all about. In reconstructing genealogies, the Incas were creating an image of history that alluded to a past which the Incas and those whom they vanquished held in common. By manipulating the idiom of kinship, expressed through shared structures of descent and the common Andean religious practice of the deification of ancestors, the Incas tried to capture the past of tributed *ayllus*. The lords of Cuzco were creating a history that would legitimize their domination. As tributed kin groups consented to the Inca version of their history, they were falling victim to the delusions of Inca ideology and Inca rule. But the Incas were not always successful. The hatred of anything Inca which tributed *ayllus* expressed to the conquistadors (H. Pizarro 1968; Xerez 1968; Sancho de la Hoz 1968; Trujillo 1968)—something the Spanish would later use to advantage as they conquered the Incas—points to Cuzco's failure to impose its world view on others.

THE HIERARCHY OF GODDESSES AND WOMEN

The Incas transformed structures of gender parallelism which shaped human and divine relations in the *ayllu* into institutions of imperial politics. The Moon dominated the female side of the Inca cosmos, and the queen, as her closest human descendant, dominated all other women. Her control was realized through religious structures that took their form from the women's organizations of kin-based communities. Chroniclers give us few clues into the queen's political entourage, while contemporary scholars have given her political activities short shrift. Hunting down remnants left in the chronicles, we will piece together this imperial cloak of women's domination over women.

First, let us look at the imperial goddesses. According to the cosmological order of the empire, the Moon held sway over divine and mortal beings of like sex. Blas Valera tells us:

> The Moon was the sister and wife of the Sun, and Illa Tecce [Viracocha] has given her part of his divinity, and made her mistress over the sea and winds, over the queens and princesses, and over the process in which women give birth; and she is queen of the sky. They called the Moon "Coya," which means queen [1950:136].

47

Imperial ideology made Mamacocha (Mother Sea) a descendant of the Moon. She was proclaimed the "mother" of all waters: streams, rivers, and mountain springs expressed her powers. Aware of how much his Cuzco parishioners adored Mamacocha as the source of irrigation water, Pérez Bocanegra advised Catholic priests to ask their Indian confessees:

. . . do you speak to the fountains, lakes, and springs, adoring them and dancing for them; and dressing a small pitcher like a woman, and feeding it do you pray, "O Mother fountain, lake, or spring, give me water without ever ceasing, urinate without stopping" [1631:133]?

Andean peoples lavished rivers and lakes with seashells. Bonds of gender and kinship linked shells with the source of all water. Consequently, they were considered most appropriate offerings. Fountains and streams were given products of the sea "because it was said that the seashells were the daughters of the sea, mother of all waters" (Murúa 1946:294). Moreover, Andean cosmology tied Mother Sea to rain-producing clouds. Pérez Bocanegra included this question as well in his confession manual for priests working in the Department of Cuzco:

. . . when it does not rain and our fields are drying, do you adore the clouds and speak to them, imploring, "O Mother Sea, from the end of the world, make it rain and form dew, and I adore you" [1631:133]?

While Spanish priests are clear that women and men adored Mamacocha, they do not tell us whether women worshipped her through their own organizations. We do know, however, that women led the cult of the goddess Apurima, a principal Andean river flowing from the Department of Cuzco in the Amazon Basin. Several chroniclers make passing reference to Apurima's elaborate shrine when commenting on the spectacular suicide of her priestess, Sarpay (Asarpay). Sarpay, an Inca noblewoman, took her life by jumping into the Apurima River (now, Apurimac) from the heights where her temple was constructed. She preferred to return to her river-goddess, it was said, than witness the shrine's desecration by the advancing Spanish army (Cobo 1964, II:198; P. Pizarro 1968:491-92).

Pachamama (or an equivalent) was adored by men and women living in Andean *ayllus* for providing them with the earth's bounty; women felt a particularly close kinship to her since human birth was one aspect of the earthly procreation which she sponsored. The Incas also worshipped Pachamama. She was included in the Inca's formal design of their cosmos (see Earls and Silverblatt 1976b). During the major imperial festivals celebrated monthly in Cuzco, an image of the Pachamama joined those of Viracocha, Sun, Thunder, and Moon in the capital's large public square. There she was given offerings on a par with the other gods reverenced by Cuzqueñans (Cobo 1964, II:212; Molina 1943:44, 69).

The Incas were shrewd. Peoples in kin-based communities imaged Pachamama as the guardian of the powers of fertility which allowed them to reproduce their existence. By reverencing her, the Incas were changing the nature of her powers. *Ayllu* procreation and *ayllu* well-being, which used to be in the hands of a goddess whose source of support was localized, were now tied to the welfare of the empire's upper class. No longer a local sponsor, Pachamama had become the benefactress of the empire through her bond with the lords of Cuzco. The Incas had compromised her allegiance to kin-based communities. Although the Incas may have legitimized an aspect of community religious belief by venerating Earth Mother, that legitimization was conferred at a price. By worshipping her at festivals that representatives from conquered provinces were obliged to attend, the Incas ensured that the Pachamama's new message was not ignored.

The Incas not only appropriated Pachamama from kin-based communities, they took away her attributes and gave them to the deities and heroines of imperial Cuzco. Andean communities bestowed goddesses like Pachamama and her daughter, Saramama, with powers to generate corn. The Incas proselytized a different version. According to royal legend, an

49

Inca queen, Mama Huaco, introduced the sowing of corn to the Andes when she planted fields in the Cuzco Valley (Molina 1943:67; Hernández Príncipe 1923:53). In honor of Mama Huaco's contribution to humanity, the Inca nobility reaped her field first during Cuzco's ritualized harvest ceremonies:

> . . . and those who had been initiated into the Inca nobility went to the field of Sausiro, to bring in the corn that had been gathered there, which is under the arch where it is said that Mama Huaco, the sister of Manco Capac, the first Inca, sowed the first corn [Molina 1943:67].

By overlaying legends of origin with Cuzqueñan divinities, the Incas were divesting local goddesses of their powers to generate Andean existence. By extension, *ayllus* themselves were symbolically shorn of their ability to autonomously reproduce their existence. Inca conquest, of course, made Inca ideology a political reality. But Inca wisdom was on shaky grounds, as some conquered communities refused to accept either that reality or its ideological justification.

The Moon, as supreme goddess of the Incas, reigned over all other female divinities. Taking away some of Pachamama's luster, Cuzqueñans claimed that the Moon was the ultimate controlling force over everything female and all things concerning women. Andean commoners invested Pachamama with powers of fertility, yet the Incas insisted that the Moon dominated all earthly procreation. The Moon even controlled the tools of female labor. Women feared that their spindles and looms would turn into vipers, bears, and tigers when the Moon's integrity was threatened by an eclipse (Montesinos 1957:48-49).

The Incas pushed the Moon onto the belief systems of subjugated groups.[5] There she dominated community goddesses

---

[5] It is often difficult to assess the impact of the Inca conquest on the belief systems of conquered peoples, and the colonial accounts of lunar cults might reflect pre-Inca worship of this deity. However, when the same community, as is the case below, has a non-Inca origin myth as well as a Cuzqueñan version, the Inca imposition of a lunar cult seems all the more probable.

as she assumed their reproductive powers. Peoples from Peru's north-central sierra gave voice to an imposed belief in Cuzco's preeminent deities. Several extirpators of idolatry (the few who were sensitive to the gender dualism that structured Andean religious thought) interrogated natives about their beliefs in the Moon: ". . . and he was asked if the Moon was adored as the wife of the Sun, who created women and the Saramamas and coca" (Duviols 1971:377). Hacas Poma responded to a similar question:

. . . all men adored the Sun for having created them, because it was a tradition of their ancestors that the Sun created men to his east, in Titicaca . . . and women were ordered to adore the Moon as the mother and creator of women, who watches over food and gives them clothing [AAL:Leg. 6, Exp. XI, f. 14].

The Moon, the creator of women—who counters the Sun, who created men—had stolen many of the Pachamama's powers. An Incanized version of creation transforms Saramama into a lunar appendage along with food production in general.

In the post-Inca Andes, many women turned to the Moon for help at childbirth, when they appealed to her for a good delivery and healthy offspring (Polo 1916:38). When women were in labor, noted the Jesuit Arriaga, they made sacrifices to "the *conopa* that the woman calls her own." "In some places," he continues, "they invoke the Moon" (1968:52). The Moon also began to preside over weaving, a task that defined womanhood throughout the Andes. Women, living in subjugated enclaves, were becoming convinced of the Moon's generative powers and of her dominion over their sex.

One of the ways, then, that the Incas tried to articulate the religious hierarchies which they dominated was by grafting divinities of imperial origin onto local religious structures. To have local groups claim Inca gods and goddesses as divine ancestors or as the source of their material well-being would be an ideological victory; the subjugated envisage their history and their welfare in terms of a shared ancestry with those who conquered them. The Incas accomplished this aim through various strategies, all of which were aimed at undermining the purported powers of the *ayllu*'s sacred beings. The villagers of Coscaya worshipped Mamayutas for providing them with corn and other Andean foods; these same villagers, however, were beginning to doubt Mamayuta's sovereignty. After all, was it not true that powers to create corn originated with the Moon (AAL:Leg. 6, Exp. XI, f. 14; BN:B1715)? The Incas reinforced their doubts. From Cuzco they sent prized ears of corn, which were to be worshipped alongside Coscaya's native Corn Mother. Catalina Marmita, who received the offerings women made to this divine ancestor, instructed them to adore Inca maize as well.

So the Incas sent goddesses to the provinces. Villagers of San Gerónimo de Copa worshipped the goddess Coya Guarmi (Queen Woman), known to the Copeñans as their "Mother from Cuzco" (Mama de Cuzco) (AAL:Leg. 4, Exp. s.n.). Of obvious imperial origin, Coya Guarmi took on the powers of local goddesses: she was the divine source of agricultural generation and household productivity. Coya Guarmi carried two *conopas* of chili pepper (*aji*) with her from Cuzco, and these were revered for their powers to generate the prized condiment. Coya Guarmi's native "sister" in the village of Copa was the sponsor of *chicha* (corn beer), Aca Guarmi (Chicha Woman). When these two were brought together during house-roofing ceremonies—"were made sisters," in the words of an accused idol-worshipper (AAL:Leg. 4, Exp. s.n., f. 39)—the well-being and fertility of household endeavors was ensured. Coya Guarmi also found a brother/husband, who had been renowned as a local hero, in her adopted village. Copeñans considered themselves to be their descendants.

According to village lore, Mama de Cuzco arrived at San Gerónimo de Copa accompanied by her two *conopas* of chili pepper. Once in Copa, she found family in the protector of *chicha* as well as a husband with whom she engendered the village's mortal ancestors. The Incas' world view was beginning to master the ways in which Copeñans understood their daily experiences.

Earthly power relations were woven into the imperial hierarchy of goddesses dominated by the Moon. Like the Moon, the earthly queen was called Coya (Valera 1950:136). The sacred queen was the mother of the mortal one. Thus the Inca queen had a divine edge over all other women—a cosmic superiority that matched the rights and privileges of class. The Inca vision of the cosmos recognized that not all mortal women were the same. These social inequalities of class formed the basis of a hierarchical religious structure through which the queen and other women from the Inca nobility wielded their power.

The Inca vision of the nature of the world explicitly intertwined divine hierarchy and political hierarchy. Dividing the universe into spheres of gender, the Incas remained faithful to Andean conceptions of the cosmos while incorporating the realities of class. Imperial politics transformed the nature of the gender-specific organizations that characterized religious life in the *ayllu*. Now the queen, standing at the pinnacle of imperial structures governing women, dominated women's religious activities. After the Inca conquest of the Andes, the traditional separation of religious experience along gender lines—ritually displayed by the worship of female deities and ancestors by women and male deities and ancestors by men—embodied the class character of an imperial society.

What do the chroniclers have to say about the women's organizations of the empire? Not accustomed to a split of religious activity into gender-halfs, nor expecting to find women officiating during sacred ceremonies, nor searching out women as informants, Spanish monographs of Inca life do not abound with accounts of women serving as priestesses in imperial religion. Like their colonial counterparts, today's reconstructors of Inca history have tended to ignore religious activities controlled by women. Yet these organizations were important means by which the Incas, transforming kin-based gender ideologies, extended their rule over conquered peoples.

53

In any case, however scanty the information that chroniclers have left us, it does confirm that the Coya presided over women's religious organizations in which women, priestesses, celebrated the empire's female deities.

Inca ideologies of gender parallelism place the royal daughter of the Moon at the head of all the empire's women, in counterpoint to the Inca, who as the Sun's son, presides over the empire's men. Guaman Poma, in his account of the relation between the empire's nobility and the supreme gods of Cuzco, describes their sacred tie and the religious practice which affirmed it in precisely these terms:

> During the offerings that were made at the rising of the sun, ... [when] the sun's rays penetrated the windows [of Coricancha], lighting up the entire temple ... the Inca would position himself in the middle, kneeling, directing his hands and face toward the sun or the image of the Sun, and he would pray, receiving a response from the devils or *huacas* regarding the different requests he made when saying these prayers. Behind him, his sorcerer–high priests, Uallaviza and Condeviza, executed the same ceremonies; and at the same time ... the principal lords who were present prayed, adoring the Sun. ...
>
> The Incas had another shrine where offerings were made to the Moon, called *Pumap chupan* ... where sacrifices were made in honor of the Moon, the god of women. And the Coya entered this shrine to render offerings accompanied by her sorceresses, just as the Inca; and praying, she would request what she desired [1956, I:185, 187, I:f. 432].

The Coya, as daughter of the Moon and representative of all womankind, enjoyed the same relation to her divine mother that the Inca had with his father the Sun. Like gendered mirrors, the Inca worshipped the Sun assisted by the male high priests of the empire, as the Coya prayed to the Moon, accompanied by her "sorceresses," or select priestesses. The Coya, then, as the leader of all women, gave reverence to the mother of all women, aided by female ministers who officiated in the lunar cult. The queen, with her "sorceresses," asked for divine help to ensure the continued well-being of those whom she represented. Guaman Poma himself draws the comparison between the queen, who on behalf of women intercedes with the consecrated source of female powers, and the Inca, who mediates for the empire's men. He equates them as delegates of womankind and mankind to the deities of like gender in the imperial cosmos.

Other accounts that describe women officiating in imperial ceremonies point to their special role in religious festivities honoring the goddess of all women. These narratives make it clear that women were priests of the empire's cult to the Moon. Molina's portrayal of the Inca festival of *Capac raymi* includes the following passage:

> They also took out an image of a woman, which was the *huaca* of the Moon, which was called Pacsamama [Moon Mother]. Women were entrusted with this image, and consequently when it was taken out of the house of the Sun, which is where they had her shrine, women carried [the image] on their shoulders. The reason why women were responsible for it was because they said it was a woman, which is what the statue resembled [1943:49].

Echoing Molina, Cobo is even more explicit:

> They imagined that the Moon took the form of a woman, and thus her statue, which was in the Temple of the Sun, had that form; it was entrusted to women who exercised the office of priestesses; and when it was taken out, these same women carried it on their shoulders [1964, II:159].

In addition to the shrine in Cuzco, an important temple to the lunar goddess was constructed on Coatí (or Coata), the Island of the Moon in Lake Titicaca. Here, too, a woman was the principal officiant of the Moon, whose powers she was said to embody:

> [After having constructed the Temple to the Sun on another island in Lake Titicaca . . . the Incas] judging that they

would not have completely satisfied their obligation . . . if they did not designate a woman for him . . . found a good place to realize their aim which was the Island of Coata or Coyata, a name derived from Coya; and there they built a sumptuous temple where they placed a statue of a woman . . . which represented the Moon. . . .

The priests and ministers of this shrine [of the Sun] and that of Coata communicated greatly with each other . . . and there were frequent missions from one island to the other . . . the ministers of both shrines pretending that the wife of the Sun, . . . the Moon, sent him messages which the Sun returned with caresses of tender affection and reciprocal love . . . and in order actually to represent this, in the one shrine the principal male minister represented the personage of the Sun, and in the other the woman represented the personage of the Moon [Cobo 1964, II:193].

Religious cults were integrated with the politics of the empire through the worship of the mummies of the kings and queens of Cuzco. The Incas deemed the adoration of their ancestors to be a criterion for the successful maintenance of the empire (see Conrad and Demarest 1983); imperial ideology declared that imperial ancestor worship was necessary for the well-being of all the Andean peoples. Chroniclers highlighted ancestral cults of the Inca kings. However, with analytical hindsight making us aware that the Incas explained the functioning of universe and society in terms of parallel hierarchies of gender—coupled with our knowledge that parallel rites structured imperial religious organization—the relatively scarce mention of royal ancestral cults to Inca queens takes on new weight.

Although sparse, these references show that cults to ancestor-heroines girded imperial politics and religion. In the eyes of the Cuzco elite, women, led by mortal queens, made an indispensable contribution to the sustenance of the Andean world by reverencing the empire's deceased *coyas*.

Molina, more than any other chronicler, documents the ritual importance of the empire's ancestral queens during the principal festivals held by the Cuzco elite. Processions of the mummies of *coyas*, along with those of the Inca kings taken from the Temple of the Sun, were essential to imperial ritual; and both sets of ancestors were placed in positions of honor in Cuzco's public square (Molina 1943:32, 56).

The Andean field where Mama Huaco supposedly sowed the first seed of corn was earmarked to ensure her continued veneration (Molina 1943:67). The lands of legendary heroine-ancestors, like those of king-heroes, stayed on in the service of their imperial possessors. In his discussion of the sumptuous ceremonies involved in the burial of Mama Ocllo, Cieza suggests that, as with Inca kings, the lands and treasures of the living *coyas* remained intact after their deaths to support ancestral cults devoted to them (Cieza 1959:247; cf. Guaman Poma 1956, I:98). How else to explain what Estete saw when he entered Cuzco for the first time?

> We found in certain temples on the outskirts of the city, many life-sized statues and figures of gold and silver, all cast in the form of a woman. . . . [O]f these there were more than twenty statues of gold and silver, [and] these must have been made in the likeness of noblewomen, now dead, because each one of them had in its service pages and ladies-in-waiting, as if they had been alive; and they served [the statues] . . . with such obedience and respect, as if they were really alive, and cooked for them in such elaborate fashion, as if, in effect, they were going to eat [1968:393].

Estete was not the only conquistador who was overwhelmed by the golden images of the empire's "great ladies." The secretary of Pizarro's expedition party, Sancho de la Hoz, gives a similar account in his list of objects that were melted and sent to Spanish coffers:

> . . . and ten or twelve statues of women, the same size as the women of that land, all made of fine gold, so beautiful and well made they looked as if they were alive. These were

highly venerated, as if they were the mistresses of all the world and alive; and they were dressed in beautiful and fine clothing, and they were adored as gods; and they were fed and spoken to as if they were women in the flesh. All these [statues] were entered in the royal tax of His Majesty. In addition, there was another one of silver, of the same size [1968:320].

These "mistresses" might preside over "all the world," but their place in the imperial cosmological scheme of things tied them to sacred beings of like gender. Garcilaso's description of the chapel devoted to the Moon, located in the Temple of the Sun, makes evident that the worship of Inca male and female ancestors followed ideologies of gender parallelism:

The first of these rooms [next to the main shrine of the Sun] was dedicated to the Moon, the bride of the Sun, and for this reason, it was nearest to the main building. It was completely paneled with silver, and a likeness of the Moon, with the face of a woman, decorated it [this room] in the same way that the Sun decorated the larger building. . . . They called her Mamaquilla, which means our mother the Moon. The bodies of queens were laid away in this Temple, just as those of the kings were kept in the other [1961:116].

The rulers of the Andes structured cults to their ancestors along lines of gender parallelism, while their generational proximity to the preeminent gods and goddesses of the Andes blessed their "civilizing" mission. The spatial disposition of the Inca royalty in death gave concrete form to this vision.

Inca politics and Inca religion were further intermeshed through gender-linked ancestor cults. We have already explored how the Incas tried to impose their vision of the world on the peoples they conquered, by manipulating the meanings attributed to imperial goddesses as well as the ritual structures that gave them expression. We will now want to sharpen our sights on the webs of power in which noblewomen strung their peasant counterparts.

Although both Guaman Poma and Murúa speak of the "jurisdictions" of Inca noblewomen, they unfortunately do not provide much detail about what their spheres of authority might have been (Guaman Poma 1956, I:90-105; Murúa 1946:267). But they do offer some clues. Like the Inca who had to demonstrate his ability to rule as a precondition for selection, the woman who ultimately was to become queen had to prove herself capable of leadership and responsibility. Rights to the office of Inca were not inherited. The man who wore the *mascaypacha*, or royal insignia, had to prove himself the most able from a pool of noble contenders. This selection process was often phrased in terms of the Sun's designation of the Inca ruler out of a group of claimants to the title (Guaman Poma 1956, I:219). The Coya was "chosen" in a similar manner. When one Inca, Capac Yupanqui, married a woman who later became insane, he asked the Sun's permission to wed someone else who would be truly capable of helping him govern (Guaman Poma 1956, I:75, 95, 219).

According to Murúa, when Inca kings had to leave the capital in order to lead their armies in battle, queens ruled in their absence (1946:97, 99). This chronicler, more attuned than most to the women of the Inca nobility, provided another indication of the Coya's role in the government of the empire. If the Inca's privy council, composed of delegates from the empire's four provincial subdivisions, could not reach an accord, the matter was turned over to the queen (Murúa 1946:352). Three *coyas* in particular, Mama Huaco, Mama Ocllo, and Mama Anahuarque, were described as having important powers, advising their husbands as well as their sons in the affairs of government (Cieza 1959:247; Cobo 1964, II:67, 87; Guaman Poma 1956, I:90).[6]

---

[6] Interestingly, these three *coyas* were the wives of those Inca kings (Manco Capac, Topa Inca, and Pachacuti) who had preeminence in the structural construction of social history by which the Incas interpreted their past. That these three *coyas* were singled out by the chroniclers, in their occidental and chronological rendition of Inca history, as having significant roles in government might relate to the dictates of the Inca model of parallelism, whereby these

59

Nevertheless, the Coya is most commonly referred to as the "queen of woman," which suggests that her authority centered on jurisdiction over the empire's female constituency. As official ruler of all of her gender, the queen commanded the respect of women from the Cuzco nobility as well as from the provinces (Murúa 1946:235). During imperial festivals, the parallel structure of authority was ritually expressed by men honoring and kissing the hand of the Inca, while women paid obeisance to and kissed the hand of the Coya (Valera 1950:172).

One way the Cuzco elite could construct and cement power relations was through the exchange of women; for, as the emblem of male imperial force, the Inca enjoyed the prerogative to distribute non-Inca women in marriage (see Chapter V, below). Yet Murúa challenges any assumption that this was exclusively a male prerogative. He reports that the queen also had the authority and responsibility to marry her female subjects to the appropriate men of the empire:

> The palace of the queen was located in this enormous construction, and it was almost as large as the Inca's; and since she held a preeminent office, she went about dressed with ornaments of *cumbi* [finely woven cloth] which represented the position she held in the palace. She had shrines, baths, and gardens, both for herself and for her *ñustas*, who were like ladies-in-waiting, of which there were more than two hundred. She was responsible for marrying them to lords who achieved honorable offices under the Inca. It was truly marvelous when the great queen walked about; she was served, in every way, with the majesty shown toward the Inca [1946:181].

In its portrayal of the sumptuary privileges to which the queen was entitled, this passage suggests how the Coya wielded

---

women would be given structural equivalence to their king-husbands.

María Rostworowski de Diez Canseco (1983) discusses the employ of dualism in Andean political structures.

power over other women. The queen, like the Inca, was at the apex of a power structure that was expressed in terms of control over women's marriage rights.

The Incas set the imperial wheels of asymmetric obligation in motion by generous giveaways. Clinging to norms of generosity in order to hide relations of class exploitation behind a cloak of chiefly prerogative, the lords of Cuzco nudged those subjugated by them into the Inca-dominated networks of power. The *coyas* enjoyed the fruits of a productive base reserved for their use, which gave them the means to live lavishly and throw huge feasts—the hallmark of chiefly generosity (Murúa 1946:85, 87, 90, 94; Cieza 1959:240; Guaman Poma 1956, I:91, 104; Rostworowski 1962:135-37, 141-59; Villanueva 1970:21, 35-37, 39, 46-47, 51-52).

Moreover, provincial leaders and lower-ranking members of the Cuzco nobility also gave the queen gifts (Guaman Poma 1956, I:247). Both the receipt of gifts from social inferiors and the ability to reciprocate with sumptuous feasts, which openly displayed who was beholden to whom, indicate that the queen—independently of the Inca—was able to bind others into a web of obligation through which power relations were articulated.

We are faced with a difficult question: what kinds of links were forged by queens, and with whom? Did *coyas* use their generosity to create alliances with other noblewomen as well as with women of privileged groups in the provinces? Unfortunately, we have little direct evidence of what queens actually did with their wealth. Murúa, however, does document the queen's generosity toward her female subjects and ladies-in-waiting, many of whom were women of the Cuzco nobility and daughters of provincial *curacas* (1946:85, 87, 90, 94, 95). Was this display of largesse the sugar coating around a female structure of imperial politics?

Guaman Poma gives us a glimpse into a gender-linked chain of authority realized through obligations that the queen's largesse would have created. One of the few chroniclers of Quechua origin to write about pre-Columbian Andean society,

61

Guaman Poma often manifests a particularly Andean (as opposed to Spanish) perception of the universe (see Ossio 1973:153-216; Wachtel 1973:163-228). We should recall that he was the chronicler whose drawings of Andean social life and ritual were characterized by parallel structures; see Figures 2-4. Because his world view was flavored by native concepts, Guaman Poma's presentation of the hierarchy of power that governed the empire becomes particularly illuminating. Unlike other commentators on Andean life, when Guaman Poma describes political hierarchies, he offers parallel lists of political ranks occupied by men or women. In other words, his description of the political organization of Inca society divides men and women into two parallel hierarchies internally ranked by criteria of social status and birth (1956, I:9, 105, 123, 127, 135, II:66, 69, 92, III:11, 22-24, 46, 153, 250). The chain of power extends from the Inca and Coya to the nobility of Cuzco, to the non-Inca Cuzco nobility, to several ranks of provincial nobility, to local ethnic leaders, and finally ends with commoners who have positions of authority within the *ayllu*. According to Guaman Poma's delineation (1956, II:69, III:104, 146), the same organization of ranks existed for women as for men. Furthermore, he stresses that women and men alike were entitled to varying degrees of services, lands, and herds in accord with their status in Inca society. Guaman Poma's rendering of the organization of imperial power relations points to parallel gender-hierarchies of rank—extending from the Inca and Coya to local community leaders—as structuring the empire's politics.

Children of *curacas* were brought into the center of imperial power through the royal schools established in Cuzco for the sons of the Inca nobility and provincial headmen (Garcilaso 1961:144, 245; Murúa 1946:148, 166, 169). In these schools, young men were indoctrinated into the ideology of the empire, learning Inca history and philosophy, military skills, and techniques of government. Part of the training entailed a period of apprenticeship—or servitude—to the Inca or other men of the royal dynasty. The goal of this training was to prepare the elite for future roles in the empire's political apparatus and to create a loyal succeeding generation of provincial leaders. No *curaca* could take office without being previously schooled in Cuzco and approved by the Inca elite (Ortiz de Zúñiga 1967, I:24, 26).

Parallel institutions were established for women, although they were not recognized or designated as such by the chroniclers. Sons of local headmen were instructed in Inca lore and management through a period of apprenticeship to Cuzco noblemen; so were their daughters. The queen, and women of the Inca aristocracy as well, were surrounded by, and had authority over, young women of the Cuzco nobility and daughters of local leaders (Cobo 1964, II:141; Guaman Poma 1956, I:94; Murúa 1946:81, 85, 93, 181). These young women were learning appropriate skills and tasks of government, following the same training process as their male counterparts. In other words, service owed to female members of the royal dynasty incorporated women of varying social ranks in the empire into a structure of authority headed by the Coya. Bonds of allegiance and obligation were thus forged between women: between women of different ranks within the Inca nobility, and between them and women from the provinces who, as daughters of local leaders, would impose their newly acquired pro-Cuzco sentiments on women of the peasantry.

There is a myth in the corpus of Inca historical legend which teaches that Andean channels of authority should follow gender lines. This legend tells of the Inca conquest of the Guarco *ayllu*, which was under the jurisdiction of a woman:

Topa Inca, accompanied by lords and men of war left Cuzco ... taking with him the Coya, who enjoyed viewing her kingdom in the company of her husband. When the Inca inspector, Apu Achache [the brother of the Inca], arrived in Guarco, the ruler of the tribe, who was a widow, began to impede him from taking a census of his vassals, saying that she would not allow the Inca to rule over her dominion. Upon hearing the news, the Inca laughed and said that he

63

was being hounded by women. The Coya asked him, "What women?"; and he responded, "You and that widow, for if it were not for you, I would easily stop her from making such problems." The queen then asked the Inca to give her permission; for she proposed to subjugate that woman without costing the life of one soldier. . . . The queen took on the responsibility, and she dispatched the royal inspector . . . ordering him to tell the *cacica* that he had the Inca's and Coya's promise that they wanted to reserve the entire province for her, and that she should prepare a solemn festival for them in the sea. The widow, believing that this information was true, conceded what was asked, and she ordered all the inhabitants of the village to go out to sea on their rafts to celebrate on the specific day that was stipulated by the inspector. And once [the villagers were] in the ocean, two Inca captains entered the village and took it over; when the *cacica* and her vassals saw that from the sea, they had no alternative but to acknowledge defeat. The captains captured the *cacica* and took her to the Coya, in order to present her to the queen [Cobo 1964, II:87].

According to legend, the king would not be the appropriate conqueror of this female ruler who refused to acquiesce in the power of Cuzco: the Coya insisted on undertaking her submission. By means of a clever ruse, the queen conquered the rebellious province without bloodshed. Note, too, that when the *cacica* surrendered to the Incas, she offered homage to the Coya and not to Topa Inca. Mythically sanctioned relations of authority observed the Andean preference for gender segregation.

Relations of authority—the intricacies of allegiance and obligation that wove together the queen, provincial headwomen, and peasant women in a hierarchy of power—were consecrated in the Inca Andes. After all, the queen was the daughter of the Moon: any relation she entered into was imbued with the force of imperial religion. Like imperial politics, imperial religion was evangelistic. The Incas sent their goddesses to the provinces, and provincials proved their loyalty by organizing structures of worship around them. Peasant women established cults to Guarmi Paso (Woman Moon), and the cults drew these segments of Andean women into the queen's hierarchy of power. An extirpator of idolatry discovered them in villages of the Jauja Valley.

> . . . and [while I] was engaged in the religious instruction of Mito, I put under guard several Indian women, idolators, having discovered an idol which they call Guarmi Paso, who is adored by many Indian women from these villages [Duviols 1971:367].

The cult of Guarmi Paso did not stop at community boundaries. The loyalties made concrete in her adoration cast aside *ayllu* frontiers for imperial allegiance.

For one month out of the empire's twelve-month year, the queen ritually celebrated the power hierarchy she dominated. All the empire deferred to her and her divine mother during *Coya raymi*, the official imperial festival honoring simultaneously the Moon and the queen. *Coya raymi*, which coincided with the September equinox, marked the beginning of both the new agricultural cycle and the rainy season. It was a time when female concerns, as Andean society so defined them, were given voice. Inca ideology bestowed Inca goddesses with controlling powers over earthly fertility and human generation; so now the empire's queen and noblewomen, worshipping the empire's preeminent goddess, ritually took on the concerns of all Andean womanhood. Hierarchy was made clear.

Coya raymi was also a time when women, through their ritual organizations, displayed their strength. It was women who hosted the month's celebrations, to which they invited men:

> The Incas made sacrifices in the month of *Capac Inti raymi* [festival to the Lord Sun]; their wives and the queen, in the festival of *Quilla* [Moon] *raymi* [Guaman Poma 1956, I:187].

65

> *Coya raymi*, ... a grand festival, was celebrated to the Moon, queen of all the planets and stars of the sky, wife and mistress of the Sun; all the women took part in the celebrations and festivals that were held during the month, especially the queens, princesses, noblewomen, and other principal and noted women who were obliged to invite men to these festivals [Guaman Poma 1956, I:176].

Noblewomen rejoiced during *Coya raymi*: it was their time to host others, their time to display the power they could wield. But *Coya raymi* also pointed to the limits of that power.

Imperial ideology was ever attempting to mask hierarchies of class and of gender. Structures of gender parallelism appeared to be structures of gender equality. The royal wedding ceremony is a case in point. During this festival, the equality of queen and king and their purported joint rule over the Andes were ritually unfolded. The king presented the Coya with a gift of cloth, saying: "Just as you will be mistress over this piece of clothing, in like fashion you will be mistress over all the rest, as I am" (Murúa 1946:235).

But the queen was not the "mistress over all the rest." She may have lived sumptuously. She may have enjoyed independent rights to imperial wealth. But her rights, like those of other women, were increasingly constrained as the building of Andean empire was indebted to and paid homage to the accomplishments of men. *Coya raymi* made women's strengths manifest, but *Coya raymi* took place only once a year.

CHAPTER IV

Ideologies of Conquest in the *Ayllu*

> Although they all have their own *huacas* . . .
> they all hold the Rayo to be their principal *hu-
> aca*, to whom they dedicate all their fetuses pro-
> duced by miscarriage, breech-births, and those
> born two in one belly [twins]; they have con-
> structed shrines [with them] in the heights
> above the village. . . . They hold these [shrines]
> in high esteem and call them *conopas*, which
> means household gods.
>
> [Hernández Príncipe (1621) 1923:65]

> There were also some called "children of Thun-
> der," given birth to by women who affirmed
> they had been impregnated by Thunder and
> had then given birth. These were also marked
> out for [religious office].
>
> [Polo (1554) 1916:34]

Andean peoples ordered the world around them through
prisms of gender. Their gender ideologies, however, constructed different meanings out of distinctions of sex. If gender
parallelism played with values of equality, another gender system, the "conquest hierarchy,"[1] explicitly denied those values.

The symbolic bonding of men with conquest was deeply
embedded in Andean culture. It formed the cornerstone of a
gender ideology that held women to be inferior: the conquest
hierarchy used symbols of gender to express the relation of
conqueror to vanquished. In the *ayllu*, the conquest hierarchy
used gender as a metaphor for ranking the various descent
groups that made up a community. In the empire, the conquest

---

[1] The conquest hierarchy, as a structure of Andean organization, was first
investigated by Zuidema (1964:40-41, 168, 173; 1973; n.d.).

67

hierarchy furthered imperial politics, as noblemen's control over the disposition of women from vanquished *ayllus* was essential to the organization of the empire itself. This process of transformation, a process which generated the Inca genderization of class relations, is what we will be unraveling here.

RANKING DESCENT GROUPS

Where kinship still dominated the fabric of life, the conquest hierarchy labeled and ranked the descent groups which constituted an *ayllu*. The building blocks of this ranking structure were opposing sets of symbols: celestial forces (male/conqueror/outsider/divine) were juxtaposed with earthly forces (female/conquered/original inhabitant/divine). This symbolic duality could be extended to form a three-tiered ranking structure when "male conquerors" produced an intermediary descent group, symbolized as their children from secondary marriages with "female subjects." The conquest hierarchy, then, marked out a prestige hierarchy through which an *ayllu* ordered its constituent kin groups (see Zuidema 1964:40-41, 1973:16, n.d.:6).

Highland villagers in the Departments of Lima and Ancash phrased this classification in terms of descent from mythical ancestors. The legendary founder of a descent group known as the *llacuás (llachuás)* was said to have come from afar to conquer the original inhabitants of the region. The descendants of the first settlers were called *llactas* or *huaris (guaris)*, whose ancestors had supposedly been conquered by the *llacuases* (see Duviols 1973). *Llacuases* often claimed the god of thunder and lightning, Illapa, as kin (Hernández Príncipe 1923:26, 51); while the *llactas* adored divine relatives associated with the earth, symbolizing their local origin (Hernández Príncipe 1923:34, 37, 58, 66; Zuidema 1973:16). Whatever the particular names of community gods and goddesses, Padre Arriaga (1968:117-18) discovered these *ayllu* divisions to be common throughout the Peruvian sierra he traversed in the late sixteenth and early seventeenth centuries.[2] Here is his advice to priests sent out to eradicate idolatrous practices:

> . . . in a town in the sierra, the Indian should be asked if he is a *llacuaz* or huari, for they call huari or *llactayoc* anyone native to the town of his ancestors and who [has] no recollection of having come from outside. All whose fathers and ancestors were born elsewhere they call llacuazes, even if they themselves were born in the town. This distinction is preserved in many districts, and the llacuazes, like persons newly arrived from somewhere else, have fewer huacas. Instead, they often fervently worship and venerate their malquis which, as previously noted, are the mummies of their ancestors. They also worship *huaris*, that is, the founders of the earth or the persons to whom it first be-

[2] The particularly rich documentation of Peru's north-central Andes reveals how the conquest hierarchy was a model of social organization for many communities in that region; it thus provides a structure that helps make sense of the internal organization of *ayllus* in other parts of the Andes for which our evidence is not so plentiful. The *ayllus* in the colonial *reducción* (forced settlement) of Sarhua, in the Department of Ayacucho, for example, distinguished themselves on the basis of an "outsider"/"original inhabitant" opposition, even though they did not use the same northern terms *"llacuás"/"llacta"* to denote these differences in rank (Earls and Silverblatt 1978a). Twentieth-century Sarhuinos still use the criterion of "outsider"/"original inhabitant" to classify the two major *ayllus* that compose the community. Those who claim that their ancestors came from outside the village to live in Sarhua worship a male saint, John the Baptist, as their patron; whereas the *ayllu* which asserts that their progenitors were the village's original inhabitants adores the female Virgin of the Assumption. These manuscripts from the north-central Andes detail the structures witnessed by Spanish clerics in the late sixteenth and early seventeenth centuries. Nevertheless, we can assume that these structures reflected those which existed before the Cuzco expansion, since the Inca conquest left internal *ayllu* organization relatively undisturbed. Zuidema, who analyzed the ancestor cults that structured the seventeenth-century Ancash village of Allauca, explained how the *llacta/llacuás* division was extended to form a three-tiered ranking system. In this village, the ancestors of the *llacuases* were called *huacas*, while those of the *llactas* were designated *mallquis*; an intermediary group, descendants of the exogamic union of these ancestors, called their progenitors *huacas/mallquis* (1973:23).

longed and who were its first populators. These have many huacas and they tell fables about them. . . . For these and other reasons, there are generally divisions and enmities between the clans and factions [1968:117-18].

Llacta descent groups throughout the north-central Andes adored Huari (Guari) hero-divinities as the "first dwellers in the land" (Arriaga 1968:23) or as "the first founders of this territory" (Hernández Príncipe 1923:27). These "native" gods also bestowed gifts of agriculture to their descendents and were worshipped for their role in organizing cultivation and instituting agricultural practices and techniques. The accused idolators of Pimachi explained their devotion in this way:

. . . [they] adored and rendered cult to the god Guari . . . and before cleaning the irrigation canals, they made offerings for water and health and plentiful corn . . . and when the Indians lived without a king or anyone to order them . . . and when there was warfare between them over land to cultivate, [Guari] appeared to them and he plowed all the fields and he distributed irrigation canals to all the kin groups, so that they no longer killed each other. . . . [A]nd the Guaris, who were giants, . . . plowed and made the furrows in the fields and made the irrigation canals [Duviols 1971:369, 374].

Huaris were culture heroes who created order not only by harmoniously distributing resources, but by teaching humankind how to make better use of land and water. Andean cosmology linked them to agricultural production, fertility, and the generative forces of the earth.

The descriptions of Huari which the Spanish have left us do not present a clear picture of this deity's gender. While Huari is sometimes portrayed as hermaphroditic (Duviols 1971:374), Huari is female when contrasted as an ancestor of the descent group of "original inhabitants" to the "conqueror progenitors" of the *llacuás*.[3] For this reason, the Huari-ances-

[3] This is another example of the relativistic and contextually determined na-

tor of the *llactas* in Allauca was said to have been a goddess who had sexual relations with a descendant of the conqueror-Illapa, Apo Ingacha. The progenitress, known as Huari Carhua, was born in a lake, revealing her bonds with the mother of all waters (Hernández Príncipe 1923:37). Further, one of the renowned female ministers of Allauca, accused by Hernández Príncipe of idol worshipping, took the name of that goddess-heroine as her own (1923:37).

Andean thought gave meaning to the symbolic matrix of "femaleness," agricultural fertility, and a community's original inhabitants by contrasting it with the symbolic matrix of conquest. Projected onto internal *ayllu* organization, *llactas* were continuously counterposed to the *llacuases*. As Hernández Príncipe noted of one Ancash village whose inhabitants he interrogated:

> In this town, like the rest . . . the *ayllus* of the *llactas* and the *llachuases* are mixed together and are in conflict or in opposition; the *llachuases* say they are children of the Rayo [lightning] and Trueno [thunder], and they adore them [1923:51].

The *llacuases*, as opposed to the *llactas*, traced their origin to the god of thunder and lightning. Rayo (Spanish for Illapa) or his sons, who were also founders of *llacuás ayllus*, were said to come from afar, sometimes from Lake Titicaca. According to some legends, they were heroes of the *puna* and herding, which further distinguished them from their cultivation-oriented *llacta* counterparts (Hernández Príncipe 1923:26, 27). The *llacuases* were identified as conquerors, being the "sons" (*churi* = son, male speaker) of a masculine divinity who embodied the concept of conquest (Duviols 1971:375; Hernández Príncipe 1923:26-27). One *llacuás* descendant from the village of Allauca responded to his inquisitor:

---

ture of Andean thought. As an androgynous being, Huari possibly symbolized the interrelation of male and female forces necessary for generation and fertility.

... [he heard from his ancestors that] the *llaguazes* [*lla-cuases*] lived in the *punas* and that they came from Titicaca, and they are the sons of the Rayo and in the *puna* they sustained themselves with meat from guanacos, llamas, [and] *tarucas* [deer]; and the *guaris*, seeing that the *llaguazes* were coming, went out with drums and their ancient dances ... and (illegible) ... that they would live together for which reason they are called sons of the Rayo because they said that he had reared them [Duviols 1971:375].

The blocks of metaphor on which the conquest hierarchy rested constituted a scale of social ranking against which community kin groups were measured. In *ayllu* social structure, the conquest hierarchy was a prestige hierarchy. It functioned to order and to classify. Higher-ranking descent groups enjoyed prerogatives of status: preferred positions in ceremony, ritual deference, representation as "first among equals." Although conquest figured strongly in many *ayllus'* myths of their past, the *ayllus* that had been subjugated in legend did not comprise a conquered class, in the sense of losing control over their means of production; nor were they dominated by force (see Spalding 1967:140). Within the frame of local political organization, the "conquering" *ayllu* was not entitled to any prerogatives, by virtue of its status, over the labor or productive resources of a *llacta ayllu*. After all, the ties that bound them together were still those of kin (Spalding 1967:11-14).[4]

[4] These conclusions are supported by Karen Spalding's research in Huarochirí (1967, 1984), where there also existed abundant myths of "conqueror" *ayllus* (Ávila 1966:77-84). Again, I am presenting a generalized model of pre-Inca social structure. Some *ayllus* at the time of the Inca conquest (e.g. Chimu) were organized as states and consequently were structured by social class. In these cases, the "conquering" group did have prerogatives over the productive resources and means of production of those they conquered. More to the point, however, I hold deep reservations about the possibility of reconstructing a history of local conquest on the basis of these myths and legends of origin. Some historians (e.g. Duviols 1973), who have interpreted these myths literally, claim that they refer to actual events of the Wari Empire (circa 800) and the subsequent Late Intermediate Period, which was marked by inter-*ayllu* hostilities and conflict. I argue that the conquest hierarchy is better understood

The god of the "conquerors" was privileged to stand for the community as a whole. Part of the advantage his descendants enjoyed was rooted in their kinship to the god of lightning or his progeny. All the villagers of Recuay, including the "conquered," paid homage to Rayo as their most important divinity. The preeminence of the god of the "conquerors" was made visible through the community's ritual practice: *llactas*, whose principal ancestor-*huacas* were of local origin, as well as *llacuases* built household altars to him (Hernández Príncipe 1923:26, 27). Hernández Príncipe relates:

> Although they all have their own *huacas* . . . they all hold the Rayo to be their principal *huaca*, to whom they dedicate all their fetuses produced by miscarriage, breech-births, and those born two in one belly [twins]; they have constructed shrines [with them] in the heights above the village. . . . They hold these [shrines] in high esteem, and call them *conopas*, which means household gods [1923:65].

When the *llactas* and *llacuases* of the northern sierra ritually affirmed their friendship and alliance, they made joint sacrifices to the god of lightning, the emblem of their unity (Hernández Príncipe 1923:27). As privileged descendants of Rayo, "conquerors" could ritually stand for their community as a whole. As we will see, conditions of empire translated this prerogative of status into a prerogative of power.

Let us look more closely at the gender attributes entailed in

as a model of the internal organization of *ayllus*, a code through which various descent groups that constituted a larger political entity were differentiated and ranked. This is not to deny that the history of the Andes prior to the Inca conquest was riddled by conflict and intergroup warfare. I simply am not convinced that we can know or reconstruct that history on the basis of these myths. Three hundred years after these feats of conquest supposedly took place, three separate *ayllus* that had been forced to resettle together in the *reducción* of Ocros consciously organized a new relationship between themselves—using the conquest hierarchy as a model (Hernández Príncipe 1923:51-58).

the conquest hierarchy, for they too will critically shape imperial policy. "Conquerors" were conceptualized as male. Further, only men as "conquerors" could enter into secondary marriages with "conquered" women and thus be founders of intermediary descent groups. Myths of conquest collected by Father Francisco de Ávila in the villages of Huarochirí celebrate male hero-conquerors as founders of *ayllus* (Ávila 1966:77-84). One myth explicitly teaches that the logic of Andean social categories refuses women the right to be conqueror-founders of intermediate descent groups. This legend recounts the story of Llacxamisa, one of the five brothers who defeated the lowland Yuncas:

> The Yuncas lived in the fields of bushes of Concha. While they inhabited these lands, other men appeared from Yaurillancha. . . . Thus it is said that the men of Concha were born in Yaurillancha, that they were born in the number of five brothers, that they burst forth from underneath the earth. The names of these five men, beginning with the eldest, were Llacxamisa, who came with his sister, Conucuyo; then Pauquirbuxi, and then Llamantaya. The other two, Huaylla and Calla remained a bit behind. . . . [W]hen they arrived at the place where their brothers had gone, they found that the others had already distributed the land . . . and everything that was possible to distribute. . . . The Yuncas were living happily when the three brothers were born. . . . The Yuncas saw Llacxamisa with his stone cap and were frightened and thought they should leave: "If these three men catch up with us, they will kill us all." The Yuncas fled, abandoning their village and their fields. . . . One of the Yuncas took the wrong child with him and left behind his own son, Yasali, in the village. The three brothers had scarcely arrived when they began to distribute the houses and all the belongings and useful things. While looking for the fields, Llacxamisa found the boy. "My son, do not worry, you will live with me. If my brothers want to kill you, I will defend you. In exchange you will herd my llamas." . . . When Yasali, the shep-

herd, was taking care of the llamas, he met Conucuyo, Llacxamisa's sister. She came from Yaurillancha. They met and copulated. ... All of Llacxamisa's descendant's died. When he was about to die, he adopted the father of the children of Conucuyo—Yasali, him and his children [Ávila 1966:171-81].

Only men could be legitimate founders of lineages based on conquest; only men, as heads of conqueror lineages, could initiate exogamic unions with conquered peoples. Andean categories of social structure, coupled with Andean metaphor, attributed social power to men.

Creating kinship, Llacxamisa ("conqueror"), became the fictive father of a descent group in which marriage to a woman of the "conquered" was implied. Through this marriage, his adopted children and their descendants were raised to form a middle-ranking kin group. Conucuyo, Llacxamisa's sister, could not symbolically represent her "conqueror" *ayllu* entering into an exogamic union with a "conquered" people. The "conquered" had to be conceptualized as female. Consequently, in the myth, Llacxamisa became the father of Yasali, the "conquered," through an implicit marriage to a woman from the Yuncas. Only in this way could he properly establish a ranked hierarchy based on the association of men with conquest and women with the vanquished. The original relations that the myth established, defined through a female conqueror, violated the deeper Andean sense of the tie between gender imagery and power. Myth was compelled to change them.

WOMEN AND THE GOD OF CONQUEST

While the division of communities into *llacuás* and *llacta* descent groups often marked out lines of tension within Andean politics, these internal conflicts did not stem from the *llacuases'* ability to make demands on the production or resources of the *llactas*. Nor did this classification have any bearing on the actual structure of gender relations in the *ayllu*.

Membership in the "conqueror" descent group did not entitle men to control over women of the "conquered." Nevertheless, although the conquest hierarchy did not refer to relations between men and women as it defined *llacta/llacuás* divisions within the *ayllu*, it did direct relations between women and gods. Moreover, the special tie that existed between women and the god of conquest, when analyzed through the structured prism of the conquest hierarchy, projects a pattern that would later be utilized by the Inca elite in the process of empire building.

Many chroniclers and priests noted that women could be chosen to assume positions in native religious life through the ability of Rayo to impregnate them or have a special relationship with them. Illapa was said to speak to women while they were dreaming or to copulate with them when they were herding in the *puna* (Arriaga 1968:31, 168; Cobo 1964, II:226; Guaman Poma 1956, I:121; Murúa 1946:286). Polo de Ondegardo, in his reports to the viceroy, explained:

... Those who were in charge of sacrifices ... were elected in this way. If any male or female was born in the countryside when it was thundering, they were paid special attention ... and called Chuquiilla [a name for Illapa or Rayo], and when they were old they were ordered to take that post, for it was believed that any sacrifice made by their hands would be more accepted. There were also some called "children of Thunder," given birth to by women who affirmed they had been impregnated by Thunder and had then given birth. These were also marked out for [religious office]. The same for two or three born from one belly and finally all those whom nature gave more than what was normal or common (believing that this had a mysterious origin) were set aside for this [1916:34].

Cobo adds that

some women made it understood that while out in the country-side in a storm, Thunder made them pregnant, and at the end of eight months they gave birth to [stones] with great pain, and that in dreams they were told that the "fate" which they predicted with them would be certain [1964, II:226].

Thus, women who begot sacred stones or who had "extraordinary" births (twins, breech-births, harelipped children) had experienced a special tie with the supernatural and its deity of conquest. Andean culture called the products of their union "Illapa's children." The gods destined these children to become officiants in the service of native deities.

Upon giving birth to twins or other infants considered outside the norm of human procreation, the mother or sometimes both parents had to participate in elaborate rituals (Guaman Poma 1956, III:121; Hernández Príncipe 1923:53). The Spanish clerics who witnessed these rites often mistook them for rites of penance because of the fasting and abstention which was part of the ceremony. Arriaga comments:

they believe that twins are a sacrilegious and abominable thing, although they say that one of them is the son of lightning. They do penance on this account as if they had committed a terrible sin. Usually the father and mother both fast for many days, . . . eating neither salt nor pepper nor having intercourse at that time. In [other cases], both father and mother lie down on one side and remain without moving for five days. One foot is folded under them, and a lima bean . . . is placed under the knee, until with the effect of perspiration it begins to grow. For the next five days they do the same thing on the other side, all the while fasting as described. When this penance is over, the relatives go hunting for a deer, and after cutting it up they make a kind of canopy of the skin. The penitents pass beneath this with ropes around their necks, which they must wear for many days [1968:53].

Fasting and abstention from intercourse signaled all Andean religious ceremonies, including rites of passage, which were imbued with sacred meaning. Arriaga's commentary detects the ritual celebration of the change in status experienced by parents who participated in the birth of twins, Illapa's children.

Guaman Poma describes the rites he witnessed in the village of Asquem, when a woman, along with her child conceived by Rayo, were ritually celebrated by the village's inhabitants. After "penance," fasting, and a one-month period of isolation on a mountain peak away from the village, the child was sacrificed to the "Rayo Santiago."[5] Afterward, the mother was joyfully brought back to the village accompanied by music, singing, and dancing. The entire community glorified her new status during a five-day revelry (Guaman Poma 1956, III:121).

Hernández Príncipe's retelling of the ceremonies surrounding the first ritual hair cutting of one of Illapa's young daughters portrays how the station of human parents was transformed by their extraordinary alliance with the god of conquest:

> Seven or eight years ago, Don Pedro Ventura went to this site [caves where his ancestors were buried] with sorcerers[6] and his daughter, who was four or five years old, following the orders of one of his *caciques*. The mother of the girl as well as the *cacique*'s mother went along, bringing *chicha*, *cuyes* [guinea pigs] and other offerings, and with the consent of his great-great-grandfather, *cacique* Poma, he gave the girl a new name, one which he determined after having consulted the fates through spiders, saying that the parents of the girl had conceived her by virtue of Rayo, whose name he gave her as well as the parents of the girl, for being worthy of having such a child, erasing the Christian name which they had received in baptism, permitting them to be called by the aforesaid heathen name. And the sorcerer-priest offered a *patacon* [coin] so that in the same manner everyone in the village would make offerings as they did during this

---

[5] After the Spanish conquest, Rayo was syncretized with Santiago.

[6] *Hechicero* = sorcerer. This term was used by chroniclers and clerics to denote any officiant of an Andean religion.

celebration and hair-cutting ceremony . . . which they perform with a thousand heathen rites instead of our baptism.
. . . And having done this, they returned to these burial caves
from the village and offered the cut hair to the *cacique* Poma
[1923:53].

Both the young girl and her parents assume a new name,
Rayo. The rite of renaming celebrated the new, consecrated
bond of kinship which tied mortals to the divine ancestor of
the conqueror-founder of *ayllus*. Carrying his name, they were
bound to him. It was an emblem of their devotion. Other idol-
smashers noted that many officiants of the outlawed indigenous religion took on the name of the deity into whose service
they were dedicated; once aware of these idolatries, priests
prohibited Andean Indians from using the names of *huacas* or
calling themselves after the god of lightning (Arriaga 1968:31,
168, 169). The new-name ceremony held in Ocros ritually displayed the distinctive relation to the conqueror-deity which
the girl and her parents came to hold. We should note that the
child's hair and other ritual objects were offered to the *cacique*
Poma, who was, as we will see, an important *curaca* of this
ayllu and a direct descendant, through the male line, of one of
Rayo's sons who founded a *llacuás* lineage.

One way of making Andean sense out of this phenomenon
is through the prism of the conquest hierarchy. The renaming
ritual and hair-cutting ceremony dedicated to Rayo and one of
his descendants marked the formation of an intermediary status—equidistant between the human world and the supernatural world. It thus comprehended the same structural relations
as the conquest hierarchy when it distinguished a three-tiered
ranking system of social groups: the superior class (Rayo, masculine deity of conquest) has children in a subordinate class
(mortal women), and the product of their exogamic union ac-
quires a status which is halfway between these two groups
(children of Rayo)—the religious officiants and intercessors
between humankind and the supernatural.

More to the point, this aspect of the conquest hierarchy's attribution in provincial communities embraced the form through which the Inca elite took peasant women from their communities of birth and placed them under imperial jurisdiction. In the *ayllu*, women were consecrated to the service of Rayo—a masculine, nonlocal deity who was associated with conquest—by becoming his wives. By this means, women could acquire a quasi-sacred status as the mediators and intercessors between the human world and the sacred world.

Arriaga described such a "wedding":

> . . . In a town in the province of Conchucos, visited by Licentiate Juan Delgado, there was a girl about fourteen years of age, of rare beauty. For this reason her parents and the caciques dedicated her to the service of a stone huaca named Chanca, which had the face of a person. They married her to this huaca, and everyone in town celebrated her wedding. . . . They offered their sacrifices by the hand of this girl and considered it a proper and a lucky thing to do. They thought that sacrifices thus performed would be most acceptable to the huacas. The girl preserved her virginity as the other ministers had commanded her to do, for by marrying her to the huaca they had invested her with the sacred office of priestess. She was held in the greatest reverence and regarded as a divine and superior being [1968:36-37].

As we shall see, the Incas expressed the severance of women from their vanquished natal communities in terms of the special relation they would obtain with the Sun. They were now the wives of the Sun—the male deity who was the emblem of Inca conquest. As the Sun's wives, these women, too, became holy.

Transformations: The Conquest Hierarchy and Imperial Rule

> Not even the Inca paid much attention to the worship of the Moon, since women were in charge of the cult to her, as was the case regarding [the cult to] Mama Huaco . . . , and for this reason men would not have paid attention to that daughter of *cacique* Poma, Tanta Carhua, if it had not been for the fact that she was consecrated to the Sun. . . .[T]he young girl [Tanta Carhua] said, "Finish now with me, for the celebrations which were made in my honor in Cuzco were more than enough"; they then took her . . . to a high mountain, the crest and last outreach of the lands of the Inca, and having made her resting place, they lowered her into it and walled her in alive.
>
> [Hernández Príncipe (1621) 1923:53, 62]

AN ANDEAN INSTITUTION OF CONQUEST

Having rights over all the empire's women, the Inca chose some to be the Sun's wives. Inca noblemen's control over Andean women was inextricably linked to Inca control over all Andean peoples. True to the ideology of the conquest hierarchy, the Incas intertwined gender hierarchy and the formation of class as they consolidated imperial rule.

Imperial politics transformed the conquest hierarchy into an institution whose jurisdiction over the destiny of Andean women helped fulfill imperial needs. The rendering of chaste women to the Inca elite represented a glaring change in gender relations. I am talking here about the most famous of all Inca women: the *acllas* or *mamaconas*, the virginal "wives of the Sun."

No other group of women was the focus of so much recorded attention as the *acllas*, whom the Spanish equated with Rome's vestal virgins or with the nuns of the Roman Catholic Church. The chroniclers tell us that, once a year, a male agent of the Inca would inspect villages which had been incorporated into the empire. In the name of the Inca, he would choose chaste girls to fill the *acllas'* ranks. These girls had various destinies: those who were to remain celibate were attached to the empire's chief divinities and officiated in their rituals; others, whom the chroniclers looked upon as concubines in a sultan's harem, eventually became the emperor's wives or the wives of other men to whom the Inca gave them. In any case, until their futures were decided for them by the empire's male elite, the *acllas'* sexuality was guarded. They were separated from their communities of origin and housed in the *acllawasi*, located in the state-run capital of each province. There they were taught "women's tasks"—spinning, weaving, and the preparation of *chicha* and special foods. (See Cieza 1959:95, 192, 213; Cobo 1964, II:134, 231-32; Guaman Poma 1956, I:137, 216-18; Murúa 1946:156, 248-55; Polo 1917a:91-92; Valera 1950:167-70.)

The chroniclers tell us that the *acllas* were organized hierarchically. Andean notions of physical perfection as well as the social rank of an *aclla*'s family determined her status. Many were the daughters of the headmen (*curacas*) of peoples conquered by the Incas. Moreover, an *aclla*'s final destination was shaped by her rank: the most prestigious wives of the Sun were destined to be chaste priestesses of the solar or other imperial cults, if they did not enter the Inca's entourage as secondary wives. Lower-ranking *acllas* served less important deities or were bestowed by the Inca as rewards to other men. Although many remained in the *acllawasi* of their provinces, the most esteemed were sent to Cuzco. At the time of their initial selection some, those who were considered to be the embodiment of physical and moral perfection, were offered as sacrifices in crucial state rituals.

Father Bernabé Cobo, who dedicated many pages of his chronicle to describing the *acllas*, wrote:

> They were chosen in this manner: a judge, named by the Inca, was sent to every province with the task of choosing young girls, watching over them, and sending them to Cuzco when they were of age. . . . [H]e was called *apupanaca* [literally "head of the *panaca*," the royal descent group]. He chose the most beautiful, and they were called *acllas*. . . . There was a home for them in each governing center [of the empire]. . . . They were reared there until they were fourteen years old in the company of *mamaconas*, who were "chosen" women, dedicated to the service of their gods, like nuns; and they taught these girls all of the feminine tasks like spinning and weaving wool and cotton, preparing food and *chicha*. . . . They were maintained by rents from land consecrated to their religion; and there were also major-domos who were responsible for providing them with what they needed and for vigilantly watching over them to ensure that they remained virgins.
>
> The commissioned official, who selected this tribute each year for the festival of *Raymi*, chose girls from these houses who were thirteen or fourteen years old . . . and took them to Cuzco, in accord with the number each province had to send that year. Brought together in that city, they were presented to the Inca, who then distributed them according to the needs at that time, and in this order: some were sent to the monasteries of the *mamaconas* to replace those who died, and these professed to that condition, living perpetually in seclusion and in chastity, dedicated to the service of the temples of the Sun, Thunder, and [all] the gods who were entitled to the service of women. Another large number were designated to be killed in the sacrifices made in the course of the year—such as those for the Inca's health or when he went personally to war—and it was a requirement that these

be virgins. The most noble and beautiful were reserved to be his servants and concubines, and a large quantity of them were distributed among his captains and relatives, thus remunerating the services they performed for him with this sort of price. He also distributed them to the *caciques* of each province. In each principal village and capital where there was a temple dedicated to the Sun, there was built next to it a house of seclusion, *acllaguasi [acllawasi]*, the home of the chosen where many virgins, called *mamaconas*, the Noble Mothers, lived. . . . [I]n some, the number reached two hundred.

Girls ten to twelve years old were enclosed in these monasteries, not because of their own devotion, or that of their fathers, but because of the will of the Inca and the rites of his religion; and these [girls] were gathered as tribute throughout the entire kingdom . . . and they were the most beautiful and noble. . . . These tributed girls lived with the *mamaconas* until they reached the age when the Inca disposed of them. They were called *acllas* because they belonged to the entire empire and there they learned things regarding their religion, rites and ceremonies, as well as the duties appropriate for women. . . . Their daily occupations were to care for the service and cult of the temples; they spun and wove very fine cloth . . . to dress the idols and offer as sacrifices and make into clothing for the Inca. They made highly esteemed *chicha* to offer to the gods. . . . Those who lived in the temple in Cuzco . . . offered food to the Sun . . . saying, "Eat, Sun, what your wives have cooked." . . . They sometimes left Cuzco, to be present at other places when offerings were made to the Sun and if they left [Cuzco] to make these sacrifices, it was because they exercised a great role, as the wives of the Sun. . . . They had to remain virginal; if they were caught [with a man] both were killed, unless it was the Inca, who occasionally spent nights there. . . .

The manner of consecrating these virgins to their gods was that they were betrothed to them, with special ceremonies, and from then on they were called, and considered to be, their wives. Some had a higher status than others; and in each house there was one with a higher rank, who was held to be the wife of the Sun, or of the god to whom she was consecrated, and this one was always of the noblest lineage, such that in the principal temple of Cuzco, the wife of the Sun was usually a sister of the king himself [Cobo 1964, II:231-32].

Students of the Inca empire have offered various interpretations of the *acllas*; but most have considered their virginity—or, better said, the fact that their sexual behavior was controlled by the Inca elite—to be of secondary importance (see Zuidema 1964:225). John Murra equated the *acllas* or *mamaconas* with other groups of peasants who were alienated from their communities of origin to work full time for the Inca elite. The *acllas* were the state's weavers, and they were renowned throughout the empire for their extremely fine cloth, used in ceremony and distributed as gifts (Murra 1956:228). I do not want to deny their crucial role in the Inca economy (see Silverblatt 1976 and 1981:12-45). The significance of the *acllas* for the Inca empire, however, did not lie solely in their function as imperial weavers. To get a handle on that significance, we have to begin by taking seriously the imperial ideology that clothed their selection: the *acllas* had to be virgins when chosen; and they were, in name, the wives of the Sun—divine symbol of the conquering empire—or the wives of the Inca. By not playing down Inca ideology, we are forced to look at the *acllas* as participating in a set of social relations which bounded and structured an imperial political system.

I am arguing here that the rendering of virgins to the Inca's service—provincial girls alienated from their communities as wives of the Inca or wives of the Sun—marked one of the major structural transformations to emerge as the Incas built their Andean empire. Further, the Inca mode of institutionalizing virginity was a critical dimension of the process whereby the Cuzco rulers forged control over other Andean cultures. That is, the institution of the *aclla* or *mamacona* was intrinsic to imperial political and ideological structures which ordered relations of conquest.

INCAS, WOMEN, AND THE HIERARCHY OF CONQUEST

The ability of a male agent of the Inca to enter villages and confiscate *acllas* implies something about relations between the Cuzco elite and women in general. So we might begin by asking how the Incas could, at least in theory, claim the right to determine the disposition of all the empire's women, and on what grounds they did so.

Here I would like to reiterate and extend some of Zuidema's insights into Andean and Inca social structure (1964:40-41, 168, 173 and n.d.). As we have seen, Zuidema coined the term "conquest hierarchy" for a structure marking out the ranks of social groups that together constituted a larger sociopolitical unit at the *ayllu* level (Zuidema 1973 and n.d.). The male/female opposition upon which the conquest hierarchy rested was used to indicate a symbolic relationship between a group of conquerors and those who were conquered. Further, the relation between these categories was expressed via terms of marriage alliance: male conquerors wedded conquered women, and an intermediary status between the two was conceptualized as the product of their union. This paradigm stipulated rank and formed a logic through which social categories were ordered. I would add that although these conceptual categories, as applied in local-level political organization, probably had no basis in a social relation of male elite dominance over women, the ranking scheme contained the potential for defining women as conquered subjects who could be manipulated by conquerors. Glaringly, as the Incas consolidated their control over the Andes, the significance of the conquest hierarchy was transformed to define a hierarchy of power—not simply one of prestige.

The Incas used the conquest hierarchy to structure the political organization of the empire (Zuidema 1964, 1972). Its semantic logic dictated that the elite be conceptualized as "male conquerors" of all non-Inca populations, symbolized as "conquered women." In keeping with the paradigm, elite males, in addition to endogamous marriages, could contract secondary alliances with non-Inca women from subjugated groups. Their progeny—equidistant between the elite and the peasantry—held a middle position in imperial political ranks. As Zuidema has pointed out (n.d.:5), the Inca legitimized his right to determine the marriage of conquered women by claiming that all women were his sisters (see Garcilaso 1961:305). Royal marriage was between brother and sister; and as his sisters, all women entered the category of potential spouse. In effect, then, the imperial politicization of the conquest hierarchy allowed the Inca to consider women as alienable goods. Although most marriages between commoners were contracted without state interference, this construct, I contend, was the means by which the Inca or his male agents selected certain young women and placed them under the empire's jurisdiction. The institution of the *aclla*, in terms of the analysis presented here, was generated by the imperial deployment of the conquest hierarchy.

Chosen Women as Political Pawns

One of the most important functions of the Inca as "potential spouse of all women" lay in his ability to create or buttress political alliances through the receipt and distribution of *acllas*. And, as I have mentioned, many were distributed as secondary wives to men of the Inca nobility—to the state's bureaucrats and warriors—to ensure loyalty to the Cuzco regime. Others were given to headmen of conquered or aligned non-Inca populations in order to cement political ties (Garcilaso 1961:132; Cieza 1959:60, 74, 160). Women, now under the Inca's direct control, were distributed as rewards to grease the political and economic apparatus of the empire.

We should not forget that these "rewards" were loaded. There is no question that the interests of the Inca rulers were cultivated within the walls of the *acllawasi*, and that those

87

acllas who were distributed as secondary wives to provincial headmen represented Cuzco's designs. Constant reminders of Inca elite power, they would serve to check any anti-imperial sentiments a *curaca* might harbor.

Since the Inca, the embodiment of imperial authority, was in principle the only person empowered with the right to transfer women, the possession of more than one wife was a privilege that only the state could bestow. Imbued with the prestige of power, having secondary wives became a singular honor (Cobo 1964, II:120, 122, 133). Cobo, talking about the rewards that the Inca might grant his subjects, commented that the "most esteemed" of all the gifts distributed by him

> were the young women which the Inca had gathered as tribute. . . . For to receive a young woman, given by the hands of the Inca, was held as a singular favor, because there was nothing which these Indians esteemed more than to have many wives, and they could not have another wife in addition to the legitimate one, except by dispensation of the king [1964, II:120, 133].

If men felt especially honored by the reward of a wife by the state, many also perceived it to be in their best interests to give their daughters in marriage to the Inca. For local headmen could thereby ensure the state's favor as well as obligate Cuzco. The story of the marriage of the Inca Lluqui Yupanqui to the daughter of the headman of the Oma *ayllu* is a case in point:

> Lluqui Yupanqui . . . decided to marry . . . and to do this he called Pachachulla Viracocha, who was one of the lords of Guaro, and ordered him to go to the village of Oma, a little more than two leagues from Cuzco, to ask that a daughter of one of their lords be his wife; and this lord, after receiving the message, was extremely flattered and with the consent of the rest of the headmen, gave her to him.
>
> The name of this lady was Mama Carhua, and she was so beautiful that her father did not want to marry her to any-

one, judging that no one could be worthy of her. But when the principal leaders of Oma saw that it was the Inca, the son of the Sun, who asked for her, they took this marriage to be a great blessing. They sent her with an entourage to Cuzco, and all along the road they placed flowers and set up platforms and hung elaborate banners. It took four days to get to Cuzco because the Inca had ordered them to stop every half-league to celebrate her and have banquets in her honor. When she approached, the king went out to receive her with much dancing and singing, accompanied by all the nobility of his court [Cobo 1964, II:69].

Since the marriage of a daughter to the "son of the Sun" meant that the father would receive political, economic, and ritual benefits, Garcilaso's comment should not surprise us:

If [an Inca prince] happened to desire some pretty woman, the Inca knew that he had only to ask her father, who not only would not refuse to let him have her, but would also consider this opportunity to give satisfaction to his sovereign as a great honor and good fortune [1961:63].

Women, "from among the many who were kept in each province in the name of the Inca" (Cieza 1959:61), had become objects in the empire's machinery of government. Through them, the men who gave them or to whom they were given, as well as their *ayllus*, became bound into imperial power relations. The acceptance and donation of women was an honor that was difficult for many *curacas* to refuse.

We should not lose sight of the fact that men (as sexual objects) were not rendered to the imperial elite. On the contrary, the conquest hierarchy was predicated on the ability of the Inca and, by royal dispensation, of other men to engage in polygynous marriages, a privilege not extended to women. Neither the queen nor any other woman could legitimately marry more than one man at a time. The Coya, therefore, could not initiate a "conquest hierarchy"; she could not engage in the multiple marriages necessary to cement a hierarchy of social groups founded on conquest and forged by means of secondary marriage alliances.

CHOSEN WOMEN AS EMBLEMS OF CUZCO'S POWER

Let us turn from political mechanics to political ideology in order to clarify how the institution of the *aclla* became an emblem of Cuzco's dominance as well as a manifestation of its power. First of all, the imperial control of local marriage in general—an aspect of its control of the disposition of women—was an expression of Inca political domination. Many chroniclers commented that the Incas celebrated yearly mass marriages in the villages they conquered (Guaman Poma 1956, I:179; Ortiz de Zúñiga 1967, I:53). I contend that when a male representative of the Inca elite formally "distributed women for marriage," he was ritually affirming the theoretical control the Inca could exert over all women. For in spite of Inca ritual, marriages contracted between men and women of vanquished groups were in effect conducted according to pre-conquest marriage practices. As Murúa observed, "the parents of girls married them to whomever they wanted, but with the permission of the king" (1946:418). Thus, the yearly distribution of peasant women under the auspices of the Inca was a symbol of Cuzco's potential dispositionary rights over all women—and by extension over the entire population that was now subject to imperial rule. These mass marriages were a yearly ritualized reminder of imperial domination, expressed through the idiom of the Inca's control over the distribution of women in marriage.

We should reconsider, then, the semantics of the conquest hierarchy, for it was through this social optic that relations of conquest were expressed: conquerors, represented as male, marry the conquered, symbolized as female. Imperial legend tells us that the first Inca, Manco Capac, received women as secondary wives from all the tribes he subjugated (Zuidema n.d.:6). Peasants from the Lima highlands told the priest Francisco de Ávila that the Inca Huayna Capac demanded that adult men from throughout the empire send him an "hermana" (sister) for his concubinage (Ávila 1966:92). Note the character of the olive branch which the Incas sent to a people they had vanquished in battle:

> . . . finally at the end of the three years, the Huarcos were becoming weakened and as the Inca knew it, he sent them emissaries once more to tell them that they all ought to be friends and comrades, and that all he wanted was to wed his sons to their daughters, and base all confederation on equality [Cieza 1959:343].

Marriage became a metaphor for conquest; and the fused relations of marriage and conquest were expressed with the symbols that structured the social categories of the conquest hierarchy: the Inca would wed his *sons* to the *daughters* of conquered people. Marriage alliances might wear a cloak of equality, but the cultural cipher which gave those marriages meaning was an ideological expression of imperial power relations.

In contrast to most non-Inca women, however, the *acllas* were directly touched by the Inca's theoretical control over all whose gender they shared. It should be clear, in light of what mass marriages and marriage alliance signified, that those women who were actually selected as wives of the Inca or Sun, were participating in an institution—anchored in the conquest hierarchy—that dramatically underscored the symbolic representation joining male elite control over marriage and political conquest.

The *aclla* then, as an institution, was an imperial precipitate of the structural forms through which the Incas consolidated their conquest of the Andes; the chroniclers confirm this. Upon conquering a new territory, the Incas demanded that a temple be constructed for the Sun, the divine emblem of the conquering empire, and that *acllas*—in the name of the Inca and the Sun—be selected from the newly subjugated populations (Garcilaso 1961:238, 299, 301, 302, 307). The astute observer Cieza de León reaffirmed that after subduing a new region the

Incas immediately saw to it that a temple be constructed for the Sun, an *acllawasi* built, and women assigned to it in the name of the Inca:

> [After a victorious campaign] ... when the Inca had appointed a governor with a garrison of soldiers ... if the provinces were large, he at once ordered a temple built to the Sun and women assigned to it as in the others [1959:160].

This dual pattern—the building of a temple to worship the Sun (divine symbol of the Inca imperial system) and the construction of residences for the chosen women (primarily of local origin and often daughters of vanquished *curacas*), who would enter into the divinity's service—marked the subjugation of every new territory. Thus the temple to the imperial solar cult, accompanied by the delegation of *acllas*, exemplified relations of conquest and were permanent signs of an *ayllu*'s subjugation to Cuzco.

Moreover, when a group rebelled against Inca domination, one of the first signs of submission demanded by the Incas was that the defeated render women to the Cuzco elite as wives of the Sun (Murúa 1946:191). Inca power was displayed by means of the seizure of *acllas*, who were then distributed throughout the empire by the lords of Cuzco. In fact, one of the most severe punishments the Inca victors imposed on rebellious groups was to demand wives of the Sun. An insubordinate faction of the Colla kingdom was ordered to give food and women to the Cuzco garrison (Cieza 1968:207). Murúa described the punishment meted out to the Huancavelicas, Cayampitaetos, and Pastos:

> because they were very rebellious people and had rebelled against Topa Inca and Guayna Capac ... [the latter] ... took many of their unmarried women and distributed them throughout the entire kingdom, placing them in [the empire's] storage houses [1946:191].

The "storage houses" that Murúa refers to were the *acllawasi*, the homes of the *acllas*. Thus "marriage" could be converted into punishment and an obvious display of dominance. In this manner, the estrangement of women from their *ayllus* of origin to become wives of the Sun laid bare the power of Inca rulers as conquerors.

Not surprisingly, vanquished peoples also perceived the rendering of women to the empire as a form of tribute owed the victorious king. We have already seen the word tribute applied to the appropriation of provincial women in Cobo's description of the *aclla*. However, "tribute" was also the word used by the *curacas* of polities as distant as the Lupaka and Chupachu, when asked by Spanish inspectors in the sixteenth century to describe the demands made on them by their Inca rulers. In his list of tribute owed to Cuzco, Pedro Cutinbo, a governor of Lupaka, included the Indian men who were drafted for imperial corvée labor along with the "virgins" who were sent to serve the Inca and the empire's gods (Díez de San Miguel 1964:39, 81, 93, 106). Ortiz de Zúñiga, who inspected the Chupachu, recorded that Inca tribute encompassed "the *indias* for the Inca, daughters of *caciques* for *mamaconas* and others for the service of the Temple of the Sun" (1967, I:47). These women, born into the Chupachu and then estranged from their communities of origin by Cuzco rulers, were then sent to the Inca provincial capitals of Guánuco and Bombón, as well as to the principal *acllawasi* in Cuzco itself (Ortiz de Zúñiga 1967, I:37).

It was often the daughters and female relatives of *curacas* who were demanded as "tribute" by the representatives of the Inca (Ortiz de Zúñiga 1967, I:37, 47; Cieza 1959:294; Garcilaso 1961:315; P. Pizarro 1968:497; H. Pizarro 1968:126). While establishing bonds between Cuzco and the conquered provinces, the hierarchical and unequal nature of these alliances formed through "marriage to the Inca" exemplified relations of conquest; and they were perceived as such by many local headmen (Cobo 1964, II:134).

One of the more obvious means by which marriage to provincial women symbolized conquest was the state's insistence that the secondary wives of the Inca, and their daughters, retain the names of their provinces of origin. The social category *ñusta*, often translated as "princess," required that these women, who were not full descendants of the Inca royalty, be called by the name of their natal land (Guardia Mayorga 1971:103; Cobo 1964, II:84; Pachacuti Yamqui 1950:224).

Given the semantic structure of the conquest hierarchy, secondary marriages contracted with non-Inca women became a continuous metaphor expressing the dominance of Cuzco. Upon conquering an *ayllu*, the Inca ordered that its principal *huaca* be brought to Cuzco, where it was then kept with the mummy of the sovereign who was responsible for this victory (Polo 1917a:96); in a not dissimilar gesture of domination, when a secondary wife of the Inca was buried in Cuzco, earth was brought from her original homeland and placed in her grave (Polo 1917a:111). Moreover, on top of the grave was emblazoned the royal insignia of the Inca (Murúa 1946:258).

The *acllas* were no longer considered to be members of the communities in which they were born; the ties of kinship that formed the fabric of the *ayllu*'s social identity were no longer extended to them. The *acllas* had been transformed into conquered subjects of Cuzco. Even in death, the Inca's *acllas* exemplified their conquered status along with that of their provinces of birth.

Embodying relations of conquest, *acllas* ritually validated the status of their fathers, who became intermediaries in imperial politics. The dramatic history of one *aclla*—who, through her sacrifice to the cult of the Sun, consecrated the bond between her father, a *curaca*, and the Cuzco regime—illustrates this process. The event took place in Urcon, an *ayllu* located near Recuay in the Department of Ancash. We owe its description to Hernández Príncipe, who early in the seventeenth century was sent to this sierra zone in order to eradicate idolatrous practices. His account was to serve as a guide for other priests undertaking similar missions.

Tanta Carhua's sacrifice to the solar cult of Cuzco and her subsequent deification signaled her father's, i.e. Caque (*Cacique*) Poma's, new position in the imperial power structure.

For by dedicating Tanta Carhua to the primary god of the Incas—the divine symbol of the conquering state—Caque Poma was formally recognized by Cuzco as the *curaca* of his *ayllu* and as the link connecting his community, Urcon, with the empire's political center. The ritual took place at the *Convite de capacocha* (Festival of the Sacrificed), during which youth from all over the empire—who held positions analogous to Tanta Carhua's—converged in Cuzco. Not only did this ritual process mark Caque Poma's elevation in status, it also affirmed that subsequent *curacas* representing Urcon to the empire's power structure would be chosen from among Caque Poma's lineal descendants. Thus the sacrifice of Tanta Carhua ritually asserted her father's, and her father's descendants', new role as the nexus between Urcon and Cuzco while dramatizing the community's subordination to Cuzco:

> This Caque Poma had a daughter ten years of age whose extreme beauty was extolled throughout, and ever since she showed that she was going to be [beautiful], he dedicated her to be sacrificed to the Sun, which meant to the Inca, [so] that by Caque Poma's going to Cuzco he would get the royal notification that within a few days he would receive the "throne" (*dúo*) and title of *cacique* on account of his aforementioned daughter [Hernández Príncipe 1923:62].

When listing Caque Poma's ancestors and descendants, Hernández Príncipe had this to say about him:

> . . . it will be necessary to mention [Caque Poma] several times because of his having dedicated and sacrificed his only daughter to the Sun at the famous festival of the *capacocha*; and the Inca gave her the name Tanta Carhua, and by means of this privilege, the governorship has passed down from one to the other, until [it was assumed by] this one who is at present ruling [1923:52].

Hernández Príncipe warned other priests who were trying to root out Andean idolatries to beware of the relationship between the *capacocha* and the position of *ayllu* headman:

you would be well advised to inquire about the way in which it was done, because it is certain that you will find among the *caciques* and governors that it was by means of them [the *capacochas*] that they received the governorship [1923:63].

The festival of the *capacocha* was celebrated in Cuzco during *Inti raymi. Inti raymi* was the state festival in honor of the Sun. The *aclla-capacochas*, who represented the four divisions of the empire, traveled to Cuzco. Accompanied by the principal *huacas* of their homeland as well as by their *curacas*, the *capacochas* led the political and divine representatives of conquered provinces in a pilgrimage of homage to their Inca rulers. After the *acllas* gave reverence to the chief gods of the Incas—the Sun and Lightning—and to the mummies of the royal dynasty, the Inca, in turn, honored the *aclla-capacochas*. Some of the *capacochas* were sacrificed to the Sun or to Huanacauri, the legendary brother of Manco Capac (founder of the Inca dynasty), whose shrine was associated with the rites of passage through which youth of the Inca nobility entered manhood. Those who remained were sent back to their provinces of origin. There they would be sacrificed to the Sun, following the ritual established in Cuzco. In addition to raising the *capacochas'* fathers to a position in imperial government, the Inca ordered members of their vanquished *ayllus* to worship them and to assign lands and priests for these royally inspired cults. The *capacochas* sacrificed in their provincial homelands were designated by the Inca as the *huaca* guardians, or divine custodians, of their communities, now under Cuzco's rule.

Let us turn to Hernández Príncipe's extraordinary description of these events:

It was the custom, in their paganism, to celebrate the festival of the *capacocha* every four years, choosing four children, between ten and twelve years old, without a blemish, of consummate beauty, children of the nobility. . . . They would celebrate the festival; and these four *acllas* who are the "chosen" were privileged, they were taken to Cuzco from the four parts of Peru: Collasuyo, Antisuyo, Contisuyo, and Chinchaisuyo. All left in good time, traveling on all the roads; it was a sight to behold, how they were greeted, walking in procession with their *huacas*; the *capacochas* arrived in Cuzco accompanied by the principal *huaca* of their homelands and by their *caciques* and *indios*. They entered Cuzco together, just around the festival of *Inti raymi*. Everyone from Cuzco who anticipated their arrival went out to receive them. The [*acllas*] entered by the main square, and the Inca was already seated there on his golden throne; and in order were the statues of the Sun, [and of] Lightning-Thunder, and the embalmed Incas who were [attended by] their priests. They marched around the principal square twice, worshipping the statues and the Inca, who with a joyful countenance greeted them; and when they approached him, [the Inca] spoke with secret words to the Sun, saying . . . "Receive these chosen ones for your service." The Inca offered aged *chicha* to the Sun, specially brewed for this occasion, which the Coya, accompanied by princesses, had brought in two golden pitchers. The Inca rubbed a ground powder over his entire body, to partake of his divinity. The high priest slaughtered a white sheep [i.e. llama] whose blood he mixed with the dough of flour and of white corn, called *sancu*, and he administered communion to the Inca and those of his counsel. . . . He distributed morsels of the llama to the Sun. The Incas feted the "chosen"; and this festival lasted for days, and they slaughtered one hundred thousand llamas.

When this festival was over, they took the *capacochas* who were to remain in Cuzco to the *huaca* of Huanacauri or to the house of the Sun, and putting her [*sic*] to sleep, they lowered her into a cistern without water, and underneath, to one side, they made a small space; they walled her in alive, asleep. . . . The Inca ordered that the rest [of them] be taken back to their homelands, and they did the same with them, privileging their fathers and making them governors; and [he ordered] that there be priests to attend her for the devotion that would be made each year [to the] *capacocha*, who

97

served as guardians and custodians of the entire province [1923:60-61].

Tanta Carhua, leading a procession of the principal *huacas* of her province and accompanied by her father and other headmen from her homeland, was celebrated as an *aclla-capacocha* by the Inca in Cuzco. Returning from the festivities held in her honor, she was buried alive within a hilltop in Aixa, which were royal lands bordering the *ayllu* of Urcon. Overwhelmed, ecstatic, exhilarated by her experience in the imperial capital, Tanta Carhua must have partaken of the divinity which was bestowed upon her by the son of the Sun. The elders of Ocros told Hernández Príncipe of Tanta Carhua's last words and of her final acts:

... the young girl said, "Finish now with me, for the celebrations which were made in my honor in Cuzco were more than enough"; they then took her from the site of Aixa, to a high mountain, the crest and last outreach of the lands of the Inca, and having made her resting place, they lowered her into it and walled her in alive [1923:62].

Tanta Carhua's burial in the "lands of the Inca" that bordered those of her natal *ayllu* solemnized Cuzco's domination over her community.

The Inca decreed that the *capacochas* returning to their native lands be adored as divinities, the protector *huacas* of their communities. In accordance with the Inca's decree, a cult was formed for the adoration of Tanta Carhua. Lands were earmarked for the support of this cult; herds were set aside. Priests were designated to officiate at festivals in her honor and to represent Tanta Carhua to the headmen of the surrounding *ayllus*, who were especially devoted to her. These ministers were her kinsmen—the descendants of her youngest brother:

Each year they cultivated fields for her festival, and they sacrificed *cuyes* [guinea pigs], and from an *usnu*, which is a platform, they gave her drink.

But although those of her *ayllu* Urcon adored her, as well

98

as others who lived in the hills which are in view, the *caciques*, her owners, adored her and communicated with her by means of witches since it was difficult to go to this site. The first [witch] was Condor Capcha, the youngest of Caque Poma's seven sons and the *capacocha* Tanta Carhua's brother, . . . and he was succeeded in office by his kinsmen [Hernández Príncipe 1923:63].

The old people of Ocros told Hernández Príncipe (1923:62) that they would turn to Tanta Carhua when they were sick or in need of help. After praying to her, Tanta Carhua would respond to them through her priests, giving advice to those who worshipped her. These priests, when speaking in Tanta Carhua's name, would simulate her voice by talking in falsetto as if they were women.

The rituals that were performed in Tanta Carhua's honor underscored the relationship between the *aclla* and her father. When Tanta Carhua was invoked, so was Caque Poma, for whom an ancestral cult was also established. Tanta Carhua was called to in these words, "Come here with your father, Caque Poma" (Hernández Príncipe 1923:63).

In his zeal to eradicate the pagan practices of this community, Hernández Príncipe hunted for Tanta Carhua's tomb:

I went with much fear and distrust . . . and tired and fed up by the precariousness of the track, I lost my courage . . . but [finally] I recognized the site because of the sacrifices of llamas and the altars from where she was invoked and because of the elders who told me that from this point, and from there, the now-dead ministers spoke to her. . . . We labored there for almost the entire day . . . and [in a shaft], made in the manner of a well, very well leveled out, in a space like a cupboard at the bottom, [we found] the *capacocha* seated, in the way of her pagan ancestors, with jewels in the shape of tiny pots and jugs and silver pins and silver charms, very beautiful. She was, by now, decomposed; and so was the fine clothing in which she was dressed, when she came to this site [1923:62].

99

Thus ends the history of the *aclla-capacocha* of Urcon. Tanta Carhua had become one of the most venerated *huacas* of her region. She had become a goddess. Perhaps, because she was a woman, Tanta Carhua embodied the forces of fertility to her adherents; for her powers were related to corn production and health. Nevertheless, the basis of Tanta Carhua's cult lay in her exemplification of the new relations that had been formed between her homeland and Cuzco. She was the means by which her father, and by extension the other local headmen of the region—her most ardent adorers—were linked to the center of imperial power. The *aclla*, Tanta Carhua, the incarnation of relations of conquest, was transformed into a divine object in Cuzco's cult of the Sun.[1]

The delegation and appropriation of *acllas* was the symbol par excellence of the force of Inca domination. The *acllas* were permanent signs of an *ayllu*'s subordination to Cuzco. If one of the clearest manifestations of Inca dominion lay in their right to take women from conquered communities, then, not surprisingly, the vanquished despised this glaring manifestation of their powerlessness. This intrusion on the part of Inca rulers became a blatant symbol of an *ayllu*'s loss of freedom and autonomy. One *curaca*, when pressured by the Incas to be incorporated into the imperial system, expressed this equation—the loss of liberty and the rendering of women to the empire—in the following manner:

> Foreign tyranny is at our gates. . . . If we yield to the Inca, we shall be obliged to give up our former freedom, our best land, our most beautiful women and girls, our customs, our laws. . . . [W]e shall become for all time [this tyrant's] vassals and servitors [Garcilaso 1961:319].

Of all the obligations and demands that the conquering Incas could make on this headman, that which he regretted most

---

[1] Zuidema (1973, 1977b) has also discussed the *capacocha* rites in his analysis of Hernández Príncipe's manuscript.

was to "give into [the Inca's] service his daughters and most beautiful women" (Cieza 1959:296).

Virginity, Holiness, and Conquest

Several characteristics distinguished the *acllas* from other people who were extricated from their natal *ayllus* and placed in full service to the state. Foremost, perhaps, was the demand of chastity: the *acllas* as potential wives of the Inca or Sun had to be virgins when chosen. According to Garcilaso, this explains why they were selected at such a young age, before reaching puberty (1961:105). Cobo reiterates that the *apupanaca*, the male agent of the Inca who was empowered to nominate *acllas* in the provinces, would choose only virgins, "for it was a requisite, without which he would not select them" (1964, II:134). Moreover, once chosen, the *aclla*'s chastity was vigilantly guarded (Garcilaso 1961:105; Cobo 1964, II:134). The *acllawasis* were policed by male gatekeepers who had the task of ensuring that no man, except the Inca or those granted royal dispensation, could enter them (Murúa 1946:422).

Those *acllas* who did commit adultery were severely punished. The chronicles abound with stories of the severe verdicts meted out to women and their "partners in sin" who dared break the Inca interdiction against sexual relations. "Those who committed adultery (which was considered a great sacrilege) were hanged or burned alive," stated Cieza (1959:21-22). The noblemen of Cuzco, who were his informants, told Cieza that

> four of them made evil use of their bodies with certain of the gatekeepers whose duty it was to guard them, and when this was learned, they were seized, together with their partners in adultery, and the high priests ordered them all put to death [1959:214].

Significantly, control over women's sexuality was an imposition associated only with this institution governed by the

Cuzco male elite,[2] for the imperial prescription of chastity for the *aclla* contrasted sharply with the *ayllu*'s norms regarding premarital sex. The chroniclers were well aware that premarital sex was both accepted and encouraged by the Andean peasantry (Arriaga 1968:55, 58; Cieza 1945:156; Polo 1917b: 202). Pedro Pizarro, commenting on the sexual practices he observed among Andean peasants, remarked:

> Peasant women are faithful to their husbands after they marry; but before then, their fathers did not pay any attention if they were good or bad; nor was it considered to be shameful among them [1968:579].

The Spanish Jesuit Arriaga expressed his horror of the sexual customs he encountered in the sixteenth century:

> Another common abuse among the Indians of today is to have carnal knowledge of each other several times before marriage, and it is rare for them not to do so. . . . In a town that I was passing through an Indian boy asked me to marry him to his betrothed. One of her brothers, however, objected strongly, giving no other reason except that they had never slept together [1968:55].

Another Jesuit, Acosta, adds:

> There is another grave error . . . which is deeply rooted in the heart of the barbarians. Virginity, which is viewed with esteem and honor by all men, is deprecated by those barbarians as something vile. Except for the virgins consecrated to the Sun or to the Inca, all other women are considered of less value while they are virgin, and thus, whenever possible, they give themselves to the first man they find [1954:603].

---

[2] For an interesting treatment of the relation between the development of state societies and prescriptions of female virginity, see Ortner (1978). See Ortner and Whitehead (1981) and Brown and Buchbinder (1976) for discussions of the relations between gender and prestige, and Dubisch (1986) for discussions of gender and power in Greece.

Thus, the requirement that the *aclla* remain chaste was a demand which, in the Andes, could only have expressed the interests of the Inca rulers who governed the institution.

In this regard, again, it is significant that the *acllas* were no longer considered members of the communities in which they were born. For these women had been transformed into subjects of Cuzco (Murúa 1946:258). The *acllas* were forbidden to all men—including those from their native lands—except the Inca or those whom he favored. By precluding the *acllas'* ability to marry men from their natal *ayllu*, by guarding their virginity, the Inca ensured that their procreative potential would be determined by the rulers of the empire.

Secondly, the *acllas* played crucial roles in imperial religious life. As opposed to other state retainers, these women were imbued with holy qualities. The estrangement of the *acllas* from their homelands was expressed in terms of their potential function in Inca sacred ceremony: they were designated as wives of the Sun, or wives of the Inca, the incarnation of the Sun in this world. This denomination was a key factor in determining their special status. The Sun's wives were not merely factory workers for the state; the *acllas* were the Sun's priestesses.

Paradoxically, even though the "marriage" of the *acllas* to the Inca or to the Sun was a central element in the construction of a political hierarchy based on conquest, these women were highly revered throughout the empire. Murúa described their lifestyle as well as the esteem with which they were held by the Inca and other male members of the Cuzco nobility:

> . . . in general, all of these aforementioned women [regardless of the rank they held within the institution] lived the life of great queens and ladies, and a life of tremendous pleasure and amusement, and they were very highly regarded, esteemed, and loved by the Inca and by the Great Lords [1946:259].

The testimony of a Spaniard who witnessed the extraordinary respect shown toward the wives of the Inca Atahualpa was recorded in a legal suit of 1555. His account is evidence of Inca norms stipulating that *acllas* be held in extreme reverence and of the elevated social rank they occupied:

> Atahualpa had his wives . . . and he treated them as such . . . and thus they were held to be and were known as his own wives, for they were set aside and designated as such. . . . They were honored and held in awe and respect . . . to such a degree that this witness saw and was given to understand that no principal *cacique* or Indian, except if he were going to serve and honor them, would dare look at their faces . . . and thus Indian men and women greatly venerated them, and this witness saw that they kept this custom even many days after Atahualpa's death . . . and this law was held to be supreme among the natives [Oberem 1968:89].

This special behavior and reverence was derived from the *acllas'* unique status in Inca religious life. As wives of the imperial god of conquest, these women, as Cobo remarked, "belonged to the entire empire" (1964, II:146, 156). Their role as imperial priestesses in a patriarchal cult—a cult to which some of them were sacrificed—was an expression of their holiness.

What did it mean to be a priestess of the Sun? The *acllas*, we discover, exercised pivotal roles in all of the empire's celebrations in honor of this god and—by extension—in liturgical practices dedicated to the other gods of the empire, who were under his command (Cobo 1964, II:232-33). The *acllas'* importance in state ceremonies was marked by the positions they occupied in Inca ritual space. During imperial festivities, the *acllas* or *mamaconas* would walk in procession with the empire's male priests—the priests forming one line while the *acllas* formed one parallel to them (Murúa 1946:387). Together they would perform sacrifices and make offerings to the state's *huacas* and implore them to foretell the events of the coming year. As priestesses, the *mamaconas* could voice and interpret the predictions of the gods (Cieza 1959:192). In addition, along with the priests, the *acllas* bore the burden of upholding the morality and normative order of the empire (Cieza 1959:213).

Thirdly, as the embodiment of relations of conquest, the *acllas* were delegated certain ceremonial tasks in which bonds between Cuzco and the provinces were reinforced and accentuated. This role was perhaps best exemplified during the festival of *Situa*, when the priests and warriors of the Inca dynasty ritually purified Cuzco. During the entire month in which *Situa* was celebrated, *mamaconas* distributed bits of holy bread to the "foreigners"—those of non-Inca origin—and to the gods accompanying them in the imperial capital. They also took holy bread to other provincial deities and *ayllu* headmen throughout the Andes. This communion solemnized the renewal of alliances and the exaction of a loyalty based on obeisance to the Inca conquerors and their god:

> This month the *mamaconas* of the Sun brought out a great quantity of balls of bread made with the blood left from certain sacrifices; and they gave a morsel to each of the foreigners [in Cuzco] ... and they also sent them to the foreign shrines of the entire kingdom, and to several *curacas* as a sign of confederation and loyalty to the Sun and to the Inca [Polo 1916:23].

But the *acllas* were more than officiants of Inca ritual: they were holy. As wives of the Sun, they partook of his divinity. The *acllas* were called "sainted people"; they were known as "sacred mothers" throughout the territory of the Incas (Cieza 1959:182; Cobo 1964, II:232). A fable recounted by Murúa reveals how the *acllas* were adored by the Inca's subjects. When the wives of the Sun living in a provincial *acllawasi* walked about the countryside, people knelt in front of them, venerating them "like goddesses on earth" (Murúa 1946:427).

In a society in which social category was made manifest by sumptuary privilege, the divine status of the *acllas* was marked by the similarity of privileges they received to those granted to the Sun and his priests. The *acllawasi* in Cuzco was described by Garcilaso as being in every particular as luxurious as the

CHAPTER V

Temple of the Sun (1961:130). Objects sanctified by Inca culture, such as the ears of corn grown in the islands of Lake Titicaca, were "divided . . . between the temples of the Sun and the convents for virgin women, throughout the Empire, so that all should receive their share of this miraculous grain, which seemed to have come from heaven" (Garcilaso 1961:122). Thus by virtue of their divinity, "the wives of the Sun and mistresses of all the land" (Murúa 1946:421) were granted the same privileges, the same material indices of holiness as the Sun.

Similarly, during the period of civil war, between the Inca half-brothers Atahualpa and Huascar, that preceded the Spanish conquest, the two sites in Cuzco that were spared by Atahualpa's victorious troops were the Temple of the Sun and the residence of the *mamaconas*:

[Atahualpa's general] continued his pursuit until he arrived at Cuzco. They sacked the city disregarding the veneration in which it was held by the entire populace of Tahuantinsuyu [the Inca empire]; only the Temple of the Sun and the home of the *mamaconas*, virgins dedicated to him, were exempt [Cobo 1964, II:98].

These events were repeated after the Spanish conquest. During the native revolt led by Manco Inca against Spanish rule, the entire city of Cuzco was intentionally set on fire in an attempt to rout the Spanish. Only the Temple of the Sun and the *acllawasi* were left untouched (Garcilaso 1959:268). Thus, history demonstrated the sacred reverence in which the *acllas* were held.

Why, then, were the ideological structures through which an *aclla* was separated from her homeland so different from those governing the manner in which other classes of men and women became full-time state retainers? I believe the key lies in the empire's designs to intervene in the process of social reproduction itself. The Inca's latent control over women—not only their labor, but their role as the potential reproducers of society—formed a critical dimension of the process through which the empire consolidated its power in the Andes. This latent control was actualized in the institution of the *aclla*; and the stipulation of virginity, a condition whose maintenance and change was exclusively in the hands of the male elite, was a logical extension of this aspect of imperial domination.

The sexual proscription that the Inca imposed on the *acllas* was a means of negating their capacity to help reproduce their natal communities. The alienation of women deprived the *ayllu* of control over its own temporal continuity. From the perspective of the conquered, women, as the symbolic embodiment of local continuity, came to represent local autonomy. The control that the Inca theoretically could exert over women, and its particular realization in the institution of the *aclla* (where women's sexuality was in fact monitored) served to exemplify imperial control over all aspects of provincial social reproduction.

Was there a relation between the *acllas'* representation or embodiment of Inca relations of conquest and their consecration? Inca ideology, which proclaimed the *acllas* to be the most sacred women of the empire, had transformed the "conquered"—the women who stood for all outsiders—into the "holy." By making the *acllas* into the empire's "holy mothers," the Incas transformed virgins into their opposite, thus mediating, expressing, and controlling the contradictory relations that conquest engendered. Moreover, this ideology, when shared by the conquered, cloaked their fundamental loss of control over their own reproduction and autonomous social creation.

Virgin women were secluded in Inca society; superficially, therefore, the *acllas* might appear to be equivalent to nuns, vestal virgins, or the women in a sultan's harem. But the significance of virginity in the Andes was different. It can be best understood in relation to the Andean social structure, the conquest hierarchy; the meaning of virginity was tied integrally to the particular way in which gender symbolism, marriage, and relations of conquest were fused to structure the Inca domination of other Andean cultures.

107

Gender and class spiraled: gender gave form to class relations in the imperialized Andes, while the Incas molded gender distinctions into approximate images of the class relations they imposed. Gender hierarchy and class formation were merged, perhaps irretrievably, as the Incas forged their Andean empire.

Under the Spanish: Native Noblewomen Enter the Market Economy

> ... and a certain Indian woman, Isabel, disho-
> nored me with insulting words, ignoring the
> fact that I am the honorable wife of a Spaniard,
> and a woman of quality and nobility.
> [Doña Paula Mama Guaco Ñusta,
> ADC:ACC, Top. 9, Leg. 5]

The Spanish landed on Peru's northern coast in 1532. Thus began the Spanish conquest of the Andes and the process of colonization which irrevocably altered the lifeways of Andean
peoples. Conquest was not new to the Andes. The empire that
the Spanish encountered was the second large-scale imperial
system in which coastal and highland cultures had been subjugated by a more powerful Andean people. However, the experiences of the conquered under Spanish rule were radically
different from those under Inca rule. Although the Cuzco elite,
at the apex of a highly stratified society, enjoyed political and
economic privileges denied to the peasantry, institutions and
norms rooted in the Inca political economy tempered the relationship between conquerors and conquered and provided
peasant men and women with the insurance that their social
and economic needs would be met. The Incas struggled to impose their vision of the world on those whom they vanquished.
Yet, that vision was one that conquered peoples could make
sense of.

The Spanish invasion imposed alien economic, political, religious, and conceptual structures on Andean society. The
economy of Spain, oriented toward the emerging market economy of Europe, saw in its New World colonies the opportuni-

ties to accumulate great wealth; and the economic institutions imposed on the colonies reflected the need of the Spanish economy to amass profit. Thus guided by an economic system in which production was colored by the dictates of the market, colonial institutions tended to break down the kin relations that underlay pre-Columbian socioeconomic organization. The ideological underpinnings of these institutions embodied an evaluation of the universe—the quality of the relationship between society and nature, between social groups, between women and men—that was totally foreign to the Andean peoples who were colonized. Buttressed by a world view in which nature and humanity were becoming increasingly defined in relation to their market value, and by a religious ideology that divided the world into competing forces of good and evil, colonial secular and religious authorities systematically attacked the religious and social foundations of Andean culture. The colonial process, then, was an attack on indigenous social relationships, which were structured by principles of reciprocity and redistribution, as well as on the ideology that molded those relationships. It was a battle to dismantle those structures which maintained pre-Columbian indigenous society, and to replace them with organizational forms that would bind the newly conquered peoples to their colonizers. Nevertheless, the creation of a colonial society, the transformation of pre-Hispanic Andean culture and its reorientation to European modes, took centuries (see Spalding 1974).

Yet, the history of Spain in the Andes was not just a history of the decimation of native structures. For Andean peoples did not passively yield to colonial powers: they struggled, within the constraints imposed by colonial rule, to defend pre-Columbian lifeways and, thus, to defend their very existence. The history of conquest is also the history of indigenous peoples struggling to contain, modify, resist, or adapt to the dismantling effects of colonial institutions. The dialectic between the destructive external forces of colonialism and the indigenous modes of organization—their structures of defense—will be the framework through which we understand the transformations experienced by Andean culture and their concomitant effects on native women. However much the institutions of colonialism exploited Andean society as a whole, the structures Spain brought to the Andes imposed a special burden on women.

LEARNING THE NEW RULES

At the time of the conquest of the Inca empire, feudal or feudal-like institutions dominated the political economy of the Iberian peninsula. This was a crucial dimension in the creation of a colonial society in the Andes, since the same norms that regulated Spanish society were brought to the Americas as a model for the goverance of the New World's peoples. Although the Spanish did not encounter a feudal social order like their own in the Inca empire, they nevertheless were confronted with the problem of colonizing a highly stratified society in which social status and privilege were clearly defined.

The stated principle behind Spanish rule was that native custom and tradition be respected unless it contradicted the laws of the mother country (Borah and Cook 1966:957). Ideally, an amalgam of Iberian and Inca tradition should have structured colonial relations; in fact, though, the institutions to emerge were heavily weighted in favor of Spanish law and practice, since the needs of Spain dominated the formation of Peru. This is most clearly evidenced, perhaps, when we look at the institutions imposed by the conquerors in their attempt to reorganize the allocation and disposition of land and labor in the Andes.

The Spanish conquest introduced to the Andes new concepts of property ownership and land tenure, along with a complex legal system through which these forms were maintained and transmitted. Following their own feudal traditions, which were adjusted with respect to the social hierarchy of the empire they had conquered, the Spanish defined the differential rights and privileges of the social categories which were to constitute Andean colonial society. Descendants of the Inca dynasty, as

111

well as descendants of the upper strata of the provinces, were classified as the equivalent of Iberian *hidalgos*, the Spanish landed gentry (Mörner 1967:41). By virtue of their colonial *hidalgo* status, these children of the Cuzco elite and non-Inca *curacas* were entitled to certain economic privileges which were denied to the ordinary Indian (*indios del común*). These *indios del común*, commoners whose ancestors were members of pre-Hispanic *ayllus*, were equated by Spanish law to the lowest rank of Spanish society, that of "free vassal." The point to be made here is that the differential privileges which Spanish colonial law stipulated for the members of indigenous society bore directly on their capacity to participate in the colonial economy. Moreover, these privileges made it possible for members of the indigenous elite to make claims on the economic resources of Andean society which had been prohibited to them under Inca structures of economic organization (see Spalding 1974). Thus, structural changes induced by the colonial process provided radically new opportunities for the members of the indigenous elite to accumulate wealth—opportunities that could have arisen only with the destruction of pre-Hispanic forms of property relations and their replacement with mercantilist institutions.[1]

Spanish property laws were rooted in rights of private ownership of land, and the variations in privilege afforded by the colonial regime to its indigenous subjects were directly related to differences in property rights. I have already noted that Spanish law gave the Inca elite as well as non-Inca provincial rulers the status of European nobility. This status made them exempt from Spanish tribute and labor demands as well as from the regulations limiting the consumptuary rights of most Indians (Roel 1970:310; Spalding 1974:37). For the Spanish Crown also guaranteed the indigenous elite privileges of maintaining personal patrimonies in land and of receiving labor

---

[1] Spalding, in her collected essays *De indio a campesino* (1974), presents a detailed analysis of these new opportunities for mobility and wealth open to the indigenous elite.

services according to the social rank and position of authority they held.

In imposing colonial rule over the Andes, the Spanish dismantled the structures of power that members of the Inca elite had controlled before the conquest. Nevertheless, the colonial Inca elite, by virtue of their privileges as surrogate knights of Castile—which included rights to private property—were able to take advantage of the new system of wealth introduced by the colonial regime. That they were able to do so is reflected in Spalding's observation that some members of the indigenous nobility, the descendants of the Inca elite in particular, integrated the richest echelons of Spanish colonial society (1974:175).

Curacas, who were entitled to similar privileges as those who claimed royal Inca descent, played a pivotal role in the political structures imposed by the Spanish. They were the intermediaries between the Indian commoners and the Spanish, ensuring that the demands made by the Spanish on the Andean peasantry were fulfilled. Responsible for the collection of tribute owed to the secular and ecclesiastical agents of the colonial regime, as well as for enforcing the labor drafts, the *curacas* could use their position for personal gain (Spalding 1974:37-50; Roel 1970:263). For example, the titles to communal lands in which Indian commoners had usufruct rights were often held in trust in the name of their *curaca*. Manipulating this situation, unscrupulous local headmen claimed that they in fact were the owners of these communal peasant fields and could sell such land to other noble Indians or Spaniards. Indian commoners, entitled only to use-rights in communal landholdings, were classed as legal minors and were incapable of entering into contractual relations without the prior consent of a representative of Spanish authority. In contrast, *curacas* as well as descendants of the Inca elite could freely engage in business transactions in colonial society. Women of the native elite were likewise privileged members of colonial society, and we will now turn to their participation in colonial mercantilist activities.

113

I have stressed that one of the privileges bestowed on the indigenous nobility by the Spanish regime was the right to claim personal ownership of land. After the Spanish conquest, members of the native elite began to assert their private rights to particular fields which they avowed had "belonged to" one of their royal ancestors. In other words, by affirming their descent from a specific Inca sovereign, members of the indigenous elite attempted to lay claim to lands which that monarch was said to have "owned" before the arrival of the Spanish. It should be obvious that these personal claims made on the so-called private property of Inca rulers were in conflict with the traditional structures that governed land and property relations during the reign of the Incas. "Private property," as defined in European society, did not exist in the Andes; fields "pertaining to" a particular ruler were not "inherited" by a descendant (Rostworowski 1962, 1970). Although it has been suggested that a kind of private property was emerging in the later stages of the empire (Murra 1956:72), no equivalent of European property relations had crystallized by the time of the Spanish conquest. An Inca monarch, for example, might claim rights to the produce of certain fields, but upon his or her death that production reverted to the control of the sovereign's entire descent group, the *panaca*. With the implantation of Spanish property laws, however, the constraints that governed and defined the traditional relation between individuals and their productive resources were broken. Living in a radically altered social and economic universe, members of the Inca elite, drawing on their privileges derived from Spain, began to manipulate these new property forms for their personal gain. Women who claimed royal descent were no exception. Documents from the archives of the Department of Cuzco bear witness to the fact that women of the Inca elite participated in the land grab.

Women descendants of the Cuzco nobility were entitled to the privileges in land afforded by Spaniards to all members of the indigenous elite; by virtue of their royal descent, noblewomen were entitled to claim personal rights over agricultural fields. Sixteenth-century representatives of the Spanish Crown, in an attempt to systematize the distribution of land to their indigenous subjects, conducted censuses whereby rights to agricultural plots were formally distributed. One such *medición y repartición* of lands, in Cuzco's Yucay Valley, exemplifies the privileges that women of noble descent received from the Crown. Other than commoner widows, who were formally granted usufruct rights in the communal lands of their *ayllus*, the only women to be registered as recipients of plots were those who claimed noble birth. These women, however, as descendants of the Inca dynasty, did not just receive use-rights, but actual titles of ownership. They could, therefore, personally dispose of their fields according to the dictates of Spanish law (ADC:AHU, Leg. IV, V, VII).

We also have documentation revealing that, as far back as the sixteenth century, women of royal ancestry entered into commercial transactions in which the lands they had claimed or inherited were sold in the colonial marketplace (ADC:ACC, Top. 8, Leg. 1; Top. 10, Leg. 21). In the seventeenth and eighteenth centuries, the period for which notarial records are more abundant, indigenous women were frequently recorded as parties in the buying and selling of lands in the Yucay Valley and in other areas of the Department of Cuzco (ADC:AUP, Proto. 1-2, f. 33, 176, 190, 273, 403, 499, 523, 637). Almost without exception, those who entered into formal business dealings asserted their descent either from the Inca nobility or from provincial leaders who had resettled in Cuzco.

The process through which land in the Andes was transformed into a private possession—whether the owners were Spanish peninsulars or men and women of the colonial indigenous elite—severely affected the institutions that had shaped the lifeways of pre-Columbian Andean peoples. One structure undermined by the politico-religious policies of the Spanish regime and by the privatization of land was the women's organizations that governed female political and religious authority. Lands that, under the regime of the Incas, were destined to maintain political and religious institutions dominated by women passed into private hands. This transformation thus

115

curtailed an Andean tradition of independent women's politico-religious activities, albeit one controlled by Cuzco's female elite. It is perhaps ironic that women who claimed private ownership of land by virtue of their royal ancestry could use their Spanish privileges to lay claim to those very lands which had supported the autonomous female cults.

Several rich fields in the Valley of Yucay that, in the Spanish wording, had "belonged to" or "bordered on" those "belonging to" the Inca queens, were considered by Doña Angelina Yupanqui Coya to be her personal possessions. Known as Anas before the Spanish conquest, she was from the highest ranks of the Cuzco nobility: the historian Domingo Angulo said that she was the daughter of Huayna Capac, whereas Garcilaso gives her father as Atahualpa (Rostworowski 1962:135). In a document published by María Rostworowski as well as in a manuscript I discovered in the archives of the Department of Cuzco, Doña Angelina based her rights to lands in Yucay and in the heights of San Blas on her descent from Topa Yupanqui and Coya Mama Anahuarque (Rostworowski 1962:135; ADC:ACC, Top. 24, Leg. 1). Doña Angelina, a concubine of Francisco Pizarro, with whom she had a child, and the wife of the Spanish scribe and chronicler Juan de Betanzos, manipulated the access to property bestowed her through Spanish law as well as her personal relationships with Spanish men to obtain a secure position in colonial society. In a similar process, the daughters of Don Francisco Chilchi of Yucay inherited the Challaguasi fields, which had been under the dominion of the *coyas* before the Spanish conquest (Villanueva 1970:46; ADC:AHU, Leg. IV).

It was the indigenous peasantry, the *indios del común*, who suffered most from the introduction of relations of private property to the Andes. Although the Crown had formally granted Indian commoners use-rights to lands that were held under communal jurisdiction, they were to see that land base—desperately needed to maintain themselves as well as to meet colonial tribute demands—quickly eroded. In the colonial Andes, land was wealth. Thus, despite the official guarantees regarding these supposedly inalienable communal fields, those members of colonial society who could own land as a personal possession strove mightily to wrest this resource from communal control. Indigenous women who were privileged by colonial society participated in this drive to usurp land from the nonprivileged indigenous community; tragically, moreover, it was peasant women who proved most vulnerable to losing their lands.

Colonial civil tribunals heard many legal suits in which commoners contested the attempts to usurp their holdings made by those who could own private property in land. Within this corpus of legal documents, one finds records of disputes between women who, by virtue of their descent from the Cuzco or provincial nobility, made personal claims on communal land, and indigenous commoners who argued that these claims were not justified.

In Yucay, Doña Gabriela Prición's claims to certain agricultural plots in the valley were challenged by the Indian commoner Carlos Flores. Doña Gabriela asserted that several fields had been privately owned by her parents. Avowing that these fields were not under the jurisdiction of the *indios del común*, she claimed to be sole owner as her parents' legitimate heir. Contradicting her claim, Flores argued that the lands in question were part of the communal holdings titled to indigenous commoners and, as such, could be used only by one who was a "descendant of a tribute-paying Indian" (ADC:AUP, Exp. Siglo XVIII, Leg. 15-2). Lands in the Cuzqueñan parish of San Blas were the object of many legal battles carried out between those who asserted descendancy from the Inca lineage and commoners who contested their claims to private ownership. Doña Ana Choquerimay Chimo Ocllo Ñusta, who conspicuously carried her indigenous title of nobility (*ñusta*), based her claim to private ownership on descent from Pachacuti Inca. She was a party in many suits over San Blas lands against tribute-paying Indians who contested her claims (ADC:ACC, Top. 9, Leg. 8). Other women who asserted Inca ancestry, the "titled" *pallas* (a female rank indicating descent

117

from the Cuzco elite) María Sissa Ocllo, Leonor Chimo Ocllo, and Isabel Choquerimay, also engaged in legal battles with the commoners of San Blas at the close of the sixteenth century (ADC:ACC, Top. 9, Leg. 8).

As favored members of the conquered caste, indigenous women who asserted noble privileges, like their male counterparts, played an ambiguous role in colonial society. Their privileged status in colonial Peru was dependent on the dispensations granted them by the Crown; yet, these privileges were based on their descent from the superior ranks of a society their benefactors had conquered. Denied full access to the Spanish world, but privileged by it; needing to avow their indigenous ancestry to obtain these benefits, yet separated by an enormous social and economic gap from the commoners who shared their ancestry, the position of native women (and men) who formed the elite of the conquered was laden with contradictions. These contradictions were compounded as elite women became the wives of men of the caste that conquered them.

The ambiguities inherent in the position of privileged native women were succinctly manifested in a legal suit over land whose ownership was disputed by Doña Paula Mama Guaco Ñusta, and the "india" commoner, Isabel. Declaring descent from the Inca monarch Topa Inga, Doña Paula Mama Guaco Ñusta, as well as her mother Doña Madelena Mama Guaco (among others), asserted that plots of land in the hills above the city of Cuzco were their personal possession. "Indians" from the parish of San Blas challenged them. The commoners based their claim to these fields on descent from the *yanaconas*, who cultivated lands that were ascribed to particular royal sovereigns and who were traditionally given rights to certain fields for their own subsistence. In her sworn testimony to the Crown, Doña Paula Mama Guaco Ñusta voiced the following complaint, explaining that when she had gone to examine her and her mother's property in the contested region of Callixpuquio, she discovered several "indios" plowing her fields:

... and a certain Indian woman, Isabel, dishonored me with insulting words, ignoring the fact that I am the honorable wife of a Spaniard, and a woman of quality and nobility [ADC:ACC, Top. 9, Leg. 5].

Through her own words and name, Doña Paula exposed the contradictions experienced by indigenous women of the conquered caste. On the one hand, her claim to these fields was based on her direct descent from the Inca dynasty. Doña Paula, we should note, conspiciously carried the Inca title Ñusta. Moreover, her surname, "Mama Guaco," was the name of one of the most important queens in Cuzqueñan historical legend. Mama Guaco was also the appellation of her mother, Doña Madelena, and the passing down of surnames from mother to daughter along gender-specific lines is an Andean (as opposed to Spanish) pattern of surname transmission. On the other hand, Doña Paula Mama Guaco relied on her marriage to flaunt her superiority over the Indian commoner, Isabel. By dint of her marital ties with a Spaniard, Doña Paula had acquired prestige and had assumed the characteristics of one who had entered the top echelon of a caste society: crossing the barrier of caste, the wife Doña Paula became "honorable" and a "woman of quality."

SPANISH LAW VERSUS ANDEAN CUSTOM

Spanish law and Andean custom conflicted in many spheres. One of these arenas of irreconcilability had to do with the status of women vis-à-vis land tenure and property rights.

Spanish law classified married women as legal minors. This meant that any legal transaction into which a woman entered had to have the prior authorization of a man, who acted as her "tutor." All transactions involving goods that a woman inherited or brought into a marriage through dowry had to be conducted with the consent and permission of her male tutor. Although women had customary rights over these goods, they were legally under the tutelage of their husbands. According to

119

Spanish law, wives could not freely dispose of their property, and Andean custom contradicted the law in this area. Andean tradition, still followed today, maintained that women, regardless of marital status, held independent rights over all goods, including lands, that might be inherited or otherwise acquired. The concept of joint or common property did not exist.

Conflicts generated by this contradiction surfaced in more than one litigation filed in the Cuzco archives; many pointed to the different status that law and custom bestowed on women owing to rights over the disposition of goods. In these litigations, women of the indigenous elite protested against unilateral economic transactions that their husbands had negotiated. Ana Suta Pongo Piña was party to one suit over the propriety of the sale of an agricultural field. Doña Ana, as a descendant of native rulers, had inherited several fields in the Yucay Valley. Her husband, taking advantage of his tutor status, sold some of the land his wife had inherited, without asking her permission. Formally protesting the validity of the sale, Doña Ana argued that her husband had conducted the transaction without her knowledge and consent (ADC:AUP, Exp. Siglo XVIII, Leg. 11-2; also see BN:B1488).

The will left by Juana Chimbo contains perhaps the strongest statement of the rejection by native noblewomen of the impositions and constraints of Spanish law. This married woman preferred to deed her inheritance to Clara Payco, "for having served her like a sister," and to Antonia Chimbo, her goddaughter, who was "more like a real daughter." Juana Chimbo denied her husband any inheritance, justifying her choice of heirs in the following stipulation: "because I have no kinsmen, and my husband has no rights whatsoever over my lands" (ADC:ACC, Top. 10, Leg. 21).

Spanish law worked to women's disadvantage. This prejudice must have been felt acutely by indigenous women who, by tradition, enjoyed dispositionary rights over their lands. Despite the imposition of Spanish systems of land tenure and inheritance, however, men and women of native origin could manipulate Spanish forms to incorporate pre-Conquest patterns. Thus we find colonial documents that reveal ways in which indigenous inheritance patterns were maintained, albeit within the official constraints imposed by Spanish law. In 1595, for example, when lands were formally distributed to the indigenous elite and commoners of the Yucay Valley, Don Alonso Topa Cusigualpa, who claimed Inca ancestry, was granted lands for his personal use. Included in the designation of fields titled to him, was one "topo" [*tupu*] of land that had been formally granted to his wife. Thus Leona Tocto Sicsa, under her husband's name, was officially allocated a plot of land that she had inherited from Beatriz Sicsa (who in all probability was her mother). In this manner, the pre-Hispanic tradition of parallel transmission rights to land—from mother to daughter—was recognized in colonial land allocations. We should note, though, that Doña Leona did not directly receive title to her land; rather, it was allocated to her by means of her husband, in accord with the constraints of Spanish law which required him to maintain powers of tutelage over his wife's possessions. A similar case was registered in a late-sixteenth-century record in which the Crown formally granted titles to land. Don Alonso Puirana, *cacique* of the *ayllu* of *yanaconas* in Yucay, was granted two and one-half "topos" of land, "one of which was given him for having been married to the daughter of Gualparoca," a descendant of the Inca dynasty (ADC:AHU, Leg. V; also see Zuidema 1967a).

Married noblewomen of indigenous descent who were entitled to personal possessions in land thus had to manipulate Spanish law, which classified them as legal minors, in order to maintain the customs which had once molded the transmission of their ancestors' property rights. If they wanted to dispose of their property in accord with traditional patterns of inheritance, indigenous noblewomen had to conduct transactions through their male affines. One case in point: a noblewoman, resident in the Valley of Yucay, willed land to one of her daughters who had not yet attained majority (ADC:AUP, Proto. y Exp., Proto. 1-2, f. 700). In her will, Doña Ursula Corimanya stipulated that her son-in-law, Don Januario Yuga-chiguan, be her daughter's (his wife's) tutor. This son-in-law was also granted tutorial rights over the lands of his wife's young sister. Doña Ursula declared Don Januario responsible for all future business dealings involving her estate, such as the collection or payment of debts. Although she also had a son, Doña Ursula, by legally entrusting her son-in-law with the handling of her estate, was in fact delegating the responsibility to her elder daughter. With male affines as a cover, Doña Ursula was attempting to follow indigenous norms in which economic obligations and benefits were transmitted along lines of gender. Nevertheless, we should remember that while women could in this fashion try to maintain the patterns that characterized the lives of their ancestors, the imposition of Spanish legal codes provided men with the opportunity to take advantage of their wives and other female kin and affines. Hence the anger and indignation registered by Doña Ana Suta Pongo Piña and Doña Juana Chimbo in colonial litigations.

The history of European conquest reveals how the privileged among colonized peoples will exploit new opportunities for personal gain, generated by colonial relations, which did not exist in their traditional cultures. Again, women who claimed descent from the Cuzco elite were no exception. Yet, we must remember that in spite of their privileges, these women were subjugated members of a patriarchal colonial society. Although the *coyas* may have been renowned during the reign of the Incas as the agronomist-geneticists of the empire (Murúa 1946:87; Silverblatt 1981:25-34), the special schools established by the Spanish for descendants of the indigenous elite were open only to men (Arriaga 1968:12; Hernández Príncipe 1923:78; Esquivel y Navia 1901:42). Today we marvel at the extraordinary weavings produced by women of the Inca lineage; yet, their colonial daughters could not gain entry into indigenous artisan guilds (Spalding 1974:177, 83). Before the Spanish conquest, the Inca queens headed a political network that connected women throughout the empire, but the Crown denied native noblewomen positions within the structures of colonial government established for descendants of the Inca elite (Roel 1970:310). The memory of very different life experiences and potentials for action, of what it meant to be a woman in Andean society before the arrival of the Spaniards, was not lost among upper-class women of the conquered caste. It should not surprise us that these women clung to the memory of their ancestresses' past, that they flaunted their identification with that memory through dress and posture. Thus Rowe, describing colonial paintings drawn more than two hundred years after the Spanish invasion writes:

> . . . in several of the women's portraits, their dress so accurately replicates Inca style, that if it were not for the way in which the landscape was represented in the background, we would have to conclude that we were dealing with personages living at the time of the Conquest [1976:23].

The identification that female descendants of the Inca dynasty felt with their past was to burst forth in political movements which in part attempted to re-create the social and political organization of the vanquished Inca empire. Women of noble birth played crucial roles in the great indigenous rebellion of the eighteenth century led by Tupac Amaru and his wife, Micaela Bastides. One of the most powerful and devoted leaders of this rebellion was the *curaca* Tomasa Tito Condemayta, who held the post of provincial chief of Acomayo, in the Department of Cuzco. Not only an active planner and counselor of military strategy and logistics, Doña Tomasa was an officer in the insurgent army. Indeed, she was at the head of a brigade of women soldiers who achieved fame by successfully defending the Bridge of Acos against Spanish troops (Valcárcel 1947).

However, this indigenous rebellion—which sought to overthrow the insidious institutions of the colonial social order—embodied contradictions reflecting the ambiguity of a mass movement led by the privileged. The arrest of colonial abuses might give rise to a more just society; yet, the society that the elite envisioned was still a hierarchical one, in which they

123

would maintain an amalgam of the privileges derived from their Inca past and from the despised Spanish regime (Flores 1976:278-80). We cannot know precisely how the peasant followers of this movement judged its leaders who glorified their Inca ancestry. Certainly the abuses they suffered at the hands of the privileged members of their own group were as deeply loathed as those imposed by peninsulars. Thus, while some women of the native elite were praised as heroic participants in the fight against the colonial regime, others were despised for their participation in, and manipulation of, colonial institutions for personal gain. One of the severest attacks by the indigenous peasant followers of Tupac Amaru was that against the houses and estate of Doña Antonia Chuquicallata, a wealthy woman from the native nobility of Azángaro (Flores 1976:282).

Although some indigenous women, those who claimed descent from the privileged ranks of pre-Columbian society, were able to take advantage of the new sources of wealth opened up by the Spanish conquest, their history represents only a tiny percentage of the Andean peoples. The great majority of the colonized were brutally mistreated under colonial rule. Moreover, even though men and women of the peasantry both suffered under the Spanish yoke, we shall see that the burdens placed on women were not only different, but more intense.

Women of the Peasantry

> The priests want money, money, and more money, so they force women to serve them as spinners, weavers, cooks, breadmakers. . . . The priests and *corregidores* make false accusations, declaring that Indian women are living in concubinage, and that they have committed a sin against God; these accusations are usually made because of the insinuation of the priest . . . especially if these women have had a child, or answered him defiantly, or if they did not want to work for him voluntarily. Then they oblige the women to work without pay, as if it were a punishment or penance. . . . Women had honor . . . during the epoch of the Incas in spite of the fact that they were idolatrous, but now the clergy and the parish priests are the ones who first violate them and lead them to sin.
>
> [Guaman Poma (1613) 1956, II:175, 34]

ECONOMIC BURDENS

The Inca and Spanish systems that garnered labor and tribute from the peasantry were as different as the principles that oriented their respective economies. The surpluses required to support the empire's nonproductive members were acquired by taxing the labor of the peasantry, under a system in which the elite were obliged to feast and redistribute goods to the laborers and were prohibited from appropriating any goods produced on the peasantry's lands or provided from their herds. Further, the rulers of the empire were culturally bound to ensure the well-being of those drafted for periodic corvée labor in the mines, army, or state-run public works. Built-in institutional and ideological mechanisms tempered the relationship between rulers and commoners, while the norms of reciprocity that operated in the kin-based *ayllus* ensured that families whose members were temporarily obliged to leave the *ayllu* to perform services for the empire were supported and cared for. The Inca designation of the household as the minimal unit liable for tribute was consonant with the Andean norm of the necessary interdependence of male and female labor, and it helped guarantee that any commoner on whom tribute obligations fell would still have the support of the spouse as well as kin or affines to soften the burden of services demanded by the state (see Murra 1956:164-71).

The goal of Spanish tribute and labor demands, on the other hand, was intrinsically tied to a radically different economic system. Goods were produced not for use, but for their exchange value on the European market. No built-in mechanisms existed to ensure the well-being of the laborer or to restrain the exploitation of nature. These existed only as a means to accumulate wealth for *criollo* and peninsular authorities, merchants, clerics, and the coffers of Spain. It was because of the intensive labor needed to produce the goods valued in European and colonial markets that the new regime was so devastating to indigenous society and so fundamentally inhumane. "What is carried to Spain from Peru," noted one Spaniard in the seventeenth century, "is not silver, but the blood and sweat of Indians" (Taussig n.d.:50).

Under the colonial system, in contrast to the Inca system of tribute appropriation, all indigenous men of "common origin" between the ages of eighteen and fifty—regardless of marital status—were subject to tribute demands. These demands often took the form of labor services. Indian peasants were forced to work in mines or *obrajes* (proto-factories, sweatshops) or were obliged to perform personal services for colonial authorities— for the magistrates (*corregidores*), clergy, or *encomenderos* who had almost unlimited access to the labor of the indigenous peasants in their jurisdiction.

Taxation was also part of colonial tribute. In the early years of colonial rule, taxes consisted of levies on goods; however, with time, peasants were required to fulfill their tribute obligations in money. In addition the Church, as an institution, was entitled to charge tithes based on a percentage of all produce of European origin. Priests could also collect personal fees for the celebration of masses, marriages, baptisms, and other Catholic rites. Particularly resented by the peasantry was the quasi-legal *repartimiento de mercancías*; this forced distribution of merchandise, imposed by the *corregidores*, obliged commoners to purchase often useless goods at highly inflated prices. All these taxes, fees, and purchase obligations which were imposed on the peasantry had the effect of forcing Indian men and women to participate in the market economy (Spalding 1974:116).

As Spalding has pointed out (1974:50-52), the indigenous peasantry perceived the Spanish tributary regimen to be doubly exploitative, compared with the pre-Conquest Andean system. The Spanish Crown expropriated lands that had once served to underwrite the Inca empire's civil and religious institutions, thereby removing the land base which the peasantry could have used to meet tribute demands. Nevertheless, Spain demanded that Indians pay for the construction of state facilities and for the maintenance of the new state religion as well as contribute toward the support of the mother country and its colonial governing apparatus. This revenue had to come, then, from the produce of the peasantry's own lands, which under the Inca regime could not be taxed by Cuzco.

In addition to ignoring the Inca decree—that production from fields or other material factors under peasant jurisdiction was inviolable—the Spanish tribute system disregarded the deeply embedded Andean concept of the household unit, the complement of female and male labor, as the minimal entity liable for tribute. Those *curacas* who were still obliged to operate within the arena of Andean values had to distort this indigenous norm in order to meet colonial tribute demands. Some betrothed young men before they had reached the appropriate age—determined in Andean culture by productive ca-

127

pacity—for marriage and entrance into adulthood. Others obliged men to wed girls who were well below the accepted age in order to maintain the appearance that they were tributing married men. But this ruse was shattered in practice: the young men were physically incapable of fulfilling their economic obligations, while the girls were too young to contribute adequately as partners in a male-female work team. Representatives of the Crown, sent to conduct inspections of the status of Indians vis-à-vis the colonial regime, recorded the complaints of male tribute-paying peasants who were abused by their *curaca*'s shams:

> ... the *cacique* Don Gomez oppressed them [male Indian commoners] by giving them as wives girls who were not ready to work and who could not help them. ... The *cacique* Gomez oppressed them while distributing tribute obligations, for ... some of the married men are only eighteen or twenty years old ... and if he married a fifteen-year-old Indian to a young girl, he would burden him with the same tribute obligations as he would an able-bodied native man [Ortiz de Zúñiga 1967, I:73, 78].

Moreover, other *curacas*, hard-pressed by the impositions of colonial taxation, completely ignored the pre-Hispanic requisite that tribute be levied only on married men. Indians complained bitterly to Ortiz that their headmen were taxing bachelors as well as widowers. Their discontent lay in the fact that these had no partners to help them:

> ... old men and bachelors are unjustly taxed because they do not have wives to work in the fields while they are occupied with tribute demands. ... [T]he old men and bachelors among them are forced to work to meet tribute demands, not having wives who cook for them and watch over their houses and land [Ortiz de Zúñiga 1972, II:30]. [They complained that] the *curaca* demanded tribute of single men, because single men do not have wives to help them as married men do, and [he did this] because there are few Indians and

the taxes are many, and to meet payment he could do nothing else [Ortiz de Zúñiga 1967, I:90].

As tribute demands increased, peasant women also bore the burdens of Spanish taxes. If before the Conquest only married women were responsible for weaving cloth for the empire, thereafter the *curacas* levied a tax in cloth on all. Wool was distributed to single women and widows in order to fulfill the demands for textiles imposed by colonial authorities (Díez de San Miguel 1964:75). Spanish observers, commenting on the increased workload shouldered by the native peasantry since the colonization of the Andes, were well aware that it was through the additional contributions of those who under the Incas had been exempt from labor services—namely, women and the elderly—that colonial exigencies were met. Ortiz de Zúñiga writes:

> during the time of the Inca they had less work because neither women nor old people labored with respect to tribute, and they cultivated the fields of those who worked to fulfill tribute obligations, and now everyone must do so [1972, II:35].

Under the Incas, peasant women, while not formally registered in tribute rolls, did contribute to the fulfillment of labor demands made by their rulers; but they did so in an economic system in which exactions were tempered. Under Spanish law, native women were formally exempt from tribute; however, attempts to moderate the exactions made on the peasantry were disregarded by colonial authorities. Since the Spanish needed women's labor, it was taken in spite of legal encumbrances. Thus women, illegally, were viewed by the Spanish as fair game for tribute, and *curacas*, unable to meet tribute demands through men's labor, were forced to turn to women (see Figure 7). This transformation of the peasant woman's economic station was at the heart of Guaman Poma's denunciation:

129

FIG. 7. Tribute Being Demanded from an Elderly Woman (Guaman Poma 1936:f. 886)

Indian women, widows, single women, young girls, and the elderly are not obliged to weave clothing for tribute, nor to spin or weave for the *encomenderos*, magistrates, priests, lieutenants, major-domos, Spaniards, or for any other person, except for their community, in accord with the dictates of the ancient laws and customs which they had in the time of the Incas, and by ordinance of Viceroy Toledo. The tax corresponding to clothing should be levied on the male Indian tributary and not on the Indian woman, according to a law to the effect that the woman is not to be a tributary, and it is thus determined in the general inspections which are made of Indian tributaries, in accord with the law [1956, III:130].

The Spanish tribute regimen had other prejudicial consequences on peasant women. One of its effects was to undermine traditional patterns of land tenure and inheritance whereby women maintained independent access to lands. Owing to Spanish law and the nature of the tributary system itself, men from the Spanish elite, as well as from the native peasantry, were induced to wrest from women their pre-Hispanic rights to autonomous control over productive resources.

Let us now turn to the impact of colonial decrees which were supposed to smooth out the operation of the Spanish tributary system. After the mayhem of the first forty years of colonial rule, the Viceroy Francisco Toledo systematized the forced resettlement of indigenous peoples into villages modeled on the Spanish ideal of town planning. By mandating that native peoples abandon their dispersed dwellings in the inaccessible *punas* to live in the *reducciones*, Toledo had hit upon a formula for facilitating not only religious indoctrination but, more important, the collection of tribute (Roel 1970:89-91). One of the effects of this campaign was to break down the societal relations that had governed the pre-Columbian *ayllu* and to replace them with new social forms compatible with the organization of the *reducción* (the colonial *ayllu*). This, in conjunction with the tremendous population decline that native

131

Andean peoples suffered after the Conquest, induced men and women from different colonial *ayllus* to intermarry—a marriage pattern that contrasted sharply with the pre-Hispanic norm of *ayllu* endogamy. Colonial *ayllu* exogamy had its toll on indigenous women, who found themselves doubly taxed. Because of the pressures of the colonial tributary system, women were now taxed both by the *curacas* of their natal *ayllus* in which they held land and by the *curacas* of their husband's *ayllus* (Díez de San Miguel 1964:221).[1] Toledo attempted to straighten out the confusion resulting from inter-*ayllu* betrothals as well as to moderate the injustices of conflicting tribute claims made on women who married outside. He did so by mandating that a couple be subject only to the tribute demands of the husband's *curaca* while obliging them to reside in the husband's *ayllu*. Moreover, children were now to be considered members of their father's kin group only (Spalding 1967:122).

Spanish law and tributary practices thus undermined indigenous structures of social organization shaped by principles of parallel descent. The Spanish solution to exogamy ended up strengthening patrilineal and patrilocal ties at the expense of relations expressed through matrilineal filiation and matrilocal residence. Spanish law thus tended to erode pre-Conquest descent structures and inheritance patterns which had unified women.

Sometimes, *ayllus* themselves tried to resolve the potential conflicts derived from intergroup marriages. One *ayllu* formula stipulated that daughters would inherit lands belonging to women who married exogamously, while sons would hold claim to their father's property (Spalding 1967:126). These *ayllus*, in other words, reverted to or upheld the Andean tradition of parallel descent.

[1] The conflicts stemming from *ayllu* exogamy lend support to my argument that Andean women traditionally had independent rights to lands, and that these rights were not lost at marriage. If married women did not have independent access to land by virtue of their *ayllu* membership, there would have been no basis for these inter-*ayllu* conflicts.

At times, even peasant men spearheaded the drive to wrest the autonomous right to land from the women who lived with them. Although male heads of household were given usufruct privileges to communal fields in the Crown's formal distribution of commoner land rights (see ADC:AHU, Leg. III, IV, V), beneath the legal surface, peasants often maintained pre-Conquest traditions of women's independent rights to resources (see ADC:AHU, Leg. III). When Spanish legal practice came to terms with indigenous tradition in Ecuador, the result, with respect to colonial tribute demands, was that produce garnered from "female lands" could not be applied toward the fulfillment of tax obligations. But as tribute burdens increased, the men from at least one village (Zuidema 1972:20) found that their lands did not produce enough to meet these exactions. One man began to use his wife's lands, which she had inherited from her mother, in order to fulfill his tax payment. His actions generated a legal battle, in which men expressed their desire to abolish the Andean tradition that afforded women autonomous rights to land. In other words, it was in the interests of the men from this indigenous village to do away with the pre-Hispanic structure of parallel transmission because it was no longer compatible with the tribute system imposed by the Spanish. Although only one example, it elucidates the ways in which the colonial tribute system eroded pre-Conquest norms of gender relations. Tragically, peasant men participated in the destruction of the principles that guided the social and economic life of their forebears—principles which guaranteed that women and men alike had independent rights to society's resources (see ADC:AHU, Leg. II).

We have witnessed the clash between Spanish law and indigenous custom and the ensuing process through which colonial institutions undermined the rights of peasant women. Spanish law defined women as minors, so lands inherited by them were under the legal jurisdiction of their spouses. Colonial laws regulating the land tenure of commoners dictated that the male head of household be granted, in usufruct, the fields to support not only himself, but his wife and children. The Crown thus gave men an advantage, and some did manipulate it to assume control over their wives' and other women's lands. But their attempts were resisted. At times, local headmen of colonial *ayllus* fought the assays of individuals who tried to usurp women's traditional prerogative (Spalding 1974:126). Women themselves protested against the attempts made to undermine their claims to independent jurisdiction over material resources (ADC: AUP, Exp. Siglo XVIII, Leg. 11-2; ACC, Top. 10, Leg. 21; BN:B1488). As colonization advanced in the Andes, indigenous men and women witnessed their communal lands being encroached upon by a Spanish and indigenous elite engaged in building agricultural estates; unfortunately, because of the unfavored position in which the colonial system placed women, they were rendered much more vulnerable than men to being dispossessed of lands and resources (BN:B1488; BN:C3967). As Guaman Poma observed, no matter how much colonial authorities and the privileged members of indigenous society robbed peasant men, "they robbed poor Indian women much more" (1956, III:98).

We have examined several ways in which colonial tributary mechanisms and economic institutions transformed the standing of peasant women and impinged on their economic capabilities. Let us further explore the special burdens that the colonial economy, tied into the European market, placed on their shoulders.

From the beginning of the Spanish conquest, representatives of the colonial regime recognized their need for access to women's labor in order to produce goods destined for colonial and European markets. One of these goods was textiles. Since the inception of colonization, peasant women were brutally exploited by *encomenderos* and, later, by magistrates and the owners of landed estates and *obrajes*. The first forms of an industrial labor draft emerged in the *encomienda* itself, when colonial "barons" demanded a tribute in cloth. In order to ensure their control over women's labor, many began locking women in *corrales* or other chambers and forcing them to spin and weave. These women were so severely exploited that, in

1549, a royal decree was issued specifically prohibiting the continuation of this practice (Roel 1970:135). However, the structure of colonial institutions, and the increasing pressures they exerted to augment tribute and wealth, overpowered decrees meant to moderate the peasants' load. Thus, this 1549 decree became only one of many advanced (and effectively ignored) in order to alleviate the burden of the colonized.

One hundred and fifty years later, the judge responsible for overseeing indigenous affairs in Cuzco was imprisoned because he had a private jail in his house; there he had put women whom he forced to spin and to weave cloth (Esquivel y Navia 1901:185). Having a voracious desire for their labor, colonial administrators commonly abused women. The *corregidores*, most of whom envisioned their stay in the colonies as a way to make quick money, obliged women to weave clothing for them at less than half the free market rate (Rowe 1957:163). Guaman Poma gives us this description of how women were mistreated by colonial authorities who made them virtual prisoners in order to exploit their labor for the production of market goods:

> In the village of Hatun Lucanas, the *corregidor*'s lieutenant kept in his kitchen a half-dozen single maidens, as well as a dozen Indian women who were performing *mita* service, who were forced to work spinning and weaving; and he employed them as bakers and *chicha* brewers; the priest who accompanied him did the same thing. Seeing the impossibility of remedying these abuses, and so as not to be left behind, the mayor kept three Indian women in his service [1956, II:111].

Moreover, the structure of the colonial institutions which extracted surpluses from the peasantry was such that it forced women to sell their labor. Spanish tribute demands and taxes were so high that the compensation men received for their work was insufficient to fulfill their tax obligations. Consequently, women were obliged to enter the labor force; often, that meant work in the textile sweatshops. The economist Virgilio Roel has pointed out (1970:137) that the exhorbitant demands of the colonial tax structure propelled women to weave in the *obrajes*. They had little choice. So while their husbands and male kin were away laboring to fulfill colonial *mita* obligations, women particularly, out of necessity, had to work for the *obrajes* in their homes—in exchange for grossly depressed wages—in order to meet tribute levies.

Caught in a similar trap, women who accompanied their husbands on work drafts away from the village were also obligated to sell their labor. The most common and loathed of colonial labor drafts was that for work in the mines. As *mitayos*, peasant workers were paid wages; it has been calculated, however, that the wages men received were equivalent to about one-sixth of the money needed for subsistence. Since *mitayos* were often accompanied by their wives and children, Rowe suggests that one way of compensating for this difference between earning capacity and basic needs was for the laborer's wife and children to work as well (1957:173). Having to work for bare survival, women could be treated as virtual slaves by colonial men of business.

The years following the Spanish conquest were shaken by a tremendous population decline (Cook 1975:xii; 1981). The native mortality rate alone placed added burdens on the living, as colonial tribute demands were not adjusted to account for demographic changes (Roel 1970:207-210). Thus, Toledo in 1572 registered 1,068,697 tribute-paying Indians, who contributed approximately 1,384,228 pesos per year to colonial coffers. Twenty years later, Viceroy García Hurtado de Mendoza still collected 1,434,420 pesos, even though the number of tribute-paying Indians had declined over two-thirds to 311,252 (Roel 1970:229).

Although the entire indigenous peasantry witnessed an alarming increase in tribute levies, the burdens were not shared equally by men and women. Men had a way out. By leaving his community of origin and taking up residence in an urban center, in another village, or on one of the growing number of haciendas, a man could avoid both *mita* and tribute obligations.

The high incidence of rural migration and escape (*fuga*) was a dramatic demonstration that peasant men preferred to abandon their natal communities than to be subject to such demands (Roel 1970:137, 334). Since tribute and labor quotas were not reformulated in relation to demographic changes, the weight on those who remained necessarily increased. In effect, then, women (along with the elderly and children)—those who stayed behind—increasingly shouldered the load of colonial tribute and labor services. By law, women were exempt from *mita* drafts and from paying tribute. In fact, however, by the end of the sixteenth century and throughout the seventeenth and eighteenth centuries, women were not only liable to be drafted for labor services, but were paying tribute as well (Guaman Poma 1956, III:33, 64, 90, 133; Roel 1970:208).

More bluntly than any other commentator on colonial society, the indigenous chronicler Guaman Poma de Ayala depicts in painful detail the systematic destruction of the institutions which governed social existence in the Andes prior to the Spanish conquest. Basing his critique of Spanish colonial society on a comparison with the quality of life enjoyed by indigenous peoples before and during Inca rule, Guaman Poma describes how the indigenous institutions governing political, economic, and social life were transformed and perverted by the pressures of the new regime. Within this context, Guaman Poma outlines the vulnerable position in which Andean women were placed as the norms and structures governing intergender relations before the Conquest—when women and their labor were highly respected and valued—were eroded by European values and institutions. He gives example after example of how native women, whether married, single, or widowed, were forced to work under highly exploitative conditions for colonial administrators, landowners, magistrates, and clergy. Guaman Poma poignantly underscores the fact that Western institutions, particularly when placed in a colonial context, were especially brutalizing and dehumanizing to colonized women (1956, II:224, 251, 220, III:55, 98, 270):

It is customary for priests to exchange parishes; thus, any priest who wants to take revenge on a *curaca* or on Indians will change with another priest whom he will order to rob and cruelly punish the Indian men and women of his parish. They are rounded up and locked in a building by the priest's replacement, especially single women, widows, and even married women; they are forced to weave and spin; in this way they take their vengeance out on poor Indians. . . . The parish priests force women to spin and weave, particularly widows and single women. Under the pretext that they are living in sin, the priests force them to work without paying them for their labor [1956, II:157, 152].

Nor does Guaman Poma spare indigenous political authorities. These male officeholders, intermediaries between the world of the conquerors and the world of the colonized, often allied themselves with their Spanish masters to the detriment of their fellow Indian commoners. Following suit, they too began to abuse women in ways that would have been unthinkable before the Conquest:

The village mayors, aldermen, and constables invoke much harm, imposing punishments; because of this, those who are wronged detest them, especially the poor Indian women who are mistreated. . . . [T]hey become *curaca* or *ayllu* leaders without having titles or rights [to these posts]. Then they form a gang of Indian toughs, with whom they begin to rob and commit banditry, going from house to house and taking all they can from the poor Indian men, and much more still from the poor Indian women, making off with all their goods, and the *corregidores* give their consent, because it is done under the pretext of charging *mita* [1956, III:55, 98].

SEXUAL ABUSE

The injustices suffered by indigenous women were not limited to economic exploitation. It was not just the fact that women's lands and herds were more easily confiscated, or that they were forced to work under virtual slave conditions, or that they increasingly bore the brunt of the Crown's taxes and labor drafts that prompted Guaman Poma's rage. Native women were also sexually abused. For a society in which pre-marital sex was encouraged, but only under circumstances in which both partners consented; in a culture where relations between men and women were conceived of as *ayni* (balance), the rape and forced concubinage of women carried out by Spanish and indigenous authorities was an abomination:

> In the mines, Indian women are employed as cooks and are made into concubines; under the pretext that they have to work in the kitchen, some daughters of Indian men are kid-napped and are forced into service, being raped by the men who run the mines or by their assistants, who even dare to rape married women, and in order to do so, they order their husbands to go work in the mines at night . . . so they can freely commit these atrocities [Guaman Poma 1956, II:117].

For many indigenous women, the theft of their lands and their bodies was a dual yoke thrust on them in the dehuman-izing process of Spanish colonization:

> In the Indian villages, the *encomenderos*, their sons, broth-ers, and major-domos rape single women, married women, all women, whom they pervert, converting them into pros-titutes. These men, as well as their servants, blacks, *mesti-zos*, and Indians [*yanaconas*] wreck the lives of these women, destroying their possessions, land and food [Gua-man Poma 1956, II:144].

In Guaman Poma's eyes, priests were the most vicious per-petrators of the dehumanization of women (see Figures 8 and 9). The terrible irony of their hypocrisy—their damning of in-digenous practices as idolatrous, while they created a "sancti-fied" colonial hell for women—was denounced repeatedly by the chronicler (1956, II:191, 141, I:49). Under the guise of teaching women the catechism or delegating penance, priests

139

FIG. 8. Andean Woman Forced to Weave by a Dominican Monk
(Guaman Poma 1936:f. 645)

FIG. 9. Priest Abusing Office by Forcing Marriage (Guaman Poma 1936:f. 573)

forced women to serve them as laborers, mistresses, and prostitutes:

> ... Priests are supposed to educate boys only, but they get girls as well, and the parish priests take advantage of this in order to have concubines at their disposal and consequently dozens of children, augmenting the number of *mestizos*. Moreover, under this pretext, they force Indian women to work, isolating them from Indian men, saying that in this way they train the women and make them Christians, and that is also why the number of Indians in this kingdom does not increase, nor will it ever increase. ... The priests want money, money, and more money, so they force women to serve them as spinners, weavers, cooks, breadmakers. ... The priests and *corregidores* make false accusations, declaring that Indian women are living in concubinage, and that they have committed a sin against God; these accusations are usually made because of the insinuation of the priest ... especially if these women have had a child, or answered him defiantly, or if they did not want to work for him voluntarily. Then they oblige the women to work without pay, as if it were a punishment or penance. If they complain ... and the complaint has been made to the royal inspector, they order the women to his house, where they are forced to work even more. Thus, there is no one who takes these women's side. If they continue to complain, they pay no attention, claiming that the women are living in sin ... and in this way these authorities take revenge on the Indian woman who preferred to be with an Indian man. ... Women had honor ... during the epoch of the Incas in spite of the fact that they were idolatrous, but now the clergy and the parish priests are the ones who first violate them and lead them to sin [Guaman Poma 1956, II:61, 175, 34].

Guaman Poma's words reveal the colonial pressures which destroyed the fabric of indigenous social life, as well as the ways in which women, exploited for their labor and abused sexually, were manipulated by men holding positions of authority in the Spanish world (see Figure 10). He witnessed the population decline of those of his caste, and he identified the disintegrating powers of colonialism—powers which undermined the socioeconomic and cultural order of Andean peoples—as the primary cause. And he also saw that, in this process of disintegration, indigenous women were rendered particularly vulnerable; for in the unrestrained milieu of colonial society, Western norms and institutions governing gender relations could develop to grotesque extremes.

The transformation of indigenous women into prostitutes was one of the tragic by-products of this imposition of Western gender traditions onto Andean society. Guaman Poma describes the terrible process whereby indigenous women were beguiled and seduced by men of authority, then used by them and debased by them. The tragedy, though, lies in the fact that these women became caught in a trap from which there was no escape, becoming outsiders and pariahs to their own communities. Dependent on the Spanish and their collaborators, most women had little choice but to participate in their own debasement:

> Now, women who are handed over to the priests and other Spaniards do not want to marry Indian men, nor do the men want to marry them; and for this reason young women are converted into common prostitutes, and married women into bellicose prostitutes and adultresses, who live outside their communities. . . . [F]acilitating and protecting illicit relations . . . their very fathers and mothers reach an accord with the parish priests, who first rewarding these girls and deceiving them, violate them and afterward hand them over to other Spaniards who convert them into prostitutes, and as such they are handed over to other men, followed by the *fiscales* [Indian agents of priests], sacristans, and cantors; and finally, completely practiced in this manner, they go to the *tambos* [inns] to look for Spaniards, with whom they sin and since all the young boys see them, they go looking for

143

FIG. 10. Sexual Abuse of Andean Woman by Spanish Officials (Guaman Poma 1936:f. 503)

them, and thus they can no longer get married in their own village [1956, III:115].

Guaman Poma related this phenomenon to the deterioration of native cultural relations as a whole. Furthermore, this deterioration, as he saw it, ultimately threatened the very ability of indigenous society to survive. This is why Guaman Poma warns against the growing mestizization of indigenous society—the "growing number of *mestizos* and *cholos*" (1956, II:61, 93, 96, 100, 214, III:75, 115)—which he directly links to the visible abandonment of native villages, as well as to the alarming decline in the indigenous population.

The gross distortion in the character of interpersonal life, which Guaman Poma roots in the colonization process as a whole, seemed all the more sordid when compared with the quality of life that marked pre-Columbian Andean societies. The increased drunkenness that he observed, the high incidence of wife beating and personal violence in general, were manifestations of the deterioration of a once ordered and humane indigenous culture. He comments:

At present, in this life, more Indian drunks exist than in the old times. In the epoch of the Incas, there were none [to speak of]; for they were immediately subjected to [traditional] justice. The Inca ordered . . . that those who were terrible drunks, who spoke in an evil way, who slapped women in the face, who fought with anyone or with their wives, be brought to justice [1956, III:98].

The interpersonal tensions decried by the chronicler were generated by the colonial forces which gnawed away at the traditional balances in Andean society. Guaman Poma points to many aspects of native life which were subsequently undermined, and the breakdown of kinship and marriage norms was one. Perhaps he exaggerates in the following passage, but the collapse of the rules underlying Andean kinship reflected the inability of kinship relations in general to maintain the social existence of native communities:

145

Once drunk, they become idolators and fornicate with their sisters, mothers, and married women; and women, when they are drunk, they themselves search out men without worrying if they are with their fathers or brothers [1956, III:102].

The breakdown of the constraints of pre-Columbian social relations could be manipulated by some women of the indigenous peasantry. They used the contacts that their sexuality offered to gain favors from men in positions of power, while casting aside their communities' traditions of authority. Prostitution or concubinage was a path that some native women chose to add a measure of security to their meager lives. But, as Guaman Poma pointed out, this path had repercussions on the lives of those women who chose to remain in the *ayllu* and follow Andean custom:

Receiving favors from Spaniards, [these women] take advantage of this to become great braggarts, prostitutes, and evil women. They fear neither God nor authority.... Living with Spaniards . . . they become fond of receiving gifts; they serve neither God nor the king; they do not obey judges or their *caciques*, their fathers, mothers, or husbands. ... [T]hey no longer want to marry Indian men [1956, III:95].

. . . The *encomenderos* . . . are absolute lords, reserving some women for their personal service whom they make their lovers, and [these women] no longer help in meeting tribute demands or labor obligations, thereby prejudicing and disadvantaging the well-being of the community, placing all the workload on other Indian women. The *encomenderos* fornicate with single women and widows, and they exempt them, because of this, from all work, such as making clothing, attending fields, herds, and other things, [thus] prejudicing the honorable women who find themselves burdened with tasks; while the former give birth to *mestizos*, the poor Indian women find themselves obliged to work more [1956, II:147].

There was another side, then, to the dehumanizing gender relations of colonial society. Women might sell their bodies for security and advantage, but they did so in a context in which the structures defining relations between men and women were controlled by men; they were only pawns, dependent on the men who ultimately debased them. Colonial pressures were destroying the *ayni*—the mutual obligations and complementarity—that characterized much of the interaction of women and men before the Conquest. The imposition of colonial institutions on indigenous society often promoted all the worst aspects of Western norms governing gender relations: native men came to "own" their female relatives. Indeed, men desperate to avoid service in the mines or elsewhere, or men unable to meet their tribute quotas, pawned their female relatives to Spaniards (Guaman Poma 1956, II:127). A priest, Fray Buenaventura de Salinas, appalled by the absolute degradation that indigenous women suffered, included the following account in his chronicle of the New World:

> [*mitayos*] pawn, rent their daughters and wives to the directors of mines, to soldiers, and to *mestizos* for fifty or sixty pesos in order to free themselves of their obligation to work in the mines. [A priest] had banned a soldier from his church, for the soldier had entered it in order to collect his pawn, a lovely Indian youth, sixteen years old. [The soldier] then went to the priest and magistrate demanding justice, saying: Lord Magistrate, Isabel ... has been pawned for seventy pesos by her father whom I freed from labor service, and until my money is returned, I do not have to turn her over; rather, I can make use of her as I wish. And thus the magistrate let him take her ... while she was sobbing, crying that the Spaniard wanted to force her to live with him, that how was it possible that the Church did not help her at all, and that having been born free in her native land, they made her a slave to sin [Roel 1970:109].

No wonder Guaman Poma thought "the world was turned upside-down" (1956, II:62, 154, III:84).

CHAPTER VIII

Political Disfranchisement

> ... the *corregidores*, priests, and *encomenderos* ... take from women and their daughters, who should legitimately govern, the rights they had since the time of the Incas, dispossessing them of their titles in order to favor rich Indian men.
>
> [Guaman Poma (1613) 1956, II:92]

In the years just after the Conquest, the Spanish debated incorporating members of the Inca elite into colonial government. Final Spanish policy was against this plan and dictated the complete dismantlement of the power structure headed by the Cuzco nobility (Kubler 1946:341-47). However, once Spanish control became entrenched in the Andes, colonial authorities still faced the problem of how to govern (and profit from) the native peasantry. The pre-Hispanic *ayllus* were very dispersed, thus impeding the collection of tribute as well as the indoctrination of *indios* into the new imperial religion. The Spanish, moreover, were sensitive to the dangers that the *ayllus* might pose to their regime if allowed to function as they had before the Conquest. The pre-Hispanic *ayllu* would keep indigenous traditions alive, and the colonists were quite aware that this might threaten the success of their enterprise. For these reasons, native peoples were forced in the mid-sixteenth century to regroup into nucleated settlements called *reducciones* (Roel 1970:94).

Colonial administrators had to elaborate a plan that would hitch indigenous peasantries to Spain's political and economic machinery. The Spanish model of political control modified the existing politicoeconomic traditions of indigenous commoners to fit the needs of the colonial enterprise. A system of

148

indirect rule was imposed: the colonial authorities recognized *curacas* as leaders of their respective communities (the colonial *ayllus*), while also installing political and religious institutions for local government which were patterned after those of Spain (Kubler 1946:341-47).

THE CURACA'S NEW ROLE

Curacas became the designated intermediaries between the worlds of the conquered caste and their masters. They, like the Inca elite, were granted a colonial social status equivalent to that of the European nobility. Consequently, they were relieved of tribute obligations and had the privilege of maintaining private estates. These privileges, however, were given with obligations attached. In exchange for the benefits of noble rank, *curacas* were expected to ensure that the colonial demands on the peasantry were met. The *curaca* was responsible for collecting tribute and taxes, organizing and selecting workers for colonial labor drafts, collecting the goods and salary owed the parish priest, the tithes owed the Catholic Church, and the construction and upkeep of the village church (Spalding 1974:37).[1]

Owing to their position in the colonial politicoeconomic structure, and their consequent alliance with Spanish authorities, *curacas* could take personal advantage of the new channels for mobility and the new sources of wealth introduced by Spain. Often they did so to the detriment of the communities they were supposed to represent and protect. To the extent that the *curacas'* authority was derived from the external colonial power structure, they could disregard Andean norms of reciprocity and mutual obligation which had customarily mediated the relation between local headmen and *ayllu* members (Spalding 1974, 1970, 1973). The deterioration of these traditions, which also flavored pre-Hispanic gender relations,

---

[1] See Stern (1982) and Spalding (1984) for excellent local histories of native responses to colonialism.

had consequences for the relations that were to emerge between *curacas* and peasant women.

We have seen how colonial village headmen participated in the economic exploitation of these women. Guaman Poma accused the *curacas* of exploiting the labor of women under their jurisdiction as well as abusing them sexually. Pérez Bocanegra forewarned priests in his confession manual for curates having native parishioners that some *curacas* illegally charged women tribute and forced them into concubinage (1631:269, 271). Taking advantage of the new means at their disposal, *curacas* deprived women of their rights to land (ADC:AUP, Proto. 1-2; ACC op. 8, Leg. 2). Another ploy used by the *curacas*, who increasingly began to participate in the colonial mercantile economy, was to convert lands under their control to monoculture for the internal Peruvian market. *Curacas*, abusing their function as official spokesmen for their communities, in effect became *hacendados*. In this process, the female members of their *ayllus* were often most vulnerable to losing water rights as well as land. In 1737, community members of San Pedro de Tacna brought suit against their *curaca* for illegally expropriating their lands. They claimed he was forcing them off communal property to facilitate the creation of a private *ají*-producing estate. In testimony, witness after witness remarked that the *curaca*'s primary target was peasant women (BN:C3967).

The Colonial Erosion of Women's Power

Although the Spanish formalized the *curaca*'s role as intermediary between Spanish society and the indigenous peasantry, they were not faithful to the pre-Hispanic structures which allowed women as well as men to occupy positions of *ayllu* leadership. Theoretically, the colonial regime sanctioned pre-Conquest mechanisms through which *curacazgos* were transmitted (Rostworowski 1961). In practice, though, colonial administrators did not recognize the pre-Columbian hierarchies of authority which delegated important governing and political functions to women. Nor were they sensitive to other matrilineally phrased patterns of succession to positions of local leadership. As a consequence, the opportunities women once had to exercise authority in the *ayllu* were undermined, as the traditional mechanisms determining their selection gave way to Spanish customs.

One of the clearest examples of this process comes from Peru's northern coast. Here pre-Columbian patterns of succession were eroded very early in the colonial period (Rostworowski 1961). The first Spaniards to arrive in Peru wrote that women, known as *capullanas*, governed the North Coast ethnic groups of Peru (Anónimo 1906:160). It seems most probable that *capullanas* succeeded to office matrilineally. For when Francisca Canapaynina, a descendant of the coastal nobility, laid claims to the *curacazgo* of Nariguala, she amassed testimony to prove that, before the Spanish conquest, women could rule. However, by 1613, testimonies are already shadowy regarding how women came to power. Some witnesses, backing Doña Francisca's contention, asserted in very general terms that "women could hold office like men." Others, again her supporters, also affirmed that women could rule; but they employed a different argument. By tradition, they said, a female descendant could succeed to office if a *curaca* left no male heir (Rostworowski 1961:29). Thus, by 1613 Doña Francisca's supporters were, in effect, citing Spanish inheritance patterns to justify the legitimacy of their claim. The pre-Columbian structures were already losing their force.

Moreover, by 1625, Doña Francisca was no longer named as the *curaca* of Nariguala. Rather, her husband, Don Juan Temoche, was registered as *"curaca* and governor" of this *ayllu* (Rostworowski 1961:29). In other words, Temoche had begun to exercise control of the *curacazgo* which originally belonged to his wife; as a married woman, Doña Francisca could no longer autonomously govern her *ayllu*. Indigenous traditions were collapsing in ways which prejudiced women's long-standing prerogative to assume positions of independent authority.

The case of Doña Francisca was not an isolated one. In the

Cuzco region, as well, Spanish legal constraints and traditions impinged on the ability of native women to hold power autonomously in their *ayllus*. Although women were recorded as being the *curacas* of several *ayllus* in the Cuzco Valley, one must be aware that by the eighteenth century (the period for which I have documentary evidence) their rights to office were based on Spanish customs of succession. Women succeeded to *curacazgos* if their fathers had left no male heir. Furthermore, once married, their right to govern autonomously was compromised.

Such was the history of Doña Martina de la Paz Chiguantupa, the *cacica* of the Indian commoners from Ccollquepata, in what is today Paucartambo Province. Her father's sole legitimate heir, she became *cacica* upon his death. Doña Martina wanted to name a woman, Doña María Juárez, as her second-in-command, or "segunda persona," who would be responsible for the collection of tribute. But she could not give this authority to María Juárez directly, for the constraints of Spanish law dictated that, as a married woman, Doña María could exercise this post only through the tutelege of her husband (ADC:AZ, Escribano A. Chacón y Becena, Proto. 260-147).

This history repeats itself in Yucay. Doña Isidora Días was registered as the *cacica* of one of Yucay's *ayllus* (Paca) in 1770. In 1778, Melchor Haller de Gamboa sued her husband, Don Felipe Tupayache, for distributing lands to an Indian commoner which Don Melchor claimed were his. Responding to Haller de Gamboa's suit, Doña Isidora indignantly asserted that she—not her husband—had given the peasants rights to communal lands, since she was still single at the time of this land distribution (ADC:AUP, Exp. Siglo XVIII, Leg. 11-2). In subsequent notarial records, the *curaca* of Paca *ayllu* is registered as Don Felipe Tupayache (ADC:AUP, Leg. II, f. 102v). The imposition of Spanish traditions on indigenous patterns of succession denied native women the chance to fill positions of autonomous authority in their communities; once married, women lost their ability to hold local office as husbands "assumed" their *curacazgos*.

In the course of colonization, the erosion of pre-Columbian patterns of governance deeply prejudiced women's political potentialities. Both Doña Isidora and Doña Martina were *curacas* by virtue of Spanish inheritance patterns. The indigenous women who once would have held posts by virtue of Andean structures of gender parallelism no longer had the chance. Guaman Poma explains:

> ... the *corregidores*, priests, and *encomenderos* ... take from women and their daughters, who should legitimately govern, the rights they had since the time of the Incas, dispossessing them of their titles in order to favor rich Indian men [1956, II:92].

Peasant Women and the Loss of Political Legitimacy

In addition to legitimizing native *curacas* by incorporating them into the colonial establishment, the Spanish also introduced political and religious institutions for local government, modeled after the municipal organizations of Spain. The civil apparatus consisted of a *cabildo* (town council) and the annual election of an *alcalde* (mayor), a *regidor* (alderman), and *aguaciles* (constables). In the religious domain, the Spanish created a hierarchy of lay assistants to the parish priests: cantor, sacristan, and treasurer (*fiscal*). As Spalding has pointed out, there were advantages for natives who decided to assume these positions and ally themselves with the provincial representatives of Spanish authority: exemption from *mita* service and dispensations from tribute (1974:73). Also, since the authority on which these offices rested lay with the colonial power structure, those holding office could to some degree disregard the customary norms regulating power and wealth in traditional Andean communities.

Like *curacas*, men in village government or in the service of the parish priest could, within limits, ignore pre-Columbian structures that molded social and political life in the *ayllu*. Backed by men of power in the Spanish religious and civil establishment, these native functionaries were able to disregard traditional Andean norms which constrained the activities of those who exercised authority in the *ayllu*. Outside the restrictions of traditional society, some men who assumed these positions in the colonial *ayllu* began to exploit the opportunities their offices offered. Often this exploitation took the form of abusing indigenous women in ways inadmissible by pre-Columbian standards.

Guaman Poma repeatedly accused *ayllu* civil and religious functionaries of taking unfair advantage of their posts. In league with Spanish officials, they would exploit labor and rob now-vulnerable women of their *ayllus* (1956, II:61, 111, 112, 122, 124, 152, 153, 175, 191, III:75). And male officials did much more than participate in the economic exploitation of peasant women, as lackeys of the Spaniards and *curacas* whom they served and imitated. As the norms and structures of Western society penetrated the colonial *ayllus*, men—the "owners" of their female kin and affines—manipulated native women in order to acquire these offices of relative advantage. Guaman Poma asks the question:

> Some married Indian men voluntarily take their wives, others . . . their daughters, sisters, or nieces, to the parish priest, and deposit them in their kitchen. Why? Because in this way the priests make them mayor, treasurer, or sacristan; Indian men are now accustomed to receiving favors in this way [1956, II:194].

Thus, as traditional structures increasingly gave way to the pressures of colonial Spain, some indigenous men turned to these positions in local government and religious institutions as a way of easing the burdens colonial society placed on them. Betraying the norms of their ancestors, men used the women who were closest in order to take advantage of the benefits which the colonial power establishment dangled in front of them:

> . . . after the priest had punished the aforementioned treasurer, he asked him for one of his daughters, telling him that

she would be more honored by being the wife of a priest than of an Indian, a tribute-paying man; and furthermore he would support him publicly before his *curacas* and mayors . . . and he would give him wine to drink, bread, and meat . . . and moreover he would keep the office of community treasurer for the rest of his life [Guaman Poma 1956, II:161].

As traditional structures yielded to such pressures, those structures which were meant to form the backbone of political and religious organization in the colonial *ayllu* became increasingly illegitimate in the eyes of many native peasants. Only peasant women, though, were forced to bear the dual burden of sexual and economic exploitation, perpetrated by indigenous men who were supposed to be their representatives. Many women must have profoundly questioned the legitimacy of the institutions which allowed their male leaders to abuse them with impunity.

Nevertheless, this is only part of the story. At the same time, *ayllu* members struggled to shape the governmental structures imposed by the Spanish to fit their traditional concepts of political and religious life. The purpose of the Toledean laws was to undercut pre-Columbian practices; yet this aim was often thwarted as the *ayllus* remodeled and adapted Spanish forms to Andean modes of organization.

The resilience of the colonial *ayllu* notwithstanding, women still found themselves in a disadvantaged position. All the formal posts imposed by the Spanish were reserved for men. Consequently, the municipal and lay offices of the Iberian peninsula could be modified or reworked in terms of the masculine components of pre-Columbian politico-religious institutions. But the women's organizations so crucial to the life of the Andean *ayllu* before the Conquest could find no equivalent Spanish forms to legitimize their existence. Even though the community apparatus of government which the Spanish imposed was being transformed by many colonial *ayllus* in accord with pre-Columbian principles of politico-religious organization, the emerging synthesis did not favor the continuance of parallel authority structures controlled by women.

Although colonial society undermined the preservation of women's ritual organizations, in some communities women (and men) discovered ways to circumvent these pressures. Some women found means—often devious—to continue participating in the official structures of community government. The Jesuit priest Pérez Bocanegra describes the development of a process in which women who held native religious posts began to link their activities with Christian practices. Inadvertently, Pérez discovered that Indians would confess to native clerics—women as well as men—before confessing to their Catholic parish priest:

> Let the priest who hears confession be forewarned that in this town of Andahuaylillas, and in other towns as well, some Indian men and women, who call themselves "elder brothers" and "elder sisters" [*hermanos mayores y hermanas mayores*], do certain things, and they are considered enlightened because of certain *quipus*, . . . which they bring with them to confess, which are like lists and memorandums of what to confess. For these Indians, particularly the Indian women, teach other women to confess by means of these knots and signs, which are multicolored, in order to classify sins and the number that were committed . . . in the following way. . . . [B]efore a penitent Indian man or woman goes to confess to the priest, he [or she] has already confessed every sin to these Indian women and men, whether they be sins he has committed, or others that he never committed, . . . and to do this, these male and female confessors tie knots in their cords which are called *caitus*, and they are the sins which they were told, and they go adding and putting in their knots others which were never committed, ordering [the penitents] and teaching them to confess a sin, when it really is not a sin, and vice versa. And commonly the [elder brothers and sisters] tell them to make an infinite number of false declarations and confess what they never did . . . and I

have brought this to light by my constant questioning . . .
until they finally admit: "This is what the brothers and sisters told me to say" . . . according to these knots; and they
call these general confessions . . . and thus they do not confess the sins they have committed, for they do not tell the father confessor about these sins, rather only those which
these Indian men and women have shown them [on the
knots]; and after confessing with the priest, they go and tell
these Indians what the father told them and the penance he
gave them, making fun of him, saying that he does not know
how to interrogate the penitent or that he does not know
their language [1631:111-13].

Thus, under the guise of Catholic ritual, indigenous
priests—men and women—were carrying out an important
rite of pre-Columbian Andean religious practice, the Andean
confession. Recording the "sins" of their *ayllus* on *quipus*
(knotted strings used as a mnemonic device), the native clergy
would then tell the penitent which "sins," selected from those
of the entire community, to reveal to the Catholic priest. Pérez
Bocanegra, of course, was appalled by many aspects of this de-
viance from Catholic orthodoxy. It was not only the fact that
women could be confessors in native rites that horrified him.
More important, concealing their "heretic" activities by send-
ing people to confess to the Catholic clergy, native priests and
priestesses were able to preserve the practice of indigenous
rites—rites which embodied concepts of sin, guilt, and responsibility that were radically different from Catholic dogma.
Pérez found to his dismay that Catholicism was treated as a
farce by his indigenous constituency, who could wear the new
religion like a cloak to conceal their idolatry and heresy.

Note that the confessional process which native priestesses
headed still harbored pre-Columbian patterns of religious organization. Pérez was well aware that these heterodox confessions were structured by gender divisions: "the Indian women
. . . teach other women to confess by means of these knots."
Pérez Bocanegra's instruction manual was written to aid cler-

157

ics in their campaign against Indians who dared to continue following the religious practices of their pagan ancestors. Consequently, elder brothers and elder sisters, the *hermanos* and *hermanas mayores*, were objects of the Catholic clergy's attack; to judge from Pérez's manual, the ensuing campaign was particularly harsh in its drive against women idolators (1631:114).

In the sixteenth and seventeenth centuries, women found themselves doubly threatened. They were hounded by the Church as well as by indigenous governmental and religious authorities who allied themselves with the colonial regime. These local-level officials, their power derived from alliances with Spanish authorities, no longer felt bound by the mutual obligations and normative rules that governed traditional Andean social relations; they threatened and abused women in ways that were illegitimate under pre-Columbian social and moral codes. Moreover, the local political and religious institutions imposed by the Spanish denied women direct access to the official channels of authority regulating community life. Declared Lucía Suyo Carhua, accused by the extirpators of idolatry of being a sorceress and priestess of heresy, "Now, don't you see, the universe has turned inside-out; for we are being persecuted" (AAL:Leg. 2, Exp. XIV, f. 2v).[2]

---

[2] In Spanish Lucía says, "*el tiempo* está al revés"; but, in Quechua, she would likely have used the word *pacha*, denoting both space and time (space-time). She is metaphorically expressing the collapse of the Andean social and physical order as well as the social mechanisms through which that order was maintained.

Cultural Defiance:
The Sorcery Weapon

> I did not [publicly whip three women] so much
> because of the fact that they believed in super-
> stitions and other abominations, but rather be-
> cause they encouraged the whole village to mu-
> tiny and riot through their reputation as
> witches who went neither to Mass nor to cate-
> chism classes, and who publicly disobeyed me,
> their parish priest, as well as their mayor.
> [Rt. Rev. Don Juan Antonio Riva de Neira,
> BN:C4142]

Europe in the seventeenth century was convulsed by witchhunts. Under the guiding force of the Jesuit order, the propa-
gators and defenders of the Counter-Reformation, trials were
held to weed out "witches," the heretical enemies of the Roman Catholic Church. It is no accident that the same order that
was responsible for Catholicism's Renaissance witchcraze also
lead the drive to "extirpate idolatry" in seventeenth-century
Peru. The European experience profoundly influenced its Andean counterpart: the ideology of the demon hunters in Europe shaped the ideology of the extirpators in the New World;
and, as in Europe, the trials to eliminate idol worshippers had
deep effects on the social and religious life of those groups
caught in the witchhunt net.[1]

---

[1] For a seminal study relating the worship of the devil in the New World to
the conflict of modes of production engendered by the capitalist penetration of
precapitalist economies, see Taussig (1980a). He has pointed to the dynamic
through which the European cosmovision became grafted onto indigenous
perceptions of the universe, and this chapter has been greatly inspired by his
work. June Nash (1979) has made important contributions to our understand-

As we shall see, women—i.e. Renaissance Europe's definition of women—held a central place in the Church's demonological philosophy.[2] Uncompromising expectations regarding the nature of women, their capacities, their responsibilities, and their position in society were transported to colonial Peru. On the Andean stage, these expectations were to play an important role in transforming Andean society's perception of itself—and, concomitantly, its definition of "the feminine"—as well as in remapping the spheres of activity in which indigenous women could participate.

THE EUROPEAN WITCHCRAZE

All witchcraft comes from carnal lust, which in women is insatiable . . . Wherefore for the sake of fulfilling their lusts they consort with devils . . . it is sufficiently clear that it is no matter for wonder that there are more women than men found infected with the heresy of witchcraft. . . . And blessed be the Highest Who has so far preserved the male sex from so great a crime [Sprenger and Kramer 1970:47].

So wrote Jacob Sprenger and Heinrich Kramer in their *Malleus maleficarum,* or *Witches' Hammer,* the book which was the Church's main reference work on demonology as well as the authoritative guide to the conduct of witch trials. Published at Cologne in 1484, the *Malleus* represented the systematization

---

ing of the history, life experiences, and religious beliefs of Bolivian mine workers. Moreover, her monograph presents pioneering detail about their beliefs in the "*tío*-devil" of the mines. Discussions of witchcraft, cosmology, and social structure are always indebted to the work of Mary Douglas (1966, 1970). Genovese's brilliant analysis (1974) of the complex dialectic between culture and power in the U.S. South is a model for studies of ideology. Also see Warren (1978) for a fascinating look at the creation of ideologies of subordination in highland Guatemala. Studies of Spanish witchcraft include Caro Baroja (1965, 1970, 1975) and Lison Tolosana (1979). My analysis of women and European witchcraft is indebted to Thomas (1971) and Trevor-Roper (1972).

[2] The question of the relation between women and witchcraft in Europe has also been examined by Garrett (1977, 1979); see, too, the ensuing debate (Balfe 1978; Honegger 1979; Moia 1979).

of Church doctrine regarding witchcraft and heresy. It is also a clear expression of its attitudes and expectations regarding women: women were the vehicle through which the devil operated on earth; personages who, because of their innate weaknesses, were easily induced to consort with the devil. And it was, after all, through alliances made with the devil that God's kingdom would be destroyed.

The "science" of demonology, which attained its most complete expression in the work of the Dominican friars just cited, had not always been at the disposal of those who would zealously guard Catholic orthodoxy. The systematized definition of Satan's kingdom and powers was a product of the late Middle Ages. This is not to deny that folk beliefs in the efficacy of casting spells, in the power of charms and incantations, in the ability of individuals to manipulate supernatural powers to cause illness or create climatic changes, were deeply rooted in the European peasant society. Moreover, it is possible that certain pre-Christian pagan beliefs—in fairies or spirits of nature, the notion of night-riding with Diana or Herodias—survived Christian evangelism of the Dark and Middle Ages. Still, these scattered folk beliefs did not constitute an articulate and organized series of principles involving the devil and the structure of the devil's reign. Nor did these beliefs include the concept of a demonic pact (Trevor-Roper 1972).

Indeed, the distinguishing characteristic of medieval European witchcraft ideology is the concept of a pact made with the devil. For it was precisely by means of this most unholy of alliances that sorcerers were said to derive their powers. The malevolent acts attributed to witches—their ability to harm people or to damage crops—was not of principal interest to medieval theologians. What was damning about fourteenth-century sorcerers was the heretical basis of their supposed powers. Witchcraft implied devil worship. It signified the gravest of all sins: the renunciation of God and adherence to his arch-rival Satan, the Prince of Darkness (Thomas 1971:438).

The British historian H.R. Trevor-Roper argues that it is mistaken to confuse fragments of pre-Christian survivals or

161

peasant folk beliefs with what was to become the highly systematized demonology presented in the *Witches' Hammer*. This "new mythology" of witchcraft, encompassing the great heresy of diabolic pacts and the predisposition of women to enter into them, might have had its roots in peasant credences or folk religion; but its articulation into a coherent system was the work of the medieval Catholic Church. It was Church intellectuals who articulated the content of this new heresy, detailing how witches were thought to behave and establishing the procedures through which they were to be rooted out. Trevor-Roper also points out that, before analyzing heresy, it is important to ask who articulated it: the heretics themselves or their inquisitors. He thus roots the development of demonology in the political culture of the late Middle Ages and Renaissance. As the religious organ of feudal society, the Church created an ideology in which political opposition could be defined as heresy. A denunciation of heresy or witchcraft, consequently, became a political weapon. Interestingly, the demonology of the Church, once created and imposed by the clergy, acquired a momentum of its own, becoming part of the perception of the universe shared by most Europeans (Trevor-Roper 1972:127-28).

Let us turn briefly to an overview of the concepts embodied by this demonology. Not only do these express some of the prevailing norms through which women were evaluated in European society, but they also serve as a base line from which to examine the New World version of demonically influenced heresies. In terms of the Christian cosmovision of the late Middle Ages, the normative aspects of the universe could be divided into two clearly defined and opposing spheres: the world of good and the world of evil. On the one hand, Christians—the servants of God—were upholding a moral order of virtue and goodness against onslaughts made by the servants of the Prince of Darkness. Within this conception of the world, the devil, the incarnation of evil, was a continual presence. Ever energetic, the devil was constantly at work, perpetually attempting to overthrow the kingdom of God. We should not forget that the devil was a real and familiar figure to the inhabitants of late medieval Europe. He was a figure as tangible and knowable as the patriarchs and saints (Caro Baroja 1965:71).

Who was Satan? The nineteenth-century French historian Jules Michelet interprets the devil in Western Europe as a figure who evolved from pagan beliefs, rooted in a pantheon of natural spirits, which were at the core of peasant folklore. In a time when the peasantry was viciously oppressed by landlords and the Church, the "devil" emerged in support of the downtrodden: the Prince of this World, as opposed to the remote and insensitive God of the Church (Michelet 1973:21-61). Thomas (1971) and Trevor-Roper (1972) trace the content of this new diabolic conception to the Church's reaction to the Manichean (and by implication devil-worshipping) tendencies of the Cathars and their successors—followers of twelfth-century heretical sects in the Alps and Pyrenees.

What emerges from the confessions of the accused witches of the fifteenth to seventeenth centuries is an almost stereotypical pattern of the devil, his kingdom, and the practices of his adherents. The devil assumed a variety of forms, but he was almost inevitably a repulsive, large, bestial, stinking, and dark figure. Most often the devil appeared as a cat or a goat, animals associated with perverted rituals of a sexual nature. According to one condemned sorceress, "the devil was dark-skinned, and his eyes burned like coals. . . . [He was] dressed in the hides of beasts" (Caro Baroja 1965:85). According to another contemporary,

> [he was] an ugly devil having horns on his head, fire in his mouth, and a tail in his breech, eyes like a basin, fangs like a dog, claws like a bear, a skin like a Niger and a voice roaring like a lion [Thomas 1971:475].

The description of the Black Sabbath, which appeared for the first time in inquisitional trials held at Toulouse, also conformed to the same model throughout the period of the witchhunts. Witches were said to anoint themselves with "devil's grease," made from the fat of the dead or murdered infants, and then fly to their Sabbath reunion. Hundreds of Sabbaths were reportedly held in every witch-beridden country; they were collective orgies, where huge banquets were served and sexual perversions indulged in. Followers of the devil, mostly women, were initiated into Satan's service through intercourse—the ultimate act through which the newly established diabolic pact was cemented. The devil, in turn, imparted esoteric knowledge, often including medicinal lore, to his converts, as well as a promise of material gain to be enjoyed during the initiate's lifetime (Caro Baroja 1965:85-87):

> [At the Sabbath] she found a huge he-goat, and after greeting him she submitted to his pleasure. The he-goat in return taught her all kinds of secret spells; he explained poisonous plants to her, and she learned from him words for incantations and how to cast spells. . . . He advised her to make sacrilegious communion if she could, offending God and honoring the Devil. . . . Like a true daughter of Satan, in answer to questions about the symbols of the Apostles and faith which true believers have in our Holy Religion, she averred that God and the Devil were completely equal, the former reigning over the *sky* and the latter the *earth* [Caro Baroja 1965:85].

For the most part, ecclesiastical authorities assumed that the devil's female converts did not act alone; they were overwhelmingly accused of being part of an enormous diabolic secret society. Most witches were condemned for being members of "the devil's party," which explains why the demonological literature is ridden with questions concerning the nature of the Black Sabbaths (Ehrenreich and English 1973:10). The Black Sabbath, or Witch's Sabbath, reflected the social structure of feudal society—although, from the perspective of orthodoxy, in an inverse form. The coven itself was not dissimilar to the court of a king or feudal lord, and the devil promised his adherents exactly what a baron offered his vassals: protection and help in exchange for total submission. The hierarchical structure of the devil's kingdom was modeled on the organization of civil society during the late Middle Ages (Trevor-Roper 1972:128; Caro Baroja 1965:76). During the Black Sabbath, parodies of holy sacraments were performed in which God was denounced and ridiculed while Satan was proclaimed the supreme potentate of the world. An interesting inversion of feudal social order was also expressed: the devil's priest was a woman, and her honorific title was "the Aged" (Michelet 1973:104).

The Priestess of the Black Mass was an old hag, the poor outcast object of village ridicule—the stereotype of the witch. Transcripts of witchcraft trials reveal that the condemned were usually poor and that they were predominantly women. Learned authorities concurred that the devil was more likely to win converts from the lowest levels of the feudal social hierarchy. According to one knowledgeable demonologist, these converts were "usually beggars"; in the words of another, they were "very miserable, poor, the basest sort of people" (Thomas 1971:520). Moreover, the authoritative ideologues of the time were convinced of the predisposition of women to the temptations of Satan, and therefore never doubted that women would far outnumber men in the ranks of the devil. James I estimated that the ratio of witches to warlocks was 20:1; a contemporary, Alexander Roberts, put the ratio at 100:1 (Thomas 1971:520). Women made up 85 percent of those executed for sorcery during the period of the witchhunts (Ehrenreich and English 1973:6).

The expectation that women would be more likely to commit sins of witchcraft because of natural moral and physical weaknesses was deeply ingrained in popular folk belief, justified and legitimated by Judeo-Christian doctrine. The story of the Creation and the Fall, explicit references to the impurity of women found in the Old Testament, as well as specific commands for the subjection of women found in the Epistles of St. Paul and in the works of the Scholastics were turned to as divine authorities guiding the special persecution of women in the Middle Ages (Schmitt 1978:196-97). The extirpators of witchcraft in medieval Europe could justify their persecutions by citing Biblical authority in Exodus: "Don't suffer a witch to live." Debators of Mosaic Law in the Talmud not only held that witchcraft was a crime punishable by stoning, but also carefully developed the argument that women were more predisposed to carry out such malevolent acts. Such Talmudic statements as "Women are naturally inclined to witchcraft," and "The more women there are, the more witchcraft there will be," are cases in point (Caro Baroja 1965:80). By the thirteenth century, Scholastic philosophy, basing its premises on the writings of St. Paul, had further elaborated these misogynous themes: the Truth was transmitted from Christ to man, and by man to woman; diabolic doctrine, in contrast, first infiltrated woman, who, "possessing a diminished faculty of discernment," then turned men from the straight path (Schmitt 1978:196).

However, the witchcraft beliefs expressed in early Judeo-Christian doctrine are not comparable to the demonological theory of the late Middle Ages; nor did they support anything similar to the great wave of witch persecutions carried out by Christian Europe from the fourteenth to the seventeenth centuries. As noted, it was the theologians of these later centuries who expanded upon preexisting conceptions of the incapacities and debilities of women to construct an articulate demonological theory. It was they who elaborated the supposedly inherent flaws in the nature of woman to concoct their theological explanation of the devil's pertinacity in this world and the seeming ubiquity of heretical pacts.

In the fifteenth century, the fatal flaw of women lay in their voracious sexuality. The Church explicated how woman's lust was the source from which the power of witches ultimately derived: "All witchcraft comes from carnal lust, which in women is insatiable," write Sprenger and Kramer. We have seen how witches' careers were initiated by intercourse with the devil. In developing their demonology, the writers of the *Malleus* enlarged upon the deficiencies of women, their greater susceptibility to Satanic advances. Sprenger and Kramer declare: "And it should be noted that there was a defect in the formation of the first woman, since she was formed from a bent rib, that is, a rib of the breast, which is bent as it were in a contrary direction to a man. And since through this defect she is an imperfect animal, she always deceives. . . . for *Femina* comes from *Fe* and *Minus*, since she is ever weaker to hold and preserve the faith" (Sprenger and Kramer 1970:44). Women became the enemy.

Women, especially the poor and old, widows and spinsters, were perceived as the weak point in a divinely ordained patriarchal social order. The theological literature of the time developed an elaborate scheme to explain the ability of Satan to penetrate God's kingdom, and women were singled out as the point of entry. Women, the consorts of the devil, were not just shameful and unclean, they were the means through which the divine order of God's kingdom, reflected in the divinely sanctioned social order of civil society, could be destroyed.

On the other hand, it should not be too surprising that the ideology of demonology accused women of being the ringleaders in a witchcraft-heresy conspiracy. In the rigidly stratified patriarchal society of the late Middle Ages, women (particularly peasant women) were the most dependent and vulnerable members. Under common law, a married woman could own no property. Nor were women allowed a voice in either the Church or the state. Woman's chief virtue was silence; her sole duty was obedience to her husband, and her main obligation was to manage the household, under God. The patriarchal structure of society and the family, moreover, was ordained by God and sanctioned by religious doctrine (Thomas 1971:520-30).

If women were the most dependent and impotent members of feudal society, they were also potentially the most volatile. One way in which that potential might become actual was through contracts made with the diabolic arch-rival of the established feudal order; the fears of those in power thus found expression in notions about witchcraft that blamed the most vulnerable members of society for its ills. The confessions accumulated by the Church reflect an awareness of the predicament of feudal women. Whether confessions were given freely or extracted under torture, they mirror social expectations regarding the stimuli and temptations to which presumed witches were subject. And so we find that in many cases the devil was extremely sensitive to the plight of women. Frequently, the promised benefits of a diabolic contract were related to the problems of peasant women. While rarely promising great riches, the devil assured his adherents that they would not lack food or clothing (Thomas 1971:520-21). The esoteric knowledge imparted by the devil often entailed knowledge about abortion and contraception. Women were also provided with a means for revenge and a way to wreak havoc on those in power. Inquisitors and accused alike agreed that the devil made his first appearance when he heard a woman cursing (Thomas 1971:524).

We have no evidence that any underground society of female devil worshippers, dedicated to the overthrow of the established order, ever existed in Europe (Trevor-Roper 1972:129). The confessions instead reveal a collective image shared by the accusers and their victims. Hundreds of women confessed to being witches. Since most of these confessions were obtained under torture, there can be little doubt that their extraordinary similarity is largely explained by the fact that the same questions were relentlessly asked under extreme pain, in a judicial situation where the verdict was predetermined. But the fact that some confessions were freely given points to something else: some women did believe they were witches. For them, the pact with the devil—the enemy of the established order—was a symbol of their alienation from a society which offered them little more than despair. It was their attempt to gain power in a society in which they were powerless (see Michelet 1973; Thomas 1971:521).

Even though a women's diabolic underground did not exist, one should note that women were particularly active in heretical sects during the Middle Ages and the Renaissance. As Thomas has pointed out, all the heretical medieval sects received remarkable support from women (1958:50). Given the socioeconomic conditions in which women lived, this is not surprising. The Church might discourse on Satan's tempting those most easily led astray. But to some observers of the seventeenth century this "error of women" was not so innocent; it was related to a desire to overthrow the established order (Thomas 1958:51). Commenting on the fact that women as a whole were denied an active role in Church affairs, one seventeenth-century theologian stated:

> ... hereupon they grow discontented, and fall into dislike with the present state of the Church; and that discontent layeth them open to Satan's delusions, who readily worketh upon such an advantage [Thomas 1958:51].

In the 1600s, the Spanish empire in Europe was splintering as the Protestant countries of the north battled for autonomy. This was the great period of struggle between the Reformists and the Counter-Reformists for control over Europe. Trevor-Roper (1972) sees the witchcraze in this period as the ideological battle cry under which these religious (and economic) wars were carried out. The Jesuits carried the banner for the Catholic countries, and it is thus to this century and the Jesuit-led battle to extirpate idolatry in Peru that we shall now turn.

IDOLS, DEVILS, AND WITCHES

Demonology, then, was rooted in medieval Europe; and the creation of the social stereotype of the witch, a stereotype that was the keystone of an ideological edifice for political persecution, was developed by the Catholic Church in an epoch marked by great political and social upheaval. Although this stereotype had been elaborated in a narrow, local context, once developed it acquired a life of its own. While the formal theological construct shaped the official rules by which orthodoxy and heresy were to be judged, the stereotype penetrated and became a part of European folk belief, of the popular culture. It became a standard for judgment and a cultural evaluation which was applied outside the boundaries of the specific

169

context in which it had been conceived. The Spanish conquest of Peru thus transported the devil, and his ally the witch, to the Andes.

Confronted with the startlingly different cultures of the New World, the Spanish Crown and Catholic religious authorities began the process of creating institutions that would bind these newly discovered lands to the mother country. An integral part of the colonization process entailed the campaign waged by the Church to destroy indigenous religion. Although the clerics who accompanied the first conquistadors and administrators might have engaged in disputes over the nature of the indigenous soul, and over the theological justification of conquest (Lohmann 1967:v-xxi), almost all agreed that the devil was flourishing in the Andes. How else to explain the devotion displayed by these people toward the hills, trees, stones, the sun, the moon, rivers and springs. Perhaps Christ or his disciples had not yet crossed the Atlantic, so the *indios* could not strictly speaking be accused of heresy; but certainly the devil had arrived. Indeed, not only the first Catholic evangelists, but the earliest Spanish conquerors and bureaucrats immediately felt the presence of Satan in the Andes, tempting and seducing the Indians into worshipping their *huacas*, their idols, their ancestors. In the earliest Spanish records, we discover that native religion was viewed as merely one more vehicle through which the devil manifested his attempts to overthrow God's kingdom. Indigenous religion was devil worship (Cieza 1968:84-88; Mena 1968:passim, Sancho de la Hoz 1968:passim; Trujillo 1968:passim).

From the beginning of the Conquest, Spanish theologians as well as soldiers and soldiers-of-fortune of less erudition saw the devil's army operating in the Andes. This perception, a direct consequence of the European cosmovision developed in the Middle Ages, led the colonizers to make some interesting conclusions about native religion. Curiously, as in Europe, this intellectual construct began to take on a life of its own, attaching itself to and penetrating the radically different pre-Columbian view of the universe (Taussig 1980a).

Once having made the association between indigenous religion and devil worship, the Spanish began to evaluate all native religious practice and theory according to European criteria. It was thus not a great leap from the discovery of idolatry to the discovery of witchcraft. Since witchcraft, in the logic of contemporary Western thought, involved a complot with the devil, and since the devil was already speaking to the *indios* through their *huacas*, witchcraft must also be permeating and rotting Andean society. If witchcraft was present, then there must also be witches with whom the devil could consort:

In Peru these witches and priests of the devil also used to daub themselves a lot [with ointment]. And it is an infinite thing, the great multitude that there was of these diviners, soothsayers, sorcerers, fortunetellers, and other myriad sorts of prophets. . . . It should be pointed out that there was one kind of sorcerer that the Inca kings permitted, and these are like witches, and they take any appearance they want, and they fly through the air and cover a long journey in the quickest time, and they see what will happen; they speak with the devil, who responds to them by means of certain stones or other things they highly venerate. . . . Some say that [to do this] they use certain ointments, . . . and they say that it is usually old women who perform this act [Acosta 1954:172].

It should come as no surprise, then, that many chroniclers describing the religious organization they discovered in Peru insist that witchcraft was practiced. And, in accord with the social stereotype of the witch—which was an integral part of the model used to evaluate pre-Columbian religious practices—those witches especially responsible for and capable of performing the blackest of black magic were expected to be women, particularly the old and poor. Those Andean witches who were the most pernicious, who had acquired powers to kill, were

almost always women . . . [Murúa 1946:301].

About these witches . . . there are a great number of them, and differences between them. Some are adept in making potions of herbs and roots in order to kill those they give these confections to. Those who perform this kind of witchcraft are almost always women [Polo 1916:28].

We have seen how the development of demonology in Europe should be understood in relation to the political context from which it sprang. Even the content of heresy was related to the socioeconomic position of women in European society. The collective fear expressed by those in power, directed toward women, was also projected onto Spanish assessments of pre-Columbian religion. For these commentators go on to note that the knowledge and power of the native sorceresses which they had uncovered was so great that even the *curacas* feared them; their powers were so terrible that consequently the Inca kings had them put to death:

. . . and these witches are tremendously feared, even by their own *caciques*. . . . [T]his kind of witchcraft was punished by the Incas, who killed not only these witches, but their descendants [Murúa 1946:301].

. . . Even their own headmen hold these witches in great fear. . . . The Incas proscribed this sort of witchcraft; not only did they put to death these witches, but their offspring as well [Polo 1916:28].

There must have been a tremendous discrepancy between the image of native religious practice provided by Spanish commentators and the reality of Andean religion. Perceiving Andean lifeways through lenses distorted by a centuries-old tradition of demonology, now also imbedded in Spanish folk culture, the Spanish found the devil under every rock and witches under every bed. Furthermore, both Satan and his prime allies were perceived to have the same motivation, to perform the same malevolent deeds, and to produce the same effects in the New World as in the Old.

If the Spanish interpretation of Andean religious activities were valid, we would have to presuppose that there existed in Andean culture a concept similar to the European notion of Satan—an entity who was the incarnation of evil in competition with an entity embodying good. We would also have to presuppose that this representation of evil worked its way in the world by making pacts with easily tempted, morally deficient women. I have already described pre-Columbian Andean religious thought. Andean cosmology did not have such a notion of evil, embodied in a Satanic being. On the contrary, Andean philosophy entailed a "dialectical" vision of the universe in which opposing forces were viewed as reciprocal and complementary, necessary for the reproduction of society as a whole. Nor is there evidence that women were viewed as being morally weak in Andean culture. Rather, women were perceived to be in a complementary relation with men, and their reciprocal interaction was seen as necessary for the maintenance and reproduction of social existence.

While Urbano (1979b) has shown that a concept of non-order was an integral component of Andean social organization, this notion should be understood as an element in the dynamic logic of Andean models of society and the universe as a whole. As a concept, it is very different from the Christian construct of the devil developed in the late Middle Ages. Similarly, dangerous qualities might be associated with *huacas*. As representations of suprasocietal forces, Andean divinities embodied powers that instilled fear; they could be destructive. But these attributes are not demonic in the Christian sense of the term. If we analyze pre-Columbian concepts of sickness, moreover, we discover that Andeans never defined disease in terms of complots made with evil forces. Rather, concepts of disease and health were intrinsically related to a normative structure in which the maintenance of "balance" (*ayni*) between social, natural, and supernatural forces was a predominant ideal. Sickness was perceived to be a product of the breakdown of cultural norms regulating the balance between social groups, between society and nature, and between society and supernatural forces (Silverblatt and Silverblatt n.d.). The god Huari

173

did cause illness in the highland communities of the Department of Lima; however, he did so because the sacred tie between humanity and the Andean divinities had been broken. In the words of one "witch-curer-idolator":

> ... our god and creator Huari has sent you this spider so that you eat it, because you have not adored him, nor have you served him, and he has formed many snakes in your body, which are the cause of your suffering [Duviols 1971:387].

Yet, pre-Columbian Andean society did include members who were specialists in medical knowledge: these men and women were renowned as herbal specialists, bone setters, and curers. Others were said to be able to predict the future, often using coca or tobacco as instruments to aid in divination. Both curing and divination rites entailed the worship of native deities (Arriaga 1968:116, 32-35; Murúa 1946-231; Polo 1916:31-36). In Europe, the devil was said to give his adherents knowledge of herbal lore as well as powers to foretell the future. Should not the Spanish have assumed that Andean curers and diviners derived their knowledge from diabolic pacts?

Several interpreters of Andean religion have asserted that some form of "witchcraft" did exist in the Andes prior to Spanish colonization (Rowe 1957:297-98). I suggest, however, that the evidential basis on which these assertions were made should be re-evaluated. Perhaps spells, spirits, and magic, which many anthropologists impute to all cultures (Garrett 1977:461), were also part of Andean belief systems. But the sorcery and witchcraft that the Spanish chroniclers claimed to have witnessed in the Andes—in which alliances made with evil forces were considered the most probable explanation of disease, misfortune, and death—were very likely a Spanish invention.

If the first Spanish administrators and clerics interpreted pre-Columbian religion according to alien concepts, creating witches where none had existed before, by the seventeenth century, self-proclaimed indigenous witches were confessing to having made diabolic contracts and having had sex with the devil. In addition, these "sorceresses" had a clientele which, while consisting for the most part of *indios*, also included blacks, *mestizos*, and Spaniards. The confessions to which I refer are part of the corpus of ecclesiastical documents accumulated during the great campaign to extirpate idolatry in Peru. At the turn of the sixteenth century and during the century to follow, a new battle was waged by the Church, with the support of the Crown, against the worshippers of the devil in Peru. Organized by the Jesuits—the same order which was at the vanguard of the Counter-Reformation in Europe and which headed the European witchhunts—this new campaign was as evangelical as it was political. Now, those who were responsible for rooting out indigenous religious practices knew they were confronting not only idolators, but full-fledged heretics: people who had been baptized, but who had renounced Christianity in favor of Satan. As was the case during the period immediately following the Conquest, evidence of Satanic worship was found in the continuing devotion shown by indigenous society toward *huacas*, not to mention the ubiquitous sorcery and curing (Acosta 1954:181; Pérez Bocanegra 1631:389-90; AAL:Leg. 2, Exp. XVIII, Leg. 2, Exp. XXI, Leg. 2, Exp. XXVII, Leg. 3, Exp. X, Leg. 5, Exp. VIII, Leg. 6, Exp. X). Idolatry, curing, and witchcraft were blurred. As in Europe, the campaign against heresy had obvious political motives. It was the ideological arm of the attempt to force Indians into the *reducciones*—all the better to evangelize, to maintain political control, to facilitate the collection of tribute.

Since native deities were only a façade through which the devil—the arch-enemy of Christendom and civilization, and consequently the enemy of the Spanish oppressors—operated, it is not difficult to understand why the continued worship of indigenous deities would be perceived as a form of defiance not only against the Church but against colonial society as a whole (see Taussig 1980a:42-53). Again, the European preconception of women's inherent susceptibility to diabolic influence molded the campaign to root out idolatry.

175

During this same period, moreover, the predominant cosmology of the West was beginning to associate symbolically all of "nature" with evolving cultural definitions of "the feminine": nature, like woman, was capricious, emotional, unpredictable, something that had to be dominated, conquered, and controlled (Leacock and Nash 1977:621). Western cosmology, associating women with nature, paganism, and the devil, built up an accompanying ideology in which women were classified as weak, incapable, and, as we have seen, consequently more susceptible to diabolic temptation (AAL:Leg. 2, Exp. XVIII). This ideological evaluation of women was reflected in Spanish law, which defined women as minors, in need of protectors or "tutors" to carry out business transactions. When this concept was applied to the colonies, where Indians were similarly defined as minors and incompetents needing "protection," we find a telling equation: in Spanish colonial law, the testimony of two Indian men or of three Indian women was considered to equal that of one Spaniard (Testimonio 1950:345).

By extension, if women were inherently weak and therefore more susceptible to the temptations of the devil, then, by the logic of Western thought, they were more likely to be responsible for the black magic and sorcery which threatened the foundations of Christendom and colonial rule. Women were perceived as potentially the mortal enemies of man, the Church, and the colonial political order. Thus, a social stereotype rooted in Europe became part of the ideological justification for the special hounding of women during the Peruvian witchhunts (Pérez Bocanegra 1631:114; BN:B1827; AAL:Leg. 1, Exp. VII, Leg. 1, Exp. XII).

How do we explain the fact that some indigenous women in the seventeenth century confessed to being "witches" who, through diabolic pacts, were capable of wreaking havoc on crops, of causing illness and death. As in Europe, the campaign to extirpate idolatry in Peru extorted evidence by torture. And, once again, we can expect that the content of many confessions can be explained by the kind of questions being asked—

questions framed in terms of a European understanding of witchcraft and heresy—and how those questions were asked. The procedures for the conduct of the witchcraft trials were remarkably similar in Europe and Peru. On both continents, an atmosphere of fear was created by the inquisitors as, almost to the word, they announced their upcoming inquest:

> [It is] directed, commanded, and required that within twelve days . . . the [inhabitants of a particular community] should reveal to us if they have known, seen, or heard that any person is . . . a heretic or witch [or idol worshipper] . . . or if any is suspected especially of such practices as cause injury to men, cattle, or the fruits of the earth [*Malleus*, in Ehrenreich and English 1973:71; cf. AAL:Leg. 2, Exp. XXVII].

Anyone failing to report a witch faced excommunication and punishment, and the dire possibility of being accused of practicing idolatry. Yet, there were some important differences between the two witchhunts. Accused Indians were entitled to a legal defense—a right denied to their European counterparts. More important, while the social stereotype of the witch-devil complex shaped the charges levied by the inquisitors (as well as the confessions of the accused witches) in Europe, it had permeated indigenous thought and consciousness only slightly. What did a confession mean, then, to a self-proclaimed Andean witch?

In trying to grasp this question, we must look at the colonial process through which "the Manichean cosmovision that underlay the ideology of conquest was grafted onto indigenous religious beliefs" (Taussig 1980a:40-43). This dialectical process, which Taussig calls "forced acculturation," entailed the institutionalization of concepts of evil and of the devil in precapitalist cosmological structures where such a good/evil dichotomy had not existed before. The Andean concept of *supay* is a good example (see Taussig 1980a; Urbano 1980). In contemporary Andean villages, the Quechua term *supay* is frequently translated as "the devil"; and a common curse takes *supay* as its base: *supaypa wawan*, or "child of the devil." Yet,

177

in the early Quechua-Spanish dictionary compiled by Domingo Santo Tomás in 1560, *supay* is the Quechua stem used to translate the Spanish terms "good angel" and "bad angel": *alliçupa = ángel bueno; manaalliçupay = ángel malo* (Santo Tomás 1951:40). *Supay* in its original form was morally neutral; it could refer to a spirit that was capable of causing harm or one that could be beneficial. The intrinsic ambiguity or neutrality of *supay*'s pre-Columbian significance is clearly distinct from the one-dimensional devil which it later came to mean.

Nevertheless, because *supay* could express some notion of malevolence, the term was able to be shaped to fit the European concepts of evil which the Spanish were trying to express. Not discovering a Quechua term that adequately portrayed their conceptions, the Spanish took one that only partially embodied an idea of "bad" and adapted it to signify their radically different notion of a "totally evil" force. This transformation of the meaning of *supay* was not lost on Quechua speakers; they soon came to recognize what *supay* could refer to in colonial Andean society. Cieza de León describes the behavior of the Spanish conquistadors when they arrived in Cuzco to collect Atahualpa's ransom:

> And they [the conquistadors] gave orders to the high priest and all the other ministrants of the temple that the sacred women were to remain in it, and Quizquiz turned over to them all the gold and silver. But as the insolence of the Spaniards has been so great, and they have shown so little regard for the honor and pride of these people in return for the welcome they gave them and the love with which they served them, they violated some of the virgins, and treated the men with contempt. This was why the Indians, because of this, and seeing the lack of reverence they showed for their sun, and how without shame or fear of God they ravished their *mamaconas*, which they held to be a tremendous sacrilege, later said that these people were not sons of God, but worse than *Supais*, which is the name of the devil [1959:30].

The Andean concept of *hapinuñu* was similarly transformed through this process of "forced acculturation of ideas," the dialectic between two sharply divergent systems of understanding and classifying the universe which was forged during the colonial period. *Hapinuñu*, Quechua for "breasts that grab," was defined by the colonial lexographer Ricardo, in 1586, as "phantom or spirit" (Ricardo 1951:42) and by Holguín, in 1608 as "a phantom, or spirit, who commonly appears with two large teats, who can grab with them" (Holguín 1952:151). Guaman Poma refers to "hapinuñu duendes," or spirit inhabitants of the world during an age that preceded the reign of the Incas and the arrival of the Spanish (1936:50).

The indigenous chronicler Pachacuti Yamqui also speaks of the *hapinuñu* as dwelling in the Andes during an age before Christianization. But he, in 1613, no longer describes them merely as spirits or phantoms of an earlier epoch. He explicitly links them to diabolic forces that were defeated by an Apostle, Saint Thomas, who preceded the arrival of the Spanish in the New World:

... It is said that in the age called *purunpacha* ... or *tuta-yachacha* (age of darkness) ... after the [Andes] were populated for many years, there was a great shortage of land and space; each day there were wars and battles ... and then, at midnight, it could be heard that the *hapinuñus* were disappearing, for they were crying and screaming, "We are vanquished, we are vanquished!" "Ay, I am losing my lands!" By this it is understood that the demons were conquered by Jesus Christ ... because it is said that in ancient times, in the time of *purunpacha*, the *hapinuñus* walked about visibly throughout this land, and it was not safe, because they would carry away men and women, children, and infants, like infernal tyrants and capital enemies of the human race ... and it is said that in ancient times, a poor, old, thin, bearded man had arrived, and that he was called Tonopa Vihinquira ... and that he exiled and threw out all the idols, images of the *hapinuñu* devils ... and this bearded

179

man, called Tonopa, . . . would he not be the glorious Apostle Saint Thomas [1950:282-83, 293]?

The *hapinuñu* began as a phantom spirit of a previous age; a spirit that was perhaps somewhat malevolent, grabbing people with its breasts. Pachacuti Yamqui, however, transforms the *hapinuñu* into a diabolic force: the infernal enemy of the human race, defeated, finally, by the powers of Christianity and its Apostle Saint Thomas. In contemporary Andean villages, the spirit with breasts has been transformed into a European-style witch. The *hapinuñu*, also known as *achikee*, is a female monster, feared by all because of her craving to eat children. She is called a witch by indigenous peasants in the Department of Ancash (Morote Best 1958:11-12). Moreover, she is said to have fought with God; she is, like the devil, God's enemy (Ortiz 1973:185).

I cannot overemphasize that, in the Andes, any concept of witchcraft entailing pacts made with God's enemy in order to injure others is an outgrowth of the process of "forced acculturation" discussed above. Any cultural evaluation suggesting some sort of special relationship between Andean women and demonic forces is part of this same process. Even the native chronicler Guaman Poma did not escape the imposition of Western norms on his evaluations of women. A staunch defender of the morality and capacities of Andean women, he nonetheless berates them as the "mortal enemies of mankind" (1956, III:196).

Through the confessions recorded in the idolatry trials, we can begin to glimpse the dynamic through which the European notion of the devil evolved in the Andes and became intermeshed with pre-Columbian symbolic structures, thereby altering them radically. Through their confessions, women—because of presumed special ties with the devil—offer us a suggestive picture of this dynamic. We will also see how the formation of colonial society, with the special burdens it brought to bear on indigenous women, created structures in which women began to exercise new powers, precisely because of their supposed diabolic pacts.

WOMEN AND THE ANDEAN DEVIL

Although the Spanish might have found a devil crouching behind every Andean *huaca*, they did not discover, in the seventeenth century, the devil to which they were accustomed—the ugly, repulsive monster who was the physical inversion of what European sensibilities defined as beautiful. Instead they found him dressed in different guises: he was a Spaniard, a shadow, an Indian wrapped in a shawl, a snake, a mysterious man with golden hair living in a mountain spring.

Juana Agustina (alias Yana Macho), a seventy-year-old widow accused of being a renowned witch, describes her encounter with the devil:

> . . . while sleeping with her husband, a little angel appeared. . . . [H]e asked them both if they knew how to pray and recite the Lord's Prayer . . . and the little angel placed by her head garlands of *catoto, chilcay* seeds, and an herb called *aminamin*; he told her that one bathes with these herbs and that [with them] she would have money to eat and dress . . . and this was how the witness began to make use of herbs in order to bathe other women . . . and thus the little angel appeared to her with his tiny, tiny wings . . . and with [these herbs] she has bathed Indian and mestizo women [AAL:Leg. 4, Exp. XLVII, f. 3].

Hardly the standard image of Satan confessed to by her European contemporaries. Our condemned witch may conform to one expectation of her inquisitors—knowledge of the curative properties of plants was sufficient evidence of witchcraft—yet our Christianized angelic devil does not fit. Thus, we are beginning to see that the devil in indigenous eyes was very different from the Satan of the Spaniards.

181

In fact, "the devil" often appeared to women as a Spaniard. In the words of an old *curandera* from Charcras:

... at the foot of a mountain called Pariahirca [the devil] appeared to her, dressed like a Spaniard—the devil astride a mule amidst a powerful wind—at the foot of the same mountain, Pariahirca, where there are many ancient graves of ancestors and walls of worked stone and idols of our ancestors [AAL:Leg. 1, Exp. XII, f. 6].

According to testimony recorded in Anahuanca, one curer diagnosed a patient's nearly fatal illness as the result of witchcraft; but the patient was advised not to worry, because

... Santiago would come to cure her ... and she was warned to cover her face with her shawl and to lower her head when looking at him because he would come resplendent, shining, dressed in gold, and he would burn her if she were to look at him. ... [A]nd she sensed that he had entered [her room], making a noise like the sound of spurs ... and they began to sing and chant to him: [you who] are dressed in gold, dressed in yellow, now you come crossing mountains, plains, and valleys [AAL:Leg. 1, Exp. VIII, f. 91].

The devil is a Spaniard and the devil is a Spanish saint, the saint associated with the conquest of *indios*. In both descriptions, this apparition of the devil is related to the mountains, the home of the Apus and the god Thunder: the indigenous deities who, while responsible for the well-being and maintenance of Andean society, were also associated with conquest. If Spanish evangelists and inquisitors constantly preached the diabolic origin of idolatry, transforming *huacas* into demons, their parishioners by the seventeenth century had converted their Apu-demons into Europeans or European divinities.

The word Apu connotes power. Colonized Indians explicitly recognized those humans (or divinities) who exercised power over their lives by calling them Apu. Consequently, we discover in testimonies recorded during the idolatry trials that priests and Spaniards are referred to by this term (AAL:Leg. 1, Exp. XII). Conquest was not new to the Andes, and we have already discussed certain Andean gods who incorporated or represented concepts of political power. Interestingly, the relationship between Andean peoples and these divinities—simultaneously a force maintaining social existence as well as the embodiment of political power—was marked by ambiguity (Earls 1973). The Spanish were the most recent conquerors of the Andes; and both their status and the gods who were their representatives, I believe, were encoded into the native concept of Apu. In terms of seventeenth-century Andean thought, however, neither the Spanish-dressed Apu *huaca* nor Santiago fully embodied a concept of evil. Yet both were powerful.

Very early in the colonization process, Santiago, the saint who had led the Castilian victory over the Moors and the Spanish victory over the Incas, became intermeshed with the local indigenous god of conquest, Illapa (Duviols 1971:366; Polo 1917b:189). The merged Santiago-Illapa, however, had potencies that the indigenous deity alone did not possess. Santiago, the curer in the above citation, was capable of combatting an "hechizo," a disease caused by sorcery. By the seventeenth century, Santiago—the devil killer in the popular iconography of Huancavelica, where he reigns as the representation of the mountain gods—seems to have acquired powers to wage a battle against a devil-induced disease. Perhaps here we can see the incipient implantation of the European notion of bewitchment, as well as the emergence of an indigenous solution to this colonial disease.

A fascinating trial brought against the widow Juana Icha, accused of having made explicit pacts with a devil named Apo [Apu] Parato (AAL:Leg. 4, Exp. XIV) also gives us clues to the dynamics of the evolution of the Andean devil. Testimony against Juana was given by Phelipe Curichagua, "yndio," who lived in the same village. He claimed that she was a *curandera*, whose cures included the prescription of herbal remedies as well as offerings made to various autochthonous divinities.

183

This description does not differ from the way cures are effected in contemporary Andean communities; but in the seventeenth century, remember, such cures were signs of heretical behavior.

In addition to testifying that Juana "worships the earth and the stars and cries to the water," Phelipe asserts that "she sees hell and forgives no one" (AAL:Leg. 4, Exp. XIV, f. 1v). This witness explicitly avows that Juana's powers are derived from a pact with the devil. If the devil taught her how to heal, he also taught her how to harm. Juana thus also stands accused of being able to predict illness and misfortune, as well as cause sickness and death.

Phelipe's testimony is difficult to evaluate because of the constraints imposed on the content of confessions by the ecclesiastical procedure itself. It is impossible to ascertain, for example, whether the language employed by this witness reflects a true belief that Juana made diabolic pacts, or his awareness that this kind of accusation was what the Spanish wanted to hear. In addition, Juana Icha's own testimony exemplifies the imposition on indigenous confessions of European expectations regarding witchcraft, as well as the use of torture to force confessions in conformity with Spanish stereotypes. The inquisitor consistently framed his questions so that Apo Parato, the mountain divinity that Juana worshipped as her "yaya criador" (father creator) was indistinguishable from "her devil." She was also continually pressured to confess to having had sex with him. But while Juana ultimately confessed to diabolic copulation, the descriptions of her consort and of his reputed powers are fascinating for the light they shed on colonial native thought.

Juana's devil, the Apo Parato, "appears in the form of an Indian man wearing a black shawl," and he comes to see her not primarily to satisfy sexual desires, but because he is hungry. When Juana was initially asked when the devil first appeared to her, she responded, "He used to arrive at night when I did not feed him, and when I do not feed him, he does not want to leave." Juana obliges, by "feeding him" what we would take to be the standard composition of offerings to Andean gods: "*chicha*, coca, black and white ground maize" (AAL:Leg. 4, Exp. XIV, f. 9). Juana's supposed diabolic pact would appear to be an expression of her worship of the mountain gods. The indigenous metaphor for giving offerings and showing devotion to divinities was "feeding them." And ever since the Spanish conquest, when Christian gods began to compete with native deities, the *huacas* were hungry: the normative prescription that guided the relationship between Andean people and their deities had been undermined.

The failure of native Peruvians to honor their gods appropriately, "to feed them," could be used as an explanation of the tremendous deterioration of living conditions experienced by the colonized (AAL:Leg. 6, Exp. XI)—that is to say, the *huacas* were no longer reciprocally bound to provide their human subordinates with the sustenance to maintain their social existence. But Juana's complaint lies in the fact that she did feed her *huaca*, yet he was seemingly impotent to reciprocate:

> and at other times the devil used to bring money in his sack . . . and the devil would show it to her and put it back again without giving her anything. . . . [H]e was stingy . . . and often [Juana] used to say to the devil, "Give that money to me and send me food," and the devil never responded; he would just silently go away . . . and in all the time she dealt with him, he never even gave her clothing. . . . [And when Juana] was gravely ill . . . she said to the devil . . . "Why don't you bring me something to eat?" And the devil Apo Parato replied that . . . he did not have the means to give her anything [AAL:Leg. 4, Exp. XIV, f. 12v].

How different this was from the powerful European devil, whose virtue lay in his ability to provide food and clothing to the desperate, who was so mighty that he could destroy God's kingdom. The devil Apo Parato, on the contrary, is poor and is afraid of his supposed rivals: ". . . the devil is very much afraid of Spaniards and priests, and even before Spaniards arrive, he flees, turning himself into wind" (AAL:Leg. 4, Exp.

185

XIV, f. 12v). This is a far cry from the combative *huacas* of the immediate post-Conquest period, the *huacas* of the Taqui Ongoy who were determined to wage war against the Christian gods. One hundred years of colonial rule had taken their toll, and Juana Icha echoes this indigenous despair.

There are times, however, when Juana's devil did seem to be effective. When her daughter became the mistress of "viracochas," Apo Parato intervened and stopped these disapproved-of liaisons with Spaniards. Another woman begged Juana to help her avoid a major-domo of the village priest through the intercession of Apo Parato, and the devil promised that this Spaniard "would not pursue her" (AAL:Leg. 4, Exp. XIV, f. 24). Apo Parato bewitched an indigenous tribute collector into not continuing his search for an escaped Indian who had defaulted on his tribute payments. He told the taxman, "There was no sense in tiring himself out, he was never going to find the Indian" (AAL:Leg. 4, Exp. XIV, f. 23v). Even though Apo Parato was poor, and in some contexts powerless, he seems to have been able to influence the future, albeit slyly—especially in cases of relations between Indians and their conquerors or their conqueror's henchmen.

Juana's inquisitors relentlessly pressured her to admit to capital crimes perpetrated through witchcraft and to the possession of the instruments—invariably associated with European sorcery—necessary to carry them out. She was asked repeatedly whether she

> had in [her] possession several figures of men made out of wax with several spines or pins . . . and the bodies of these wax figures were bound in such a way that they [the men] would slowly die, little by little [AAL:Leg. 4, Exp. XIV, f. 18].

Repeatedly Juana denied these charges. But she did admit that through the intervention of Apo Parato she could offer protection, as in the cases noted above. In addition, Juana was renowned for aiding men on their way to forced labor in the mines of Potosí or in the sugar refineries.

The Apu was an enemy of miscegenation and a protector of Indians: not quite the instrument of vengeance assumed by the inquisitors or by Juana's accusers, but nevertheless a symbolic force capable of intervening on behalf of Indian commoners. It is therefore not surprising that the most serious charges levied against Juana Icha had to do with pacts made with Apo Parato to murder or harm either Spanish authorities or native governmental officeholders. Interestingly, such accusations usually followed from situations in which these men had taken advantage of their position in the colonial political apparatus to abuse the Indians they were supposed to represent or protect. Phelipe Curichagua, for example, accused Juana Icha of causing the death of the village mayor because he had unjustly whipped one of her daughters. He overheard Juana's pledge that the mayor would have the devil to pay:

> . . . and this witness heard Juana say, "Didn't I tell you the devil was going to get the mayor; look, isn't that exactly what took place? And the same thing will happen to anyone who violates my will" [AAL:Leg. 4, Exp. XIV, f. 2v].

Whether Juana's powers were devil-derived or not, she could effectively challenge the political establishment precisely because of the "diabolic" powers attributed to her. As a witch in colonial indigenous society, Juana became the spokesperson for and the defender of the normative standards of village life. Juana, who "forgives no one," especially if they have "violated her will," came to embody the moral sanction of her community. An examination of the accusations made against Juana reveals that her malevolence was usually directed against people who had transgressed community norms: the mayors and headmen who, taking advantage of their position in the political structures imposed by the colonial regime, defied traditional Andean expectations regarding the behavior of community authorities. Juana's actions or accredited actions against those in power were defended by the members of her community, as Phelipe's lament makes clear:

... and Don Francisco Poma Condor, mayor, apprehended Juana and then let her go . . . and then Don Pedro Yauri, an *yndio principal* [*curaca*] of this village recaptured her, but she still escaped, and Pedro de Zárate, the priest, ordered her arrest, but to no avail . . . because the Indians of the village support her [AAL:Leg. 4, Exp. XIV, f. 3v].

Juana Icha was by no means the only woman accused of bewitching Spanish authorities, priests, and their Indian allies after having been mistreated by colonial and indigenous officeholders. Madalena Achaguato was condemned for having prepared a potion that would cause the parish priest to be removed from his post. The witch Madalena, who conspired with Canta's female governor, denounced the priest because he unjustly punished her (AAL:Leg. 1, Exp. s.n.). María Alvarado, who admitted to knowing how to cure with herbs, was also accused of bewitching men of power. The foreman of the *obraje* where she worked for more than nine years claimed that his illness was the result of a diabolic spell which María Alvarado had cast. While denying that she caused his sickness, this "witch-curer" did confess to a knowledge of love magic, which could also "calm the authorities . . . so that they do not interfere with her" (AAL:Leg. 3, Exp. XVIII, f. 7v). As in the case of Juana Icha, the *obraje*'s director did punish her. Nevertheless the foreman, who was in league with the *corregidor* and the curate, was unable to exile her from the *obraje*, because of what he claimed to be the fear in which all her fellow workers held her (see BN:C4142; AAL:Leg. 1, Exp. VIII and X, Leg. 2, Exp. XVIII, Leg. 4, Exp. XLVII, Leg. 6, Exp. VIII). One might surmise that men in authority who accused women of witchcraft were merely channeling their guilt and fear into accusations of sorcery. However, the record of support shown by Indian commoners toward these "witches," with whom they lived and worked, points to something else.[3]

---

[3] In this chapter, I am analyzing only some of the social tendencies which the witchcraft trials make evident. Presented here, therefore, is only a partial picture of what these trials say about colonial village life.

In addition to the Indian devil Apo Parato, Juana Icha independently confessed to having consulted another, named Rara Puquio. I shall turn briefly to this self-confessed devil, a mountain spring (*puquio*), because it reveals how concepts that were related to the feminine in pre-Columbian Andean thought became transformed in the Spanish colonial context. Juana Icha told her inquisitors that she, accompanied by her teacher and master, Catalina, would regularly "feed" the devil Rara Puquio:

> . . . [Juana's] teacher told her that one day when she went to the mountain spring, the spring opened up and kept her inside for five or six days . . . and she had seen a man with golden-red hair. . . . [T]his had taken place when she was a little girl pasturing her llamas, and this man with golden-red hair gave her *mazamorra* [pudding] each of those five days . . . and after she left, this man told her that she should be very careful always to bring him food, and after five months had passed, the teacher returned, bringing *sanco* [flour paste], coca, ground corn, fat, potatoes, and *chicha* [AAL:Leg. 4, Exp. XIV, f. 16].

This devil, of golden-red hair, initiated the relationship with his adherent by offering food; the *maestra* and her disciple, in good Andean fashion, reciprocated. However, although the tenor of the bond between this divinity and his mortal followers may have been typically Andean, the symbolic representation of this (super)natural force was not. The god of the *puquio* was a man. Before the Spanish conquest, bodies of water—lakes, springs, fountains—had been considered female; they were the daughters or extensions of the Mamacocha. Moreover, this god of the *puquio*, with his golden-red hair, was not Andean; he was of Spanish origin. As opposed to the Indian Apo Parato, Rara Puquio embodied truly extraordinary powers: "he could go anywhere" to carry out the commands of his adherents (AAL:Leg. 4, Exp. XIV, f. 16). Perhaps, in terms of Andean understandings evolved under the reality of colonial relations, it would be impossible for either a

189

female deity or an indigenous deity to incorporate the sort of power that this *puquio* possessed.

The trial in which charges of witchcraft were brought against Francisca Carguachuqui will also shed light on how Andean concepts were transformed by the colonial process—as well as revealing something of the new kinds of power that the structures of colonial society bestowed on its female "witches" (AAL:Leg. 1, Exp. XII). Francisca, whose age was estimated as eighty, was accused of being a curer as well as a witch who damaged crops, decimated herds, and caused illness; by some accounts, she was also responsible for the deaths of at least five people, including a priest and the owner of a large estate. As with Juana Icha, much of Francisca's testimony was coerced. Francisca freely admitted knowing how to cure with herbs, but she was time and again forced under torture to confess that her knowledge had a diabolic source. When asked to ratify her depositions, she would staunchly deny the validity of these confessions, asserting that they had been made under duress.

Francisca's testimonies revealed ways in which reputed Indian sorceresses could take advantage of the witchcraft fears that Spaniards projected onto their colonized subjects. Spaniards believed that elderly women like Francisca had extraordinary powers; consequently, they sought out old indigenous women to perform devil-derived acts. Not sharing their belief in the European devil, Francisca thought these requests absurd. But she appeased them and ridiculed them by pretending she could conjure the black arts. Thus, Francisca could take her revenge, albeit in a small way, on Spaniards and their nonsensical beliefs and assumptions.

At one point, Francisca was re-examined about testimony she had refused to ratify concerning an alleged pact made with the devil. At the urging of two Spanish women, Francisca, supposedly with the help of the devil, had fabricated a "door" so that the priest-administrator (a lover of one of the women) of the *hacienda* Uchusquillo would not be removed from his post:

Asked again with what knowledge she had done this, whether it was not by means of a pact with the black devil, and whether she said that she would not have done anything had she not been forced to do so by these ladies, and that she had done it only to please them, making fun of them all the while . . . and asked again and threatened with torture because she denied what she had previously confessed, she became somewhat ashamed and said that the devil had spoken to her . . . and told her to do what these ladies had asked [AAL:Leg. 1, Exp. XII, f. 17].

The transcript speaks for itself.

In the formal deposition made in Francisca's defense by her counselor, an interesting picture emerges of the defendant's beliefs. According to her lawyer's petition, most of Francisca's confessed crimes, including elaborate testimony describing the devil, who appeared in a variety of guises, had been extorted:

. . . in reference to the pact made with the devil [who appeared to her] as a cat . . . she says that she did not commit [such an act]; but, rather, afraid of the torture and whippings that the interpreter said she would suffer if she insisted on not revealing any more pacts with animals, he had hardly to ask her if [she made a pact] with a cat, repeating it one or two times, and she said yes [AAL:Leg. 1, Exp. XII, f. 36v].

However, although Francisca, like Juana Icha, denied most of the diabolic murders, she did admit worshipping one "devil" who aided her in causing the death of a priest and a landlord. The priest and the landlord had abused their positions, mistreating this accused witch. Francisca confessed to one diabolic pact:

. . . she spoke with the serpent . . . whom she saw when she went to gather some herbs . . . and she saw, from the mountain spring, a deformed serpent . . . with a beard that seemed like fire . . . and she was terrified and it spoke to her, demanding white and black maize to eat . . . and she did what was asked of her . . . because if she did not, he would eat her.

191

> ... [A]nd by invoking [the serpent] ... and by offering the
> serpent people to eat, who died, [she thought] that he would
> aid her sorcery ... and she said she had a pact and dealings
> with the devil ... when she spoke to the serpent, and sepa-
> rating herself from the congregation of faithful Christians
> ... she was only concerned with giving credence to the
> devil, calling it in her thoughts, for aid and witchcraft
> [AAL:Leg. 1, Exp. XII, f. 37 and 37v].

For a Spanish inquisitor, a devil in snake's clothing would be
an expected and reasonable guise for Satan to take. For an Indian subject in colonial Andean society, the devotion shown
toward a snake residing in a mountain spring is also to be expected, but for different reasons. The serpent has deep roots in
the configuration of Andean symbolic thought. The complex
of serpents residing in springs is one manifestation of the Andean concept of the *amaru*. While the *amaru* as a symbol en-
capsulates many referents, one of its principal connotations is
that of relation or alliance. This connotation can be extended
to the *amaru*'s representation of a force that erupts when relations of balance and equilibrium are not maintained in the
social and natural universe (Earls and Silverblatt 1976a).

The potentially destructive characteristics of the *amaru*
snake figure are exemplified in the mythology of the region
where Francisca Carguachuqui resided. Thus, a nearby village

> maintains the tradition that there used to be a large snake,
> like a serpent, which walked and traveled underneath the
> earth, and it toppled mountains and the serpent went about
> pilfering and eating the Indians. ... [And the Indians asked]
> the idol Capabilla to free them ... and the idol transformed
> the serpent into stone which the Indians also worshipped
> [AAL:Leg. 6, Exp. XI, f. 22v].

Although the snake with its destructive powers—capable of
toppling mountains and consuming people—was an entity
that inspired fear in the Andes, it was at the same time incorporated into the pantheon of deities to which devotion was

shown. In this sense, it cannot be qualitatively equated with the Catholic devil, the embodiment of evil, whose worship was defined as heretical. However, conceptions of evil or of the diabolic could be grafted onto this indigenous construct, and in some circumstances, it could then become devilish.

The same witness who told of Capabilla and the serpent described his curing techniques:

> . . . extracting these snakes and toads from the bodies of sick people was [necessary in] that the devil had entered their swellings and wounds, and because of these offerings and sacrifices which he performed, he extracted the devil from these wounds [AAL:Leg. 6, Exp. XI, f. 15 and 15v].

For a native living under colonialism, qualities of illness and sickness were becoming merged with the Spanish-introduced concept of the devil, a devil who took the form of a snake. Trapped in the contradictions of colonial relations, the "dangerous" and "irrational" powers of indigenous deities were becoming equated with diabolic forces. Some divinities, like the Huari of the northern sierra, introduced "devilish" diseases into the bodies of those who no longer worshipped them. The breakdown of the sacred bond between Andean gods and their native adherents was manifested in illnesses caused by snakes, toads, and spiders. But in the process, the god Huari was also transformed, taking on attributes in the colonial period that were associated with the devils of Europe. A priest-inquisitor, in a written summary of the idolatries he had witnessed, documented this transformation:

> Nowadays, the aforementioned Huari converts himself into many shapes—man-like forms or snake-like forms—and he especially converts himself into a rapid wind, and in this form he goes about, every day, governing the world, introducing diseases, snakes, and other things into the bodies of those who do not adore him or serve him, and giving health to those who do serve him, dogmatizing that he was God and the creator of the earth [Duviols 1971:388].

Yet, as Juana Icha discovered, some native deities, despite the devotion shown them, were no longer capable of providing their adherents with the means to sustain their lives. As colonial economic and political policies devastated the material and social basis of *ayllu* organization, native gods—the representation of lifegiving forces—became increasingly powerless. The devastation and despair experienced by the colonized were expressed through these Andean symbols: the *huacas* themselves, despite being "fed," began to consume their adherents. Isabel Chuqui, a seventy-year-old accused witch, claimed that it was this aspect of her *huaca*'s behavior that was demonic: "these two stones [her adored *huaca*] are the devil; they consumed my sister's children" (AAL: Leg. 3, Exp. I, f. 3v). Trapped in the irrationality of colonial relations, unable to fulfill the expectations of their native worshippers, *huacas* had become diabolic.

Returning to the one manifestation of the devil, the *amaru*, with which Francisca Carguachuqui admitted to having made a pact, we can further comprehend how indigenous concepts evolved and were transformed in the colonial context. Francisca believed she could intervene in her destiny, and that of her fellow Indian commoners, by worshipping a devilish *amaru*, a powerful and bearded *amaru*, who incorporated some of the diabolic power of her oppressors. The *amaru* in Andean thought has close associations with revolt and revolution. The last descendant of the Inca dynasty to head the resistance to the Spanish conquest in the sixteenth century was named Tupac Amaru; the leader of the indigenous revolt against colonialism that shook the Andes in the 1780s also assumed that name. It should not surprise us that this persecuted woman was worshipping the *amaru*, for by means of "witchcraft" she was attempting to bring about the destruction of the extremely distorted and unbalanced conditions that character-ized her life under colonial rule. In the Andes of the seventeenth century, as in Europe, a religious battle was merged with a political one. If the Spanish institutions and ideological structures imposed on the colonies systematically eroded the potentialities of Andean women, they also provided them with a means to undermine those same structures.[4] The Spanish created witches in Peru where none existed before.

Although the witch-heretic of Europe may have been perceived by the power establishment of late Middle Ages and Renaissance as a political subversive, she acted alone. She was an outcast in her own village. This was not so with her Andean counterpart. Witches were powerful figures in colonial indigenous society: they were actively sought as *comadres*, and their presence was required in informal village reunions in which native deities were worshipped (AAL:Leg. 5, Exp. 18, Leg. 6, Exp. 11). The Spanish decreed that witchcraft and idolatry were indistinguishable; thus, witchcraft, maintenance of ancient traditions, and conscious political resistance became increasingly intertwined for colonial Indians. "Witches," manipulating structures and ideologies introduced by the Spanish, formed crucial links in an underground politico-religious movement that was emerging in response to colonialism.

From the indigenous point of view, women became identified as the upholders of traditional Andean culture, the defenders of pre-Columbian lifeways against an illegitimate regime. As the *cuaracas* and other native allies of Spanish authority became entrenched and caught up in the contradictory roles they occupied in the colonial system, they were increasingly associated with that system's illegitimacy. Polo, Murúa, and the idol smashers noted how these men "feared" the female witches of the Andes. Were they not bound to "fear" increasingly these women who replaced them—from the perspective of native culture—as the legitimate, albeit underground, representatives of that culture? And even if it were true, as Polo states (1916:28), that Indians refused to divulge the names of these women to colonial authorities for fear of being bewitched, is he not perhaps also revealing that these women's

---

[4] Taussig (1980b) discusses the dialectic between conquest and curing in Colombia.

195

identities were being protected by their indigenous companions because of their "powers" of resistance to colonial forces?

A priest explained to ecclesiastical authorities why he publicly whipped three women:

> I did not do this so much because of the fact that they believed in superstitions and other abominations, but rather because they encouraged the whole village to mutiny and riot through their reputation as witches who went neither to Mass nor to catechism classes, and who publicly disobeyed me, their parish priest, as well as their mayor [BN:C4142].

CHAPTER X

Women of the *Puna*

> The [Indian women] are overwhelmed by trib-
> ute demands and personal labor service; for
> this reason, they are terrified and do not want
> to serve God or the king, and fleeing [the *reduc-
> ciones*] they go and hide in the *puna* [high
> tableland] and *estancias* [pasture areas in the
> *puna*]. . . . [T]hey do not confess, they do not
> attend catechism classes teaching Christian
> doctrine; nor do they go to Mass. They do not
> even know who their parish priests, *corregi-
> dores*, or *curacas* are; they do not obey their
> mayors or their *curacas* . . . and returning to
> their ancient customs and idolatry, they do not
> want to serve God or the Crown.
>
> [Guaman Poma 1956, II:147]

By the seventeenth century, colonial institutions were firmly
entrenched in Peru. While indigenous men often fled the
oppression of the *mita* and tribute by abandoning their communities and going to work as *yanaconas* (quasi-serfs) in the
emerging *haciendas*, women fled to the *punas*, inaccessible and
very distant from the *reducciones* of their native communities.
Once in the *punas*, women rejected the forces and symbols of
their oppression, disobeying Spanish administrators, the
clergy, as well as their own community officials. They also vig-
orously rejected the colonial ideology which reinforced their
oppression, refusing to go to Mass, participate in Catholic
confession, or learn Catholic dogma. More important, women
did not just reject Catholicism; they returned to their native religion and, as best they could, to the quality of social relations
which their religion expressed.

197

CHAPTER X

Priestesses of Idolatry

In the campaign mounted by the Church to extirpate idolatry in Peru, women were persecuted not only as practitioners of witchcraft, but also as key participants and leaders in the worship of outlawed indigenous cults. One of the most important religious officiants in the pre-Columbian *ayllu* led the worship of *huacas* considered to be guardian-ancestors of the entire community. Although chroniclers affirm that women before the Conquest were responsible for ceremonies devoted to female deities, the majority deny that women, for the most part, could direct communitywide rituals that were dedicated to the gods (Arriaga 1968:32-35, 67; Cobo 1964, II:225-29). In the seventeenth century, however, women not only served as assistants in communitywide religious cults to male ancestor-*huacas* (a secondary post which the chroniclers affirm women could hold), but also served as their principal officiants (AAL:Leg. 2, Exp. IV, Leg. 2, Exp. XXI, Leg. 1, Exp. II, Leg. 2, Exp. X, Leg. 3, Exp. X, Leg. 2, Exp. XIV, Leg. 4, Exp. XVIII).

Now, in the colonial period, indigenous women could become priestesses to their *ayllu*'s gods. The peculiar constraints imposed on women by colonial institutions turned them to offices in native religious organizations largely prohibited prior to the Conquest. I do not want to imply that men stopped participating—either as priests or believers—in Andean religious activities, for the traditions that the idol smashers tried to root out are still important to the Andean peasantry of today. But women frequently remained behind in their native villages as men fled to avoid tribute or *mita* service. Those men who held positions of authority in colonial political and religious institutions often had to hide their idolatrous inclinations. Moreover, the male bias of these official institutions to which women were prohibited access tended to push women toward traditional practices which were defined by the dominant regime as diabolic. Women, then, were increasingly viewed by their indigenous companions in colonial communities as the defenders of ancient traditions, and they were encouraged to assume leading roles in carrying out native ritual.

The history of one renowned female priest, Catalina Guacayllano, is indicative of the role that women began to play in the underground "idolatrous" cults that were emerging in colonial communities (AAL:Leg. 4, Exp. XVIII). Catalina was known as "la doctora," a Spanish title of prestige which indigenous peoples appropriated to bestow on their own men and women of wisdom. Catalina was revered in her northern sierra village of Otuco, in the mid-seventeenth century, precisely because she was the guardian of pre-Columbian customs. Priestess and teacher, she directed the community's veneration of its principal ancestor-deities and instructed others in the rites of the indigenous priesthood. One of her disciples, Domingo Runa Chaupis, testified about his apprenticeship to this woman of knowledge:

> . . . and this witness . . . served an Indian woman named Catalina Guacayllano for several years, . . . and she ordered him to bring *cuyes* [guinea pigs], white and black maize, coca, and fat to offer to the idol, the god Guari [Huari], whom all of the Indians worshipped every year before cleaning their irrigation canals and preparing their fields. . . . [And the offerings] were made on a small plain called Ariguanapampa . . . and the priest, Father Avendaño, removed from this plain an idol of stone, made in the likeness of man, along with five *conopas*, which had been placed at the foot of a *molle* tree [a pepper, or mastic, tree having many medicinal uses], which all the Indians from this village of Otuco as well as those from the village of Guamgri venerated, and [Avendaño] burned them, and the aforesaid [Catalina Guacayllano] put another ten idols in their place . . . and she taught him [Domingo Runa Chaupis] to be a witch, and in order to do so they brought ten *cuyes*, coca, fat, and black and white maize to the aforesaid Ariguanapampa, and in the middle where there are several piles of stones she began to sacrifice the *cuyes* with her hands, spilling the blood over

199

these stones, saying . . . "O, Lord Father, who has been burned, who gives us the irrigation canals and water, give me food; ever since you have been burned we are dying of hunger and have no food"; . . . [A]nd the aforesaid Indian woman told him she had done this all her life, had made sacrifices to the god Guari, because before there were *yngas* [Incas] and *apoes* [= *apus*, or Spaniards] he appeared . . . and distributed all the fields and irrigation canals to every village and *ayllu* . . . and it was he who gave us food and water [AAL:Leg. 4, Exp. XVIII, f. 5v, 6].

Domingo Runa Chaupis was one of several people whom Catalina Guacayllano trained as priests to continue the traditions and beliefs of their ancestors. Francisca Cocha Quilla was instructed by Catalina to lead the adoration of the *huaca* Pucara; Francisca Llacsa Chacara, to head the devotion of the gods Raupoma and Choqueruntu. She taught the ancient curing rituals to Inés Capxa Mayhuay, Francisca Quillay Suyo, Francisca Misa, and Inés Yalpo Cocha, who were from the villages of Otuco and Guamgri. While Catalina instructed men in the beliefs and practices of Andean religion—designating Domingo Runa Chaupis to minister to the god Guari is only one example—she tended to choose women to maintain the ways of the past. Her daughter, Catalina Mayhuay Colque, succeeded her.

Faced with the deteriorating lives of her people, Catalina believed that the maintenance of Andean cultural traditions was a crucial defense against the onslaughts of colonialism. She preached this doctrine in her native village as well as in neighboring communities. She also trained disciples to ensure that her beliefs would be diffused and continued after her death. Refusing to be outdone by the preachers of Catholicism who were trying to destroy the religion of her ancestors, Catalina not only defended her faith but aggrandized it. When the extirpator of idolatries Hernando de Avendaño burned the god Guari and the five *conopas* which embodied its powers, Catalina replaced them, twofold.

Catalina's activities also provide an important insight into the role played by women in the synthesis of traditional and Christian ritual that was taking place in native communities during the seventeenth century. Men were often designated sponsors, or *mayordomos*, of the celebrations held in honor of Christian holy days. The male sponsors of these festivals would slaughter llamas in the village, ostensibly to distribute the meat for the feasts which accompanied the Christian festivities. But it was Catalina Guacayllano, along with her female assistants and trainees, who collected the llamas' blood. This blood was taken to the *puna* to the sites where their *huacas* were adored, and to the *machayes*, or caves, where their ancestors were heretically buried—as offerings to the traditional sacred beings of Andean culture. Catalina's apprentice, who at the time of the idolatry trials was a priestess in her own right, gave the following testimony:

> ... this witness saw how during the festival of the birth of the Virgin Mary, when Santiago Guaripisco was *mayordomo*, he killed a llama, slitting it on the side of its heart, and the aforesaid Indian woman [Catalina Guacayllano] collected the blood and took it to Pucara, where they offered it, and this witness and the aforesaid woman said the following prayer ... "O rich and powerful lord take this, eat and drink so that the *chicha* will multiply so that those who come to the festival will have plenty." ... and as had been declared ... during the festivities to Our Lady, the [blood of the] llamas which the *mayordomos* slaughtered for the festival was collected by those Indian women, witches, and they carried it to the *guacas* [*huacas*] and *machayes* where they made offerings, and to the idol Pucara, where they danced in the pagan manner of their ancestors [AAL: Leg. 4, Exp. XVIII, f. 3v and 5].

The idolatrous and subversive activities that Catalina Guacayllano championed were supported by Otuco's *curaca*, Don Alonso Ricari. Certainly Don Alonso was not the only man to hold a position in the colonial power structure and, at the same time, encourage native ritual practices. Some men actually took advantage of colonial society's new sources of wealth to reaffirm their positions in the native community (Spalding 1967:96-135). Further, as Millones (1976) has pointed out, other *curacas* consolidated their internal political control by manipulating indigenous religious institutions (also see Salomon 1983). But the point I want to make here is that Spanish institutions made men—whether tribute payers or officeholders—wear a public, official face. Since their behavior was more closely scrutinized by the dominant regime, their ability to assume leading roles in the underground of idolatry must have been severely constrained. Also, flirting with colonial power contaminated them. As Spanish institutions made men public figures, however, they made women invisible. Hence, indigenous men, tainted by the power that colonial institutions bestowed on them, had to turn to women to maintain the heretical traditions of their ancestors (see AAL:Leg. 4, Exp. XXXII, Leg. 6, Exp. XVII, Leg. 4, Exp. XXI, Leg. 2, Exp. IV, Leg. 3, Exp. XV, Leg. 1, Exp. VI, Leg. 2, Exp. XV, Leg. 2, Exp. XXI).

Catalina Guacayllano's grave was discovered by the priest sent to Otuco to extirpate idolatry. She was given an elaborate burial in her *ayllu*'s *machay*, similar to the burials of those who held important positions in the religious and political life of the *ayllus* before the Spanish conquest (Hernández Príncipe 1923:53-55). Catalina could be recognized by the exquisitely woven ritual clothing in which she was buried:

> . . . among the bodies [discovered in the *machayes*], they recognized the Indian woman named Catalina Guacayllano, also known as "la dotora," the teacher and master of witchcraft, rites, and ancient ceremonies, because of the vestments of *cumbi* that she wore and in which she was buried, which were those she put on when she made the sacrifices to Pucara and the idols Choqueruntu and Raupoma [AAL:Leg. 4, Exp. XVIII, f. 11, 11v].

THE VIRGIN'S NEW ROLE

By the seventeenth century, another underground religious structure was emerging which assigned to women an increasingly important role in the maintenance of indigenous traditions. Celibate women, most often virgins but including widows who refused remarriage, were dedicated to the service of *huacas* and the ancestors. Virgins played a crucial part in the religious activities of Andean society long before the Spanish conquest. However, the *aclla* as an institution evolved only with the development of the Inca empire into a complex, stratified polity. It is difficult to ascertain the role of virgins in the sacred organizations of the pre-Columbian *ayllu*; but I would argue that it was minimal, or that the consecration of virgins per se existed only in an embryonic form. Yet we find various references to virgins in colonial *ayllus*—virgins whose lives were devoted to the cults of local deities or who, because of "marriage" to a particular *huaca*, were said to become its sacred spokeswomen (AAL:Leg. 2, Exp. IV, Leg. 3, Exp. X, Leg. 4, Exp. XVIIIa, Leg. 3, Exp. XV, Leg. 4, Exp. s.n., Leg. 6, Exp. XI). Like the growing number of priestesses, the growing number of virgins in native religious structures signals the development of a defiant indigenous response to colonial pressure.

In the village of Gorgor, one Asto Mallao, *soltera* (unmarried woman), was dedicated to the *huacas* and ancestors of her *ayllu*. Always accompanying the native priest and priestess who directed the worship of her community's gods, Asto Mallao spent most of her life close to the hilltop home of her deities, near the ancient village where her *ayllu* lived before being forced into the *reducciones* (AAL:Leg. 2, Exp. IV). In 1612, Asto Mallao was known only by the pagan name of her ancestors; she had never been baptized. Magdalena Antonia, the niece of one of Puquiian's most renowned "dogmatists" of Andean religion, was similarly devoted to the goddess Coya Guarmi. Testimonies recount that because she was a virgin ("had never known a man") it was considered appropriate for Magdalena to enter the service of this goddess (AAL:Leg. 4,

203

Exp. s.n.). Only Magdalena was permitted to carry the image of Coya Guarmi from her permanent shrine in Puquiian's pre-Columbian ceremonial center in the *puna* to Puquiian's colonial settlement in the valley.

The campaign to extirpate idolatry was particularly aggressive in the Parish of Acas, a parish whose principal *curaca* was a staunch defender of the customs of his ancestors. Several denunciations were made against its principal headman, Cristóbal Hacas Poma, as well as against other *curacas* such as Don Alonso Ricari (the *curaca* of Otuco) for encouraging the practice of singling out virgins or widows for the service of native gods. In 1656, Otuco's *fiscal*, who had been charged with the task of presenting accusations against his native companions, made the following denunciation:

> . . . and there is an Indian woman named Nanya, whose Christian name is not known . . . and she is not baptized, and she is a virgin, and she is never seen in the company of men because she is consecrated to the service of idols and concerns herself only with making *chicha* for their offerings, and it is said that she lives like a pagan Indian woman [AAL:Leg. 6, Exp. XI, f. 1v].

Leonor Nabin Carhua was a widow when Cristóbal Hacas Poma summoned her into the service of the *huacas* and ancestors. A witness, Juan Raura declared:

> . . . Nabin Carhua, an elderly woman . . . is dedicated to the ministry of making *chicha* to offer to the *malqui* [ancestor] Guamancama and to the idol Tarquiurau . . . and the reason why this widow, and not a young girl, was designated is because Hacas Poma said that younger girls and single women were called every day to go to catechism class, and thus they were dirty and contaminated for making *chicha*. . . . [A]nd the aforesaid widow never went to church, nor did she ever hear Mass [AAL:Leg. 6, Exp. XI, f. 42].

Leonor Nabin Carhua gave her own testimony:

... after her husband died ... Hacas Poma told her not to marry because the *huacas* and *malquis* told him she was needed for the office of making *chicha*, and to confess the other Indian women of her *ayllu* ... and ever since the day she was to enter into the service of the idols, she was never to enter the church to pray or hear Mass, because if she were to enter, she would become dirty and unable to make *chicha* for the offerings [AAL:Leg. 6, Exp. XI, f. 57].

Common to all of these testimonies concerning the role of celibate women in underground religious cults is the conscious rejection and prohibition of any consort with the world of the conquerors. These women did live a "pagan" life: they were neither baptized, not went to Mass. Leading the life of their ancestors kept them pure and consequently suitable to perform the sacred rites of their Andean past. If Spanish institutions made women invisible, an ideology of celibacy was a further defense against disclosure.

Another "pagan" virgin priestess, Francisca Guacaquillay, was discovered in Otuco by the extirpators of idolatry. Isabel Poma Cargua's testimony echoes the content of other declarations about celibate priestesses. Francisca Guacaquillay, the niece of Otuco's *curaca* Don Alonso Ricari,

has never gone to hear Mass, and the reason is that she is not baptized and is dedicated to the idols and *guacas* and is a virgin ... and she could have no carnal knowledge of any man. ... [A]nd she was concerned only with making *chicha* for the *guacas*, and it is generally known that she is a virgin [AAL:Leg. 4, Exp. XVIIIa, f. 2].

Francisca Guacaquillay concurs that she "never went to Mass, or even once attended catechism classes ... [and that she] is not baptized, nor is she a Christian" (AAL:Leg. 4, Exp. XVIIIa, f. 3v).

These testimonies allow us to glimpse a process whereby native communities were desperately trying to defend indigenous religious activities, the lifeways of Andean society, in the face

205

of the constant pressures of Spanish secular and religious institutions to undermine them. A critical component of this cultural defense was the designation of celibate women, in the
majority of cases young girls, who from childhood were
trained in the rites associated with their society's outlawed religious beliefs. Francisca, whose mother was also a well-
known "idolator-confessor, who ordered her *ayllu* not to worship God" (AAL:Leg. 4, Exp. XVIIIa, f. 28), lived an underground existence. Removing herself to the *puna*, Francisca
lived as much as possible in isolation from the contaminating
elements of Spanish society. At thirty-five she was not baptized; she had never entered a church; she had no contact with
Spanish authorities. Perhaps Christian ideology was incorporated into the fiat that she remain virgin. Perhaps her virginity
was rooted in Andean custom. But the celibacy imposed on
women who entered the service of the sacred beings of Andean
culture was a protection. It reinforced their separation from
Spanish men, and thus shielded them from the pollution which
contact entailed. More important, it shielded them from the
watchful eyes of colonial institutions: single women did not
constitute an important category for colonial censuses. Isolated in the *puna*, these women effectively vanished from the
cognizance of the Spanish world.

 In 1656, the dedication of virgins into the service of *huacas*
was a critical component of Otuco's growing attempt to defend native culture. Approximately thirty years before, Francisca Guacaquillay was the only young girl designated to be a
virgin priestess of her village's gods. But now four more young
girls were being initiated into indigenous religious lore. María
Francisca, María Micaela, María Cargua, and Francisca
María, all younger than ten, were under the tutelage of Francisca Guacaquillay. These girls, each of whom represented one
of the four *ayllus* which constituted the village of Otuco, were
being carefully trained in "the rites and ceremonies that the
consecrated Indian [Francisca Guacaquillay] commands"
(AAL:Leg. 4, Exp. XVIIIa, f. 2). The dedication of virgins into
the service of autochthonous deities was part of an expanding

native religious structure, evolved under the exigencies of the colonial experience, whose purpose was to defend and ensure the survival of Andean traditional life.

ESCAPE AND DEFENSE

The return to native religion and the increasingly important role women played in its maintenance was a form of cultural resistance. If men tried to escape from the burdens of colonialism by fleeing their natal communities, women escaped by going to the *puna*, as far as possible from the post-Conquest indigenous villages where the forces of colonial rule held sway. In the *puna*, close to the burial sites of their sacred progenitors and the shrines of their gods, women attempted to return to the ways of their ancestors. But return meant defiance in colonial Peru; cultural resistance was political subversion. Women hiding in their huts in the Andean tablelands rejected the ideology and institutions of their masters. That they would not go to Mass or learn Christian doctrine was, as Guaman Poma recognized (1956, II:147), the ideological manifestation of their rejection of any colonial authority. Not only that, but these women tried to perpetuate their culture of resistance. Ensconced in the *puna*, they shielded their children as well from the institutions of the dominant. They refused to allow them to be baptized, the sign of entrance into the Christian world:

> Moreover, nowadays, many Indian women hide their children in the pasture lands where they have their herds. . . . [O]ften they die there without ever having been baptized [Guaman Poma 1956, III:182].

Guaman Poma and other commentators give us a clue to the emergence of a woman's society in the *puna*—a society that resisted and defended itself against the oppression of colonialism. Women worked together, pasturing their herds and protecting one another from the representatives of colonial institutions. Explaining why Indian women were so afraid of

207

their parish priests and why they hid their children from baptism, Guaman Poma declares:

> . . . they fear that the priest would exile them from their native *ayllus*—they as well as their female companions—in order to compel them all to perform forced labor services [1956, II:183].

Mandatory exile to the *obrajes* was one of the commonest punishments meted out to women who were accused of witchcraft and idolatry, of returning to the traditions of their ancestors (AAL:Leg. 1, Exp. X).

Sometimes, however, witnessing the destruction of their culture, women became so desperate that they preferred to commit suicide than to live a tortured existence. The inquisitor Hernández Príncipe recounts the suicide of an elderly Indian woman who, in the company of other women, was caught carrying offerings that were to be made to their gods:

> . . . the old Indian woman who hung herself at the beginning of the inquest, deceived by the devil, [did so] because the village prosecutor bumped into her in the street and, noticing a bag she carried in her hands, took it from her by force, and he discovered that it was a bag full of offerings for *huacas*.
> . . . [A]nd the inquisitor, having asked her several questions, left her to think about her welfare and salvation, without any oppression; but she, finding herself deprived of her instruments of witchcraft—even though she was accompanied by other Indian women—was discovered to have hung herself by her own belt in the morning [1923:38].

Other women, similarly consumed by despair, preferred to kill their own children rather than allow a new generation to suffer at the hands of priests, colonial administrators, majordomos, or their own native functionaries. But mothers who practiced infanticide killed only their male children. As the Franciscan monk Buenaventura de Salinas noted, "mothers also kill their children, because in giving birth to boys, they suffocate them" (Roel 1970:11; cf. Guaman Poma 1956,

II:182). This male infanticide can be interpreted in several ways, but in part it expressed the deep disillusion which Andean women felt toward the men who had betrayed them and their culture. Desperate, finding themselves abused not only by male representatives of colonial authority but by men of their own culture, women attempted to re-create the "female component" of Andean lifeways, as well as the social relations and ideology which governed the ordered world their ancestors had known.

The creation of an underground culture of resistance in the *puna*, led by women and marked by a return to the traditions of pre-Columbian society, is foreshadowed in the following testimony. Three elderly women, fleeing to the inaccessible tablelands to avoid persecution at the hands of the priest and extirpator of idolatry Francisco de Ávila, recounted their plight:

> These women, since they were Christians, declared [to the cleric-inquisitor] that they knew nothing about *huacas*. In spite of having said this, [Ávila] made them as well as other Indian women mount llamas where he beat them until they bled. . . . These women, overcome by the torture and pain were obliged to confess that they did adore *huacas* so that the priest would stop torturing them. [These women lamented] . . . "Now, in this life, we Indian women, like those men [Castilians whose ancestors were pagan] are Christians; perhaps then the priest is to blame if we women adore the mountains, if we flee to the hills and *puna*, since there is no justice for us here" [Guaman Poma 1956, III:265].[1]

EPILOGUE

In contemporary Andean culture, the *puna* is considered women's territory and is the center of women's society. In this

---

[1] Although some anthropologists contend that the metaphorical association of women with the *puna* and of men with the village is a pre-Columbian tradition, I maintain, in light of the evidence in this chapter, that it is a product of native responses to the colonial process.

isolated tableland where they pasture their herds, women occupy positions of privilege. The *puna*, close to the home of the
mountain god Wamani, is also associated with the "wild and
savage" when metaphorically compared with the "masculine
village"—the locus of "civilization." But the physical manifestations of "civilization" in this male domain exemplify the history of colonial domination of the Andes: the church, the mu-
nicipality, the jail. And so we find a paradox. The male
members of the *varayoq*, who are obliged to guard the morality of the village, are afraid to go to the *puna*, for "if the
women in the *puna* do not like what we are doing, they will
stone us and make us return to our village." On the other hand,
the *varayoq* add: "The women in the *puna* are living in the
ways our ancestors lived years ago; they are defending our customs, they are defending our culture" (Silverblatt n.d.).

CHAPTER XI

A Proposal

> They strode over the giant cordilleras, over the
> rugged Americas, hunting for potatoes, sau-
> sages, beans, black tobacco, gold, corn, fried
> eggs, with a voracious appetite not found in the
> world since then. . . . They swallowed up every-
> thing, religions, pyramids, tribes, idolatries just
> like the ones they brought along in their huge
> sacks. . . . Wherever they went, they razed the
> land. . . . But words fell like pebbles out of the
> boots of the barbarians, out of their beards,
> their helmets, their horseshoes, luminous
> words that were left glittering here . . . our lan-
> guage. We came up losers. . . . We came up win-
> ners. . . . They carried off the gold and left us
> the gold. . . . They carried everything off and
> left us everything. . . . They left us the words.
>
> [Neruda 1978:54]

The political antagonisms unleashed by the Inca conquest of
the Andes and by the Spanish conquest of the Incas illuminated
cultural forms which contoured and articulated Andean society.[1] In the preceding pages, we have looked at the reconstruction of one cultural form—gender—which these two succes-
sive waves of empire building set in motion.

The Inca empire was born of a struggle between peoples
whose social experience was framed by kinship and a people
whose imperial enterprise would undermine that autonomy
and supplant that power of kin. Only a hundred years before

---

[1] I borrow Marx's metaphor, describing the relation between mode of production and historical process as a "general illumination in which all other
colors are plunged" (1973:106-107).

211

the arrival of the Spanish, the lords of Cuzco had succeeded in their design to conquer the communities which dotted the Andean sierra and coastal plain, from southern Colombia to northwestern Argentina. But their success was limited and constantly challenged. The Incas had made their force known—less dramatically than Spain, but just as portentously—as they fought to impose their own vision of world order on those whom they would rule. In this process, the Incas distorted the familiar, built on common expectations of human relations and cosmology, to turn community-framed notions into accepted Inca common sense. Thus, Pan-Andean gender ideologies were drafted into imperial service.

Central to the lifeways and experience of Andean women and men, gender ideologies not only gave shape to male and female identities but were the prisms through which the universe and society were viewed. Nature and the supernatural, social divisions and ranks, economic relations and environment—all these were infused by gender imagery. The Incas reconstructed these systems, so familiar to conquered Andean peoples, to fit the new relations of power they imposed.

Gender images were metaphors for complementarity as well as for hierarchy; and the Incas elaborated gender's contrariness to cloak their subjugation of others while they forged relations of subjugation. As class relations supplanted kinship, gender became a trope embracing relations of power and articulating them. Class formation, transforming cultural distinctions into reflections of its own exploitative image, took gender distinctness and made hierarchical differences. The Incas genderized class.

The formation of an Andean colony of Spain was no less than social war. The Spaniards insinuated alien economic, political, and religious institutions to create a colony that could meet the expectations of Iberia; conquered Andean peoples rebelled against, accommodated, adapted to, and ignored those institutions. Spanish gender ideologies were also basic to the making of colonial Peru; and they, like mercantilism and

212

Christianity, were profoundly foreign to Andean ways of living.

Iberian gender beliefs proclaimed women's infantility; only men could reach true adulthood and enter public life, freely sign contracts, and hold public office. Thus, although the Spanish colonial polity privileged men and women of the Andean elite, in general it prejudiced women. As a consequence, all native women experienced the erosion of deeply rooted pre-Columbian traditions that once gave them autonomous access to their society's material resources and control over their own religious and political institutions. Colonization also brought with it the horrors of sexual abuse. Spanish gender ideologies weighed heaviest on peasant women, who bore the double yoke of class and gender.

But the women of the Andes resisted such dehumanization; and the colonial experience—with its peculiar struggles over meanings of gender—colored that resistance. Rejection of the Spanish world entailed, in some measure, the use of ideological forms imported by the Spanish: thus, Iberian gender ideologies made women witches, and Andean women turned witchcraft into a means of resistance. Actively participating in a religious underground, opposed to Christianity and its secular political mainstays, Andean women defended themselves as colonized women. In this way, they helped direct the history of the colonized Andean peoples, marking paths for the defense of indigenous culture.

This book tells a partial tale: from the vantage point of gender, it re-examines the profound changes in Andean lifeways that followed upon the Inca and Spanish conquests. But this partial tale is tied to a larger project. While the dynamics of political hierarchy and gender hold center stage, the broader issues of power and culture, the ideological shadings of historical reconstruction, the ways in which dominant social orders shape interpretations of the trajectory of social life are always in the wings.

The encounter of the Incas and the Spanish in the sixteenth century—part of the global drama orchestrated by the expansion of merchant capital—intermingled Andean and Iberian history. Yet, our own intellectual enterprises have tended to hide this mutuality. The dominant ideologies of the social sciences have a selective memory that is likely to overlook Andean transformations which were spawned in the throes of pre-Conquest state building, as well as those set in motion by Spain's colonization project.

This selective memory is not merely an academic lapse. For it is part of our common sense of the past, our awareness of time and change. And that historical common sense—which is often a sentiment as much as it is an intellectual endeavor, often unstated and assumed as much as consciously articulated—presupposes that history is not made by our world's "others." "Others," including women and the colonized, are people without history.

Historical reconstructions are part of a cultural process; and as this book has explored, cultural processes, in societies divided by class, are colored by the tensions, conflicts, impositions, and challenges that class antagonisms radiate. While neither history making nor social-science making need be conspiratorial, self-critical history and self-critical social science demand an awareness that the sense of society and the past which they transmit often encourages—unconsciously and commonsensically—consent to a particular vision of the present.

History and the sciences of society imprint definitions of social reality. Though mainstream history and anthropology may have stifled the voices of many, protesters at the edge of conventional human science have called "common sense" to task. These voices remind us of the error of canonizing heroic versions of history as the collective memory of all, of forgetting their partisan nature and their power. They abhor the academic arrogance of equating reconstructions of society and history with the totality of social forces that propel human trajectories, and they put us in our place as professional codifiers of society's past and present.

214

These voices of challenge have a history, too, and that history warns against its trivialization—against accepting categories and distinctions of a given social order as eternal "others," against reducing their protests to mainstream mimicries by tacking women's history and the anthropology of women onto a list of conventional studies. It challenges us to place "others," along with ourselves, within the thicket of social process.[2] In so doing, we shall confront the obstacles which contemporary conditions of life throw in the way of our interpretation of the past and present world. Only then can we face the real challenge of changing it.

[2] Here again, I am following Fox-Genovese's (1982) insightful leads.

APPENDIX

Ayllu, Tributed *Ayllu*, and Gender

For most of the sociopolitical groups which inhabited the Andes prior to the Inca conquest, the *ayllu* was the fundament of productive relations. The word *ayllu* in its basic form means "family," and this connotation underlay the term even in its wider application to extensive political units with a territorial base. The organization of these Andean political groups, which have been called *etnías* (ethnic groups) or *señoríos* (seigniorial domains) (Murra 1964; Rostworowski 1977, 1978) was predicated on principles of descent. *Ayllu*, then, can refer to an extended family, to a larger descent group within a *señorío*, to a local "ethnic" community or political group—the connotation favored in this book—and, as the Incas would have it, to an empire.

Part of the confusion in studying pre-Columbian Andean kinship and political organization lies in the fact that the word *ayllu* could refer to several different kinds of social groups—genealogical groups as well as political groups of varying size. As a genealogical unit, the *ayllu*'s major structural element was the sibling pair, in which either sex could be the point of reference, or could become the genitor/genitrix of a kin group (Zuidema 1972:15). As a political unit, however, the *ayllu* could only have a male genitor. In other words, a male was always conceptualized as the representative of a political entity when it entered into relationships with other political groups (Zuidema 1972:21).

Before the Inca expansion, the kinship-defined social units which together constituted an *ayllu* could be delimited and ranked by the "conquest hierarchy." This ranking system, built on the symbolic juxtapositions of male/conqueror to fe-

217

male/conquered worked out a prestige hierarchy through which kin groups were ordered. The deity of the "conqueror" group, a male figure, often represented or symbolically stood for the community as a whole, and the higher rank which the "conqueror" group enjoyed was expressed through their privileged relation to this divinity.

Another common *ayllu* division, which overlapped that marked out by the conquest hierarchy, was tied to the frame of gender parallelism. *Ayllus* could be split by moieties associated with gender symbols. While *ayllu* moieties were considered complementary, the "upper," "right-hand" group—usually associated with "male"—carried a slightly higher status. Its *curaca* could stand for or represent both moieties to other *ayllus*. Conquest hierarchy and gender parallelism interpenetrated, as both privileged male symbols in contexts of political relations. An aspect of gender hierarchy—the association of male attributes with social power—was implicit and nascent in Andean ideologies governing *ayllu* structure.

Before the Inca elite conquered and incorporated other political units into its imperial system, the *ayllu* exercised ultimate control over the productive resources which formed the basis of subsistence. Rights to agricultural land, water, herds, and pasture lands were vested in the *ayllu* as a whole (Díez de San Miguel 1964:35, 100; Murra 1956:151; Ortiz de Zúñiga 1967, I:42); and by virtue of *ayllu* membership, which was phrased in terms of kinship connections, Andean people were guaranteed access to those resources which were necessary to maintain their existence (Murra 1956:53, 56, 151; Spalding 1967:63, 68). Social relations of production within the *ayllu* were ordered by kinship bonds as well. Thus, the culturally defined and morally sanctioned obligations of reciprocity (*ayni*) which constituted the motor of Andean economic life were articulated by ties of kinship.

It is most likely that a combination of systems governed access to land and other resources in the pre-Inca *ayllu*. Several chroniclers document that land was periodically reapportioned to *ayllu* members in relation to the needs and size of

218

each household (Polo 1917a:68; cf. Cobo 1964, II:121). Yet within this frame of periodic reapportionment of land, usufruct rights to particular fields were inherited (Ortiz de Zúñiga 1967:42; Díez de San Miguel 1964:35).

Perhaps the best-known account of the mechanisms through which *ayllu* land was reapportioned is that of Garcilaso de la Vega. His description is of special interest because it bears directly on our evaluation of the economic potential of women. According to Garcilaso, each male head of household received one *tupu* of land for himself and his wife. He had the right to an additional *tupu* for each dependent son, while for each daughter he had the right to only one half *tupu*. Upon marriage, the son retained the right to use the land allotted to his father for him, whereas the daughter relinquished "her" share (Garcilaso 1961:58).

Because Garcilaso's formula has been frequently cited in discussions of Andean land tenure patterns, I want to point out several inherent problems. First of all, it is remarkably similar to rules governing the allocation of land to the Spanish peasantry during the late feudal period. Garcilaso, we should recall, spent most of his life in Spain, and it should not surprise us if his account were influenced by Spanish norms reigning at the time he wrote his chronicle. Moreover, Garcilaso's formula is contradicted by information provided by other chroniclers.

The indigenous chronicler Guaman Poma de Ayala, for example, makes several statements indicating that women had independent rights to land that were not abrogated at marriage (1936:67; 1956, II:125, III:104, 125, 132, 181). Martín de Murúa affirms just the opposite of Garcilaso, writing that when a woman was about to marry, she was given lands and other goods necessary to set up a new household (1946:240). It seems that not only at marriage, but during other rituals marking changes in status, a woman received goods which would be used later in her adult life. During the hair-cutting ceremony (*ruto chico* or *rutuchikuy*) described by Guaman Poma (1956, III:129) and the ritual marking first menstruation (*quicuchicu* or *quikuchikuy*), described by Molina (1943:69),

219

girls were given various "donations" by their relatives, some of which secured their access to critical Andean resources.

Since the *ayllu* was an endogamous unit, women's inheritance of rights to land (or men's inheritance) was compatible with the *ayllu*'s having ultimate claim over factors of production. A marriage contracted between *ayllu* members would not entail the *ayllu*'s loss of jurisdiction over its resources, or its ability to make labor demands on its constituents (Spalding 1967:122).

Usufruct rights to certain fields as well as claims to other factors of production were ordered by patterns of inheritance. R.T. Zuidema has shown, along with Lounsbury, that the principle of parallel transmission lines of descent, in which men conceived of themselves as descending from a line of men and women from a line of women, constituted one of the key rules ordering pre-Columbian Andean kinship (Zuidema 1977a:240-55; Lounsbury 1964). Within this system, the basic structural unit was the sibling pair; either sex could be the point of reference or the genitor/genitrix of a descent group. The parallel descent structure of the kin group marked out lines through which classes of material goods (as well as ritual objects and obligations) were transmitted (Zuidema 1977a:240-55; Duviols 1971:373, 383; Murúa 1946:427).

Parallel transmission was not the only means through which rights to land were inherited by men and women living in the Andean *ayllu*; nevertheless, it probably constituted a predominant mechanism for the peasantry as well as for the Inca elite (Spalding 1967:126; Zuidema 1967a:49-58, 1977a:240-56). The structure of parallel transmission rights to land also had implications regarding the power of parents over the marriage choices of their children. From the bride's perspective, for example, the consent of the mother would be necessary, since part of her inheritance was activated at marriage.

Another rule which underlay pre-Columbian inheritance patterns was that of cross-transmission. According to this rule, the significant relations were between mother's brother and sister's son, and between father's sister and mother's daughter

(Zuidema 1977a:253). Common to both the principle of parallel transmission and that of cross-transmission is the creation of links which are expressed in terms of corresponding gender markers—male or female.

Kinship ties, including those acquired through marriage, structured the process through which labor outside the household was garnered. Although marriage was contracted within the community, it was permitted only between those descendants separated by more than four generations from a common ancestral pair (Zuidema 1977a:247, 250). The ritualized gift giving that cemented the marriage bond was also extended between the kin groups whose descendants had contracted marriage (Cobo 1964, II:248-49; Murúa 1946:235, 240). Thus, entire descent groups, defined theoretically by Andean rules prescribing possible marriage partners, were articulated into a network of mutual assistance in which labor demands could be made (Guaman Poma 1936:846).

Speculations regarding the origin of women's inferior status vis-à-vis men have referred to the need of societies to control women's reproductive powers (see Aaby 1977; Edholm, Harris, and Young 1977; Meillassoux 1975) and to the concomitant "objectivization" of women as objects of exchange between male-dominated lineages. Although the structures that governed the process through which families were reproduced in Andean culture varied between ethnic communities, it appears that many of the factors assumed to be at the root of the oppression of women in other societies were not developed in the Andean *ayllus*.

First of all, one of the basic kinship units that structured Andean descent groups was the sibling pair, in which either sex could take the role of genitor/genitrix. Gender itself did not denote authority, for within the kin group the designation of authority was based on order of birth, with no distinctions made according to gender (Guaman Poma 1956, III:111). The preferred marriage form was symmetrical (Ortiz de Zúñiga 1967, I:31; Murúa 1946:240, 244), and it appears that decisions regarding the appropriateness of marriage often resided with

221

both parents (Cobo 1964, II:248-49; Molina 1943:68; Murúa 1946:240, 244). Although several chroniclers indicate that men—either fathers or brothers—controlled the exchange of women in their descent group (Ortiz de Zúñiga 1967, I:31), others designate mothers as the executors of that role. While the discrepancies in the chroniclers' accounts may reflect regional variations in marriage traditions, we should not underestimate the power of Spanish preconceptions (i.e. men are the donors of brides) to color their descriptions of indigenous custom (Cobo 1964, II:249).

Bride price, which in many societies formed the material basis permitting the manipulation of women in marriage exchange, should be examined carefully with respect to its function in the Andean *ayllu*. As Cobo suggests, and other chroniclers affirm, "bride price" was equivalent to the institutionalization of a bond of obligatory aid between affinal groups. Asymmetric ties were established between groom and father-in-law and between bride and mother-in-law, while the equality of the relations between kin groups and between spouses was expressed by ritualized gift giving (Murúa 1946:235, 244; Molina 1943:68; Cobo 1964, II:248-49; AAL:Leg. 5, Exp. XIII).

The "bride price" in the Andean *ayllu* marriage exchange is best conceptualized as a ritual catalyst which cemented new ties and relations. Far from consisting of objects that represent accumulated wealth, the gifts symbolize the creation of a new network of reciprocal obligations. No one in the Andean *ayllu* could be denied marriage because of the inability to acquire a bride price. These goods—firewood and straw, or coca and dried meat—could be got by all; moreover, mechanisms existed to ensure that they could be easily obtained (Murúa 1946:240). In contrast to African lineage societies, no class of elders controlled the material means through which youth could be manipulated in an exchange process whereby women were traded for objects of material value. The process through which women have been "reified" as objects of exchange and objects of reproduction in other cultures (Aaby 1977) had not developed in the kin-based Andean *ayllu*.

In sum, with respect to the distribution of critical factors of production, women obtained access to labor, land, and other material resources by virtue of their *ayllu* membership, as did men. Nor does the kinship system, which structured the ability to claim these rights, appear to have prejudiced the capacity of women to activate them. And, at least at the level of the pre-state *ayllu*, women—*qua* women—were not "reified" as objects of exchange relations controlled by men.

To explore the impact of the Inca expansion on the potentialities of women within economic life, we must consider the ways in which the Cuzco elite affected the traditional, kinship-based system which governed access to the factors of production. Probably the best-known act that accompanied the Inca conquest and its incorporation of *ayllus* into the imperial system was the repartitioning of community lands, as a means through which surpluses could be generated to maintain the newly evolved state structures and the status requirements of the Inca elite. Consequently, a new, tripartite division of lands and herds was imposed on the *ayllus*: the produce of the "lands of the Incas" was appropriated to support the empire's administrative apparatus and upper class; that of the "lands of the Sun" was destined to support the religion of the Incas; while the "lands of the *ayllus*" were to remain in the domain of the conquered communities for their subsistence (Rowe 1963:265; Moore 1958:17-48; Murra 1956:63).

In order to justify its expropriation of *ayllu* resources ideologically, the Incas fabricated a new definition of ownership with respect to Andean factors of production. All resources—lands, rivers, llama herds—were declared to be property of the empire (Murra 1956:59-61). This not only permitted the Inca elite to use what had been under the *ayllu*'s domain in order to support its bureaucracy and religious apparatus, but it also enabled the elite to claim that any utilization of resources by the *ayllu* came by virtue of a "gift" from Cuzco. The Inca elite thus phrased its exploitative relations with the conquered provinces

223

in terms of the norms of mutual obligation which character-ized productive relations within the kin-based *ayllu*.

According to Murra (1956:151), the principles which gov-erned politicoeconomic relations between the Cuzco elite and the *ayllu* were structured along the lines of the traditional rec-iprocity and "chiefly generosity" which characterized the eco-nomic relations of the Andean community. However, the Inca expansion superimposed, by force, a new authority on the con-quered *ayllus* as they were incorporated into an imperial polit-ical system dominated by the Cuzco elite. While it would be in-correct to treat the Inca expansion as a mere extension of the norms that governed *ayllu* relations, the Inca elite were, none-theless, constrained to some degree by the expectations of the kin-based *ayllu*.

The Incas, trying to legitimize their conquest in terms of the perceptions of the conquered, created quasi-kin ties between themselves and their subjects by subsuming the lineage of the conquered as their own ancestors (Anónimo 1934:117-118; Zuidema 1972:34). It is mistaken, though, to credit the Inca's own ideology and to characterize the social relations of pro-duction in the empire as still founded in kin relations (or in re-lations between differentially ranked kin groups). The Inca conquest transformed these into productive relations that were dictated largely by the requirements of Cuzco-dominated politico-religious structures. In terms of the empire's symbolic representations, the Inca became the central axis of a now Pan-Andean civilization—forging bonds with male representatives of political units—and the embodiment of the social and supernatural relations which permitted that universe to exist. He thus manipulated an ideology, rooted in the experience of the *ayllu*, which was a force behind the new social relations of production. Although this ideology, often shared by those who were conquered, masked exploitative relations, the Incas were nevertheless constrained by this same ideology, and by the cul-tural expectations it embodied, to provide for the well-being of the populations they conquered.

Murra very cogently argues that, in spite of the change in the "legal status" of the *ayllu*'s resources, the *ayllu*'s traditional rights to the use of its fields were in practice not hindered by the Incas. So long as the "lands of the Sun" and "lands of the Inca" were set aside, so long as the *ayllu* provided labor for the cultivation of these fields, the Incas' expansion did not further impede the self-sufficiency of the *ayllu* (Murra 1956:64). For the most part, the critical resources required by the *ayllu* for its maintenance effectively remained under the control of the community, and local arrangements governing land use were undisturbed. The customary right of women to claim usufruct rights to *ayllu* land and to make demands on kinsmen or affines for labor were not affected by the Inca conquest and the imperial system of extracting surplus.

GLOSSARY

(Q) designates a word of Quechua origin
(S) designates a word of Spanish origin

acllas—"wives of the Sun," "chosen women"; virgin girls, selected by the Inca, under the domain of the Inca male elite (Q)
acllawasi—home of *acllas* (Q)
aguacil—constable (S)
ají—chili pepper (Q)
alcalde—mayor (S)
amaru—Andean symbol connoting relationship, alliance; often appears as a snake or serpent (Q)
amauta—"wise one"; Inca philosopher (Q)
Apu—mountain god in southern Andes; connotes power (Q)
aucacamayoq—soldier (Q)
Axomama—Potato Mother (Q)
ayllu—extended family or social group with territorial base; community (Q)
ayni—reciprocity, balance (Q)
beata—blessed, devout (S)
cacica—female chief, headwoman (S)
cacique—male chief, headman (S)
capacochas—humans sacrificed in Inca ritual (Q)
capullanas—women who governed ethnic groups of Peru's North Coast (Q)
cargo—burden or obligation; position in *varayoq* system (S)
chicha—corn beer (Q)
cholo—person of Indian and *mestizo* descent (S)
Chuquiilla—god of thunder and lightning; another term for Illapa (Q)

227

churi (pl. *churikuna*)—son, male speaker; man who represents his household to god of thunder and lightning (Q)

Cocamama—Coca Mother (Q)

comadre—godmother (S)

compadrazgo—spiritual parenthood (S)

conopas—household gods; models or miniatures which embodied potential to create the items they represented (Q)

corregidor—magistrate (S)

coya—an Inca queen (Q)

Coyamama—Mother of Metals (Q)

criollo—person of Spanish descent, born in the colonies (S)

cumbi—finely woven cloth (Q)

curaca—chief, headman (Q)

curacazgo—position or office of *curaca* (Q)

curandera—female curer (S)

cuy—guinea pig (Q)

encomendero—one who receives an *encomienda* (S)

encomienda—Crown grant of tribute and labor rights over specified indigenous groups (S)

estancia—pasture area in the *puna* (S)

etnía—"ethnic" sociopolitical group; designates a culture inhabiting the Andes prior to Inca conquest (S)

fiscal—indigenous agent of priest in an Indian community (S)

guarmi—woman, wife (Q)

hechicero—sorcerer (S)

hermana mayor—elder sister (S)

hidalgo—Spanish landed gentry (S)

huaca—generic term for sacred place or divinity; also designates ancestor of *llacuases* (Q)

Huari (Guari)—divinity associated with *llactas*; also (*huari, guari*) synomym for *llacta*; related in general to agricultural production, fertility, and generative forces of the earth (Q)

Illapa—Andean god of thunder and lightning (Q); see Rayo

indias de servicio—service women (S)

indios de común—Indian commoners (S)

Inti—Sun god (Q)

llacta—"village"; also designates a social group claiming descent from the original inhabitants or founders of an Indian community (Q); see *llacuás*

llacuás—designates a social group, within an Indian community, claiming descent from a conquering group not native to the community (Q); see *llacta*

machayes—traditional burial caves (Q)

maestra—female teacher (S)

malquis (mallquis)—generic term for ancestors; also designates ancestors of *llactas*, in contrast to ancestors of *llacuases* (Q)

Mamacocha—Mother Sea (Q)

mamaconas—"the Mothers"; term applied to *acllas* (Q)

mayor—elder, higher-rank (S)

mestizo—person of Indian and Spanish descent (S)

ministras—female ministers (S)

ministros—male ministers (S)

mita—rotation; rotated, corvée labor (Q)

mitayo (mitayoq)—man drafted into *mita* service (Q)

ñusta—an Inca princess (Q)

obraje—proto-factories, "sweatshops" (S)

Pachamama—Earth Mother (Q)

Pacsamama—Moon Mother (Q)

palla—Inca noblewoman or older woman (Q)

panaca—Inca royal descent group (Q)

pirhuas—storage bins (Q)

puna—high tableland (Q)

puquio—mountain spring (Q)

quikuchikuy (quicuchicu)—ritual marking first menstruation (Q)

Quilla—Moon goddess (Q)

quipucamayoq—one in charge of registering information on a *quipu* (Q)

quipus—knotted strings; Andean mnemonic devices used to record information (Q)

Rayo—Andean god of thunder and lightning (S); see Illapa

reducción—colonial forced settlement of indigenous groups (S)

regidor—alderman (S)

rutuchikuy (ruto chico)—ritual hair-cutting ceremony (Q)

Sañumama—Clay Mother (Q)

Saramama—Corn Mother (Q)

señoríos—"seigniorial domains"; applied to certain cultures inhabiting the Andes prior to the Inca conquest (S)

soltera—unmarried woman (S)

taclla—foot plow (Q)

tupu—Inca measure equivalent to a landholding capable of feeding a family for one year (Q)

varayoq—"one who holds a staff of office"; sponsor in a local hierarchy of civil-religious posts (*varayoq* system) (Q, S)

Wamanis—mountain gods in central Andes (Q)

yachaywasi—school (Q)

yanaconas—state retainers; those who gave full-time service to the state (Q)

A NOTE ON SOURCES

The ethnohistorical material used to reconstruct the Inca and Spanish colonial past falls chiefly into two categories: chronicles and administrative or judicial documentation. The writers of the chronicles, most of whom were Spanish administrators, scribes, soldiers-of-fortune, and priests, present us with narrative histories of Inca society. They have all been published; and in the Bibliography, I have noted in brackets the dates when they were originally written.

Many chroniclers deliberately wrote their reports in terms that would serve to justify the Spanish conquest to their countrymen. In any case, information offered by a chronicler's Inca informants was inevitably distorted by his own cultural lens. Consequently, students of Inca society have begun to recognize that the chronicles must be critically evaluated when used to reconstruct the pre-Columbian and colonial history of the Andes. Precautions are doubly warranted when one tries to reconstruct the role of women in the Andean world, since the andromyopia of the Spanish often blinded them to the profoundly different structures which governed Andean gender relations.

Fortunately, several chronicler accounts of life before and after the Conquest were written by men of Andean origin, notably Guaman Poma. His chronicle, a letter of protest to the Spanish Crown, decried the injustices of the colonial world by comparing the experiences of Andean people under Inca rule with their experiences as colonial subjects. In contradistinction to the Spanish chroniclers, Guaman Poma applied an Andean vision of the world to his interpretation of Inca and colonial society. He thus provides us with an indigenous model of how relations between the sexes were ordered in pre-Conquest Andean society, a way of life which was shattered by the pressures of the colonial regime. Sensitive to the reality of gender relations prior to the Spanish invasion, and to the ways in which the imposition of alien institutions and norms transformed those relations, Guaman Poma's chronicle is an important source for our purposes.

Administrative and judicial documents, derived from the records of the colonial civil and ecclesiastic bureaucracy, are housed in various Peruvian national, departmental, and community archives. These include *visitas* (censuses of indigenous communities undertaken to fix tribute quotas); notarial records (land titles, deeds of sale, rental contracts, powers of attorney, wills, donations to the Church); baptismal, marriage, and mortuary registries; and civil and ecclesiastical juridical proceedings. These documents give us a detailed look into the daily life of Spain's colonial subjects and reveal much about the conflicts between Spanish law and Andean custom. Through notarial records, for example, one can reconstruct attempts to maintain pre-Columbian land tenure patterns as well as the efforts to eliminate women's independent rights to land. Law suits shed additional light on the changes experienced by women in the colonial political economy, as they contested the expropriation of their lands or the denial of their right to occupy positions in local government. Community registries of baptisms and marriages document the persistence of Andean kinship patterns: throughout the seventeenth century, women still assumed their mother's surname while men took that of their father.

A most important source—enabling me to reconstruct local indigenous religious practices, the role of women therein, as well as the ways in which those practices were transformed during the colonial period—was the ecclesiastical suits generated by the campaign to extirpate idolatry in Peru. Proceedings dating from the early 1600s and lasting through the mid-seventeenth century are filed under the section "Idolatrías" in the Archivo Arzobispal of Lima. This campaign, an extension of the Inquisition, was levied against practitioners of native religion. Ecclesiastical authorities, sent to highland communities to investigate and prosecute the idolators, convened tribunals in which charges were brought against Indians who resisted conversion to Catholicism. The trial proceedings include lengthy testimonies by the accused, by Spanish and indigenous accusors, as well as by various witnesses and supporters on both sides. These provide a unique, if tragic, source of information on indigenous religious practices and beliefs, resistance to Catholic evangelization, and intracommunity conflicts which colonialism engendered.

Fieldwork, conducted in selected villages in the Departments of Ayacucho and Cuzco, enabled me to learn about Andean cultures first-hand. This experience provided a vital supplement to my archival reconstructions of Inca and Spanish society, as I saw how the present illuminates history. The chroniclers had interpreted the Andean world through Spanish eyes. Archival records are almost always fragmentary and, like the chronicles, are inevitably colored by bureaucratic exigencies. Fieldwork let me get one step closer to the Andean reality. It also allowed me to sense the unity of Andean culture, something that often gets lost as one goes about picking up the pieces of the past. Important for this study, contemporary Andean cultures provided me with clues about how gender relations were ordered, altered, and maintained through history. They pointed me in directions that helped me make sense of archival fragments. Further, by knowing (in my own partial way) the experiences of contemporary Andean women, I could pierce the Spanish trappings which covered my principal sources.

BIBLIOGRAPHY

CHRONICLES AND DOCUMENTS

AAL   Archivo Arzobispal de Lima
ACC   Archivo Colonial de Ciencias
ADC   Archivo Departamental de Cuzco
AHU   Archivo Histórico de Urubamba
AUP   Archivo Urubamba, Protocolos y Expedientes
AZ   Archivo Zembrano
BN   Biblioteca Nacional del Perú

Acosta, José de
1954   *Historia natural y moral de las Indias* [1590]. Madrid: Biblioteca de Autores Españoles.
Albornoz, Cristóbal
1967   "Instrucción para descubrir todas las guacas del Perú y sus camayos y haciendas" [158?]. *Journal de la Société des Américanistes* 56:17-39.
Anónimo
1906   "Discursos de la sucesión y gobierno de las yngas" [1570]. In *Juicio de límites entre Perú y Bolivia*, edited by Víctor Maurtua, vol. 8, Barcelona: Henrich y Compañía.
Anónimo
1934   "Relación del sitio del Cuzco" [1536]. In *Colección de libros y documentos referentes a la historia del Perú*, edited by H. Urteaga and C.A. Romero, ser. 2, vol. 10. Lima: Librería y Imprenta Gil.
Arriaga, Father Pablo José de
1968   *The Extirpation of Idolatry in Peru* [1621]. Translated by L. Clark Keating. Lexington: University of Kentucky Press.
Avendaño, Hernando de
1904   "Relación sobre la idolatría" [1630?]. In *La imprenta en Lima*, edited by J.T. Medina, vol. 1, pp. 380-83. Santiago de Chile: Imprenta Elzeviriana.

235

BIBLIOGRAPHY

Ávila, Francisco de
1966   *Dioses y hombres de Huarochirí* [1598?] Translation
        into modern Spanish by José María Arguedas. Lima: Mu-
        seo Nacional de Historia y el Instituto de Estudios Peru-
        anos.
Betanzos, Juan de
1968   "Suma y narración de los Incas" [1551]. In *Biblioteca
        peruana*, ser. 1, vol. 3, pp. 197-296. Lima: Editores Téc-
        nicos Asociados.
Cieza de León, Pedro de
1945   *La crónica del Perú* [1553]. Buenos Aires: Colección
        Austral.
1959   *The Incas of Pedro de Cieza de León* [1553]. Translated
        by Harriet de Onís and edited by Victor Wolfgang von
        Hagen. Norman: University of Oklahoma Press.
1968   "El señorío de los Incas" [1553]. In *Biblioteca peruana*,
        ser. 1, vol. 3, pp. 9-196. Lima: Editores Técnicos Asocia-
        dos.
Cobo, Bernabé
1964   *Historia del Nuevo Mundo* [1653]. 2 vols. Madrid: Bi-
        blioteca de Autores Españoles.
Collapiña et al.
1974   *Relación de la descendencia, gobierno, y conquista de los
        Incas* [1533-75]. Lima: Edición de la Biblioteca Univer-
        sitaria.
Díez de San Miguel, Garcí
1964   *Visita hecha a la provincia de Chucuito . . . en el año
        1567* [1567]. Lima: Casa de la Cultura.
Duviols, Pierre
1971   *La lutte contre les réligions autochtones dans le Pérou
        colonial: L'extirpation de l'idolâtrie entre 1532 et 1660*,
        appendice documentaire. Lima and Paris: Institut Fran-
        çais d'Études Andines.
Esquivel y Navia, Diego de
1901   *Anales de Cuzco* [1601-1749]. Lima.
Estete, Miguel de
1968   "Noticia del Peru" [1535]. In *Biblioteca peruana*, ser. 1,
        vol. 1, pp. 345-404. Lima: Editores Técnicos Asociados.
Garcilaso de la Vega, "el Inca"
1959   *Comentarios reales de los Incas* [1609]. Edited by José

236

Durand. 3 vols. Lima: Universidad Nacional Mayor de San Marcos.

1960   *Comentarios reales de los Incas* [1609]. Madrid: Biblioteca de Autores Españoles.

1961   *The Incas: The Royal Commentaries of the Inca Garcilaso de la Vega* [1609]. Edited by Alain Gheerbrant. New York: Avon Books.

Guaman Poma de Ayala, Felipe

1936   *El primer nueva crónica y buen gobierno* [1613?]. Paris: Institut d'Ethnologie.

1956-66 *La nueva crónica y buen gobierno* [1613?]. Translation into modern Spanish by Luís Bustíos Gálvez. 3 vols. Lima: Editorial Cultura.

Hernández Príncipe, Rodrigo

1923   "Mitología andina" [1621]. *Inca* 1:24-68.

Holguín, Diego

1952   *Vocabulario de la lengua general de todo el Perú . . .* [1608]. Lima: Instituto de Historia, Universidad Nacional Mayor de San Marcos.

Mena, Cristóbal de

1968   "La conquista del Perú, llamada la Nueva Castilla" [1534]. In *Biblioteca peruana*, ser. 1, vol. 1, pp. 133-70. Lima: Editores Técnicos Asociados.

Molina (el Cuzqueño), Cristóbal de

1943   "Relación de las fábulas y ritos de los Incas" [1573]. In *Los pequeños grandes libros de historia americana*, edited by Francisco A. Loayza, ser. 1, vol. 4. Lima: D. Miranda.

Montesinos, Fernando de

1957   "Memorias antiguas historiales y políticas del Perú" [1644]. Edited by Luís A. Pardo. *Revista del Museo e Instituto Arqueológico de la Universidad Nacional del Cuzco*, nos. 16-17.

Murúa, Martín de

1922   "Historia del origen y geneología real de los Incas" [1590]. In *Colección de libros y documentos referentes a la historia del Perú*, edited by H. Urteaga and C.A. Romero, ser. 2, vol. 4, pp. 1-253. Lima: Sanmartí y Ca.

1946   *Historia del origen y geneología real de los Incas* [1590]. Edited by Constantino Bayle. Madrid: Consejo Superior

de Investigaciones Científicas, Instituto Santo Toribio de
Mogrovejo.

Oberem, Udo
1968 "Amerikanistische Angaben aus Dokumenten des 16
Jahrhunderts." *Tribus* 17:81-92.

Ortiz de Zúñiga, Íñigo
1967 *Visita de la provincia de León de Huánuco* [1562], vol.
1. Huánuco, Peru: Universidad Hermillo Valdizán.
1972 *Visita de la provincia de León de Huánuco* [1562], vol.
2. Huánuco, Peru: Universidad Hermillo Valdizán.

Pachacuti Yamqui, Joan de Santa Cruz
1950 "Relación de antigüedades deste reyno del Perú" [1613].
In *Tres relaciones de antigüedades peruanas*, pp. 207-
81. Reproduction of edition of M. Jiménez de la Espada.
Asunción: Editorial Guaraní.

Pérez Bocanegra, Juan
1631 *Ritual formulario e institución de curas para administrar
a los naturales* . . . Lima.

Pizarro, Hernando
1968 "Carta de Hernando Pizarro a la Audiencia del Santo
Domingo" [1533]. In *Biblioteca peruana*, ser. 1, vol. 1,
pp. 117-32. Lima: Editores Técnicos Asociados.

Pizarro, Pedro
1968 "Relación del descubrimiento y conquista de los reinos
del Peru" [1571]. In *Biblioteca peruana*, ser. 1, vol. 1, pp.
439-586. Lima: Editores Técnicos Asociados.

Polo de Ondegardo, Juan
1916 "Errores y supersticiones . . ." [1554]. In *Colección de libros y documentos referentes a la historia del Perú*, edited
by H. Urteaga and C.A. Romero, ser. 1, no. 3, pp. 1-44.
Lima: Sanmartí y Ca.
1917a "Relación de los fundamentos acerca del notable daño
que resulta de no guardar a los indios sus fueros . . ."
[1571]. In *Colección de libros y documentos referentes a
la historia del Perú*, edited by H. Urteaga and C.A. Romero, ser. 1, no. 3, pp. 45-188. Lima: Sanmartí y Ca.
1917b "Instrucción contra las ceremonias y ritos que usan los
indios conforme al tiempo de su infidelidad" [1567]. In
Colección de libros y documentos referentes a la historia

del Perú, edited by H. Urteaga and C.A. Romero, ser. 1, no. 3, pp. 189-203. Lima: Sanmartí y Ca.

1917c "Del linaje de los ingas y como conquistaron" [1567]. In *Colección de libros y documentos referentes a la historia del Perú*, edited by H. Urteaga and C.A. Romero, ser. 1, no. 4, pp. 45-95. Lima: Sanmartí y Ca.

Ramos Gavilán, Alonso
1976   *Historia del celebre santuario de Nuestra Señora de Copacabana, y sus milagros, e invención de la cruz de Carabuco* [1621]. La Paz: Editora Universo.

Ricardo, Antonio
1951   *Vocabulario y phrasis en la lengua general de los indios del Perú, llamada Quechua* [1586]. Lima: Universidad Nacional Mayor de San Marcos.

Ruiz de Arce, Juan
1968   "La advertencia" [1545]. In *Biblioteca peruana*, ser. 1, vol. 1, pp. 405-38. Lima: Editores Técnicos Asociados.

Sancho de la Hoz, Pedro
1968   "Relación para SM de lo sucedido en la conquista y pacificación de estas provincias de la Nueva Castilla y de la calidad de la tierra" [1543]. In *Biblioteca peruana*, ser. 1, vol. 1, pp. 275-344. Lima: Editores Técnicos Asociados.

Santo Tomás, Domingo de
1951   *Lexicón o vocabulario de la lengua general . . .* [1560]. Lima: Instituto de Historia, Universidad Nacional Mayor de San Marcos.

Sarmiento de Gamboa, Pedro
1947   *Historia de los Incas* [1572]. Buenos Aires: Biblioteca Emece.
1960   *Historia general llamada índica* [1572]. Madrid: Biblioteca de Autores Españoles.

Sprenger, Jacob and Heinrich Kramer
1970   *Malleus maleficarum* [1484]. Translated, with an introduction, bibliography, and notes, by the Rev. Montague Summers. New York: Benjamin Blom.

Testimonio . . . de la Audiencia de Lima
1950   *Revista del Archivo Histórica del Cuzco* 1:345-46.

Titu Cusi Yupanqui, Diego de Castro
1973   *Relación de la conquista del Perú* [1570]. Lima: Biblioteca Universitaria.

239

BIBLIOGRAPHY

Trujillo, Diego de
    1968   "Relación del descubrimiento del reyno del Perú" [1590]. In *Biblioteca peruana*, ser. 1, vol. 2, pp. 9-104. Lima: Editores Técnicos Asociados.

Valera, Blas
    1950   "Relación de las costumbres antiguas de los naturales del Pirú" [1590]. In *Tres relaciones de antigüedades peruanas*, pp. 135-203. Reproduction of edition of M. Jiménez de la Espada. Asunción: Editorial Guaraní.

Villanueva, Horacio
    1970   "Documentos sobre Yucay en el siglo XVI." *Revista del Archivo Histórico del Cuzco* 13:1-148.

Xerez, Francisco de
    1968   "Verdadera relación de la conquista del Perú" [1534]. In *Biblioteca peruana*, ser. 1, vol. 1, pp. 191-274. Lima: Editores Técnicos Asociados.

MODERN SOURCES

Aaby, Peter
    1977   "Engels and Women." *Critique of Anthropology* 3:25-54.

Adorno, Rolena
    1978   "Felipe Guaman Poma de Ayala: An Andean View of the Peruvian Viceroyalty, 1565-1615." *Journal de la Société des Américanistes*, 65:121-43.
    1982   "El lenguaje de la historia en la crónica de Guaman Poma." In *From Oral to Written Expression: Native Andean Chronicles of the Early Colonial Period*, edited by Rolena Adorno. Syracuse, N.Y.: Syracuse University, Maxwell School of Citizenship and Public Affairs, Foreign and Comparative Studies Program, Latin American Series, no. 4.

Anderson, Perry
    1984   *In the Tracks of Historical Materialism*. London: Verso.

Ardener, Shirley (ed.)
    1977   *Perceiving Women*. New York: Halsted Press.

Asad, Talal (ed.)
    1973   *Anthropology and the Colonial Encounter*. London: Ithaca Press.

Atkinson, J.M.
  1982 "Anthropology." *Signs* 8:236-57.
Balfe, Judith
  1978 "Comment on Clark Garrett's 'Woman and Witches.' "
        Signs 4:201-202.
Belote, Linda and Jim Belote
  1973 "The Fiesta Cargo System in Saraguro, Ecuador." Paper
        presented at the Symposium on Andean Time, 71st An-
        nual Meeting of the American Anthropological Associa-
        tion, Toronto.
Borah, Woodrow and Sherburne Cook
  1966 *The Aboriginal Population of Central Mexico on the Eve
        of the Spanish Conquest.* Berkeley: University of Califor-
        nia Press.
Bourque, Susan C. and K. Warren
  1979 *Women of the Andes: Patriarchy and Social Change in
        Two Peruvian Towns.* Ann Arbor: University of Michi-
        gan Press.
Brown, P. and G. Buchbinder (eds.)
  1976 *Man and Woman in the New Guinea Highlands.* Wash-
        ington, D.C.: American Anthropological Association.
Burkett, Elinor
  1977 "In Dubious Sisterhood: Class and Sex in Spanish Colo-
        nial South America." *Latin American Perspectives* 4:18-
        26.
Caro Baroja, Julio
  1965 *The World of the Witches.* Chicago: University of Chi-
        cago Press.
  1970 *Inquisición, brujería, y cryptojudaísmo.* Barcelona: Edi-
        ciones Ariel.
  1975 *Brujería vasca.* San Sebastian: Editorial Tertoa.
Catacora, Sergio
  1968 "Organización social de la comunidad de San Ildefonso
        de Chuqui Huarcaya." Tesis para optar el grado de Ba-
        chiller en Ciencias Antropológicas, Universidad Nacional
        de San Cristóbal de Huamanga, Ayacucho, Peru.
Conrad, G.W. and A.A. Demarest
  1983 *Religion and Empire: The Dynamics of Aztec and Inca
        Expansion.* Cambridge: Cambridge University Press.

241

BIBLIOGRAPHY

Cook, Noble David
  1975 "Introducción." In *Tasa de la Visita General de Francisco de Toledo*, paleographic version by Noble David Cook, pp. ix-xxvii. Lima: Universidad Nacional Mayor de San Marcos.
  1981 *Demographic Collapse: Indian Peru, 1520-1620*. Cambridge: Cambridge University Press.

Deere, Carmen Diana
  1976 "Rural Women's Subsistence Production in Capitalist Periphery." *Review of Radical Political Economics* 8:9-18.
  1977 "Changing Social Relations of Production in Peruvian Peasant Women's Work." *Latin American Perspectives* 4:48-69.

Deere, Carmen Diana and Magdalena León de Leal
  1983 *Women in Andean Agriculture: Peasant Production and Rural Wage Employment in Colombia and Peru*. Washington, D.C.: International Labor Office, Women, Work, and Development Series, no. 4.

Diamond, Stanley
  1974 *In Search of the Primitive*. New Brunswick, N.J.: Transaction Books.

Douglas, Mary
  1966 *Purity and Danger: An Analysis of Concepts of Pollution and Taboo*. New York: Praeger.

Douglas, Mary (ed.)
  1970 *Witchcraft Confessions and Accusations*. London: Tavistock.

Dubisch, Jill (ed.)
  1986 *Gender and Power in Rural Greece*. Princeton, N.J.: Princeton University Press.

Duviols, Pierre
  1971 *La lutte contre les réligions autochtones dans le Pérou colonial: L'extirpation de l'idolâtrie entre 1532 et 1660*. Lima and Paris: Institut Français d'Études Andines.
  1973 "Huari y Llacuaz: Agricultores y pastores. Un dualismo pre-hispánico de oposición y complementaridad." *Revista del Museo Nacional* 39:153-93.
  1979 "La dinastía de los Incas: Monarquía o diarquía? Argu-

mentos heurísticos a favor de una tesis estructuralista."
Journal de la Société des Américanistes 66:67-73.

1980 "Periodización y política: La historia del Perú según
Guaman Poma de Ayala." *Bulletin de l'Institut Français
d'Études Andines* 9:1-18.

Earls, John
1969 "The Organization of Power in Quechua Mythology."
Journal of the Steward Anthropological Society 1:63-82.
1971 "The Structure of Modern Andean Social Categories."
Journal of the Steward Anthropological Society 3:69-
106.
1973 "Andean Continuum Cosmology." Ph.D. dissertation,
University of Illinois, Champaign-Urbana.
1976 "La evolución de la administración ecológica Inca." *Revista del Museo Nacional* 42:207-45.
n.d. Field notes.

Earls, John and Irene Silverblatt
1976a "La realidad física y social en la cosmología andina."
*Proceedings of the XLI International Congress of Amer-
icanists* 4:299-325.
1976b "Sobre la instrumentación de la cosmología Inca en el sitio arqueológico de Moray." Paper presented at the Col-
loquium on Mesoamerican and Andean World Views
and Social Organization, Université de Provence, Aix-en-
Provence.
1977 "El matrimonio y la autoconstrucción de alianzas en Sarhua (Ayacucho, Perú)." *Bulletin de l'Institut Français
d'Études Andines* 6:63-70.
1978a "Ayllus y etnías de la región Pampas-Qaracha: El im-
pacto del estado Inca." In *III Congreso: Hombre y Cultura Andina*, edited by R. Matos. Lima: Editora Lason-
tay.
1978b "Investigaciones interdisciplinarias en Moray, Cusco."
In *Primera Jornada del Museo Nacional de Historia, Et-
nohistoria, y Antropología Andina*, edited by Marcia
Koth de Paredes and Amalia Castelli, pp. 117-22. Lima:
Centro de Proyección Cristiana.

Edholm, Felicity, Olivia Harris, and Kate Young
1977 "Conceptualizing Women." *Critique of Anthropology*
3:101-30.

BIBLIOGRAPHY

Ehrenreich, Barbara and Deirdre English
1973   *Witches, Midwives, and Nurses: A History of Women Healers.* Old Westbury, N.Y.: Feminist Press.

Espinosa, Waldemar
1973   "La Pachaca de Pachu en el reino de Cuismancu, siglos XV y XVI." *Bulletin de l'Institut Français d'Études Andines* 2:35-71.
1978   "Dos casos de señoralismo feudal en el imperio Inca." In *Los modos de producción en el imperio de los Incas,* edited by Waldemar Espinosa, pp. 329-56. Lima: Mantaro-Grafital.

Etienne, Mona and Eleanor Leacock (eds.)
1980   *Women and Colonization: Anthropological Perspectives.* South Hadley, Mass.: Bergin & Garvey.

Flores Galindo, Alberto
1976   "Tupac Amaru y la sublevación de 1780." In *Tupac Amaro II, 1780,* edited by A. Flores Galindo, pp. 269-323. Lima: Retablo de Papel.

Fox-Genovese, Elizabeth
1982   "Placing Women's History in History." *New Left Review* 133:5-29.

Fox-Genovese, Elizabeth and Eugene Genovese
1976   "The Political Crisis of Social History: A Marxian Perspective." *Journal of Social History* 10:205-20.

Fuenzalida, Fernando
1968   "Santiago y el Wamani: Aspectos de un culto pagano." *Cuadernos Antropológicos* 5:118-65.

Gailey, Christine Ward
1976   "Gender Hierarchy and Class Formation: The Origins of the State in Tonga." Paper presented at the 75th Annual Meeting of the American Anthropological Association, Washington, D.C.
1981   "Our History Is Written in our Mats: State Formation and the Status of Women in Tonga." Ph.D. dissertation, New School for Social Research.
1983a   "Categories without Culture: Structuralism, Ethnohistory, and Ethnocide." *Dialectical Anthropology* 8:241-50.
1983b   "The Kindness of Strangers: Transformations of Kinship in Pre-Capitalist Class and State Formation." Paper pre-

244

sented at the 10th Annual Meeting of the Canadian Ethnology Society, Hamilton, Ontario.

1985   "The State of the State in Anthropology." *Dialectical Anthropology* 9:65-90.

Garrett, Clarke

1977   "Women and Witches: Patterns of Analysis." *Signs* 3:461-70.

1979   "Reply to Honneger and Moia." *Signs* 4:802-804.

Genovese, Eugene

1974   *Roll Jordan Roll*. New York: Pantheon.

Godelier, Maurice

1978   "El concepto de formación económica y social: El ejemplo de los Incas." In *Los modos de producción en el imperio de los Incas*, edited by Waldemar Espinosa, pp. 265-84. Lima: Mantaro-Grafital.

Golte, Jürgen

1978   "La economía del estado Inca y la noción de producción asiático." In *Los modos de producción en el imperio de los Incas*, edited by Waldemar Espinosa, pp. 285-98. Lima: Mantaro-Grafital.

Gough, Kathleen

1968   "World Revolution and the Science of Man." In *The Dissenting Academy*, edited by Theodore Roszak, pp. 135-58. New York: Vintage Books.

Guardia Mayorga, César A.

1971   *Diccionario Kechwa-Castellano, Castellano-Kechwa*. Lima: Los Andes.

Harris, Olivia

1978   "Complementarity and Conflict: An Andean View of Women and Men." In *Sex and Age as Principles of Social Differentiation*, edited by J. LaFontaine. London: Academic Press.

Hobsbawn, Eric

1984   "Introduction: Inventing Traditions." in *The Invention of Tradition*, edited by E. Hobsbawm and T. Ranger. Cambridge: Cambridge University Press.

Honegger, Claudia

1979   "Comment on Garrett's 'Women and Witches.' " *Signs* 4:792-98.

245

BIBLIOGRAPHY

Huertas, Lorenzo
1969 "La religión de una sociedad rural andina: Cajatambo en el siglo XVII." Tesis para Bachiller, Facultad de Letras, Universidad Nacional Mayor de San Marcos, Lima.

Hymes, Dell (ed.)
1969 *Reinventing Anthropology.* New York: Pantheon.

Isbell, Billie-Jean
1973 "Andean Structures and Activities: Towards a Study of the Transformations of Traditional Concepts in a Central Highland Peasant Community." Ph.D. dissertation, University of Illinois, Champaign-Urbana.
1976 "La otra mitad esencial: Un estudio de complementaridad sexual en los Andes." *Estudios Andinos* 5:37-56.
1978 *To Defend Ourselves: Ecology and Ritual in an Andean Village.* Austin: Institute of Latin American Studies, University of Texas at Austin.

Jara, Victoria de la
1974 *Los nuevos fundamentos para el estudio integral de la escritura peruana.* Lima: INIDE.

Kubler, George
1963 "The Quechua in the Colonial World." In *The Handbook of South American Indians,* edited by J.H. Steward, vol. 2, pp. 331-410. New York: Cooper Square Publications.

La Fone, Samuel
1950 "El culto de Tonapa." In *Tres relaciones de antigüedades peruanas,* pp. 287-353. Reproduction of edition of M. Jiménez de la Espada. Asunción: Editorial Guaraní.

Larco Herrera, Rafael
1934 *Cuzco Histórico.* Lima: La Crónica y Variedades.

Lathrap, Donald
1971 "Complex Iconographic Features Shared by Olmec and Chavin and Some Speculations on Their Possible Significance." Paper presented at the I Simposio de Correlaciones Antropológicas Andino-Mesoamericanas, Salinas, Ecuador.

Lavallée, Danielle
1973 "Estructura y organización del habitat en los Andes centrales durante el período Intermedio Tardío." *Revista del Museo Nacional* 39:91-116.

Leach, Edmund
1964 *Political Systems of Highland Burma*. Boston: Beacon Press.

Leacock, Eleanor
1981 *Myths of Male Dominance: Collected Articles on Women Cross-Culturally*. New York: Monthly Review Press.
1983 "Interpreting the Origins of Gender Inequality: Conceptual and Historical Problems." *Dialectical Anthropology* 7:263-84.

Leacock, Eleanor and June Nash
1977 "Ideologies of Sex: Archetypes and Stereotypes." *Annals, New York Academy of Science*, vol. 285.

Lison Tolosana, Carmelo
1979 *Brujería, estructura social, y simbolismo en Galicia*. Madrid: Akal.

Lohmann, Guillermo
1967 "Étude préliminaire." In *Juan de Matienzo, Gobierno del Perú*, pp. v-lxix. Paris and Lima: Institut Français d'Études Andines.

López-Baralt, Mercedes
1980 "La crónica de Indias como texto cultural: Policulturalidad y articulación de códigos semióticos multiples en el arte de reinar de Guaman Poma de Ayala." Ph.D. dissertation, Cornell University.

Lounsbury, Floyd
1964 "Some Aspects of the Inca Kinship System." Paper presented at the 36th International Congress of Americanists, Barcelona.

Lyon, Patricia
1979 "Female Supernaturals in Ancient Peru." *Ñawpa Pacha* 16:95-140.

MacCormack, Sabine
1985 "A Conflict of Myths: Genesis, Classical Antiquity, and the Rise of the Incas." Paper presented at the Wilson Center, Smithsonian Institution, Washington, D.C., June 1985.

Marx, Karl
1973 *Grundrisse*. London: Penguin Books.

247

BIBLIOGRAPHY

Meillassoux, Claude
    1975   *Femmes, greniers et capitaux.* Paris: Maspero.
Michelet, Jules
    1973   *Satanism and Witchcraft.* New York: Citadel Press.
Millones, Luis
    1976   "Religión y poder en los Andes: Los curacas idólatras de
            la Sierra Central." In *Primera Jornada del Museo Na-
            cional de Historia, Etnohistoria, y Antropología Andina,*
            edited by Marcia Koth de Paredes and Amalia Castelli,
            pp. 253-76. Lima: Centro de Proyección Cristiana.
Moia, Nelly
    1979   "Comment on Garrett's 'Women and Witches.' " *Signs*
            4:798-802.
Moore, Sally Falk
    1958   *Power and Property in Inca Peru.* New York: Columbia
            University Press.
Mörner, Magnus
    1967   *Race Mixture in the History of Latin America.* Boston:
            Little, Brown.
Morote Best, Efraín
    1958   "El tema del viaje al cielo." *Tradición,* no. 21:2-14.
Murra, John Victor
    1956   "The Economic Organization of the Inca State." Ph.D.
            dissertation, University of Chicago.
    1964   "Una apreciación etnológica de la visita." In Garcí Díez
            de San Miguel, *Visita hecha a la provincia de Chucuito
            . . . en el año 1567.* Lima: Casa de la Cultura.
    1967   "La visita de los Chupachu como fuente etnológica." In
            Íñigo Ortiz de Zúñiga, *Visita de la provincia de León de
            Huánuco* [1562], vol. 1, 383-406. Huánuco, Perú: Uni-
            versidad Hermillo Valdizán.
    1968   "An Aymara Kingdom in 1567." *Ethnohistory* 15:115-
            51.
    1975   *Formaciones económicas y políticas del mundo andino.*
            Lima: Instituto de Estudios Peruanos.
    1978   *La organización económica del estado Inca.* México,
            D.F.: Siglo XXI.
    1980   Waman Puma: Etnógrafo del mundo andino. In Felipe
            Guaman Poma de Ayala, *El primer nueva crónica y buen*

gobierno, critical edition of John V. Murra and R. Adorno. México, D.F.: Siglo XXI.

Nash, June
1979   *We Eat the Mines and the Mines Eat Us*. New York: Columbia University Press.

Neruda, Pablo
1978   *Memoirs*. London: Penguin Books.

Ortiz, Alejandro
1973   *De Adaneva a Inkarrí*. Lima: Retablo de Papel.

Ortner, Sherry
1978   "The Virgin and the State." *Feminist Studies* 4:19-35.

Ortner, Sherry and H. Whitehead (eds.)
1981   *Sexual Meanings: The Cultural Construction of Gender and Sexuality*. Cambridge: Cambridge University Press.

Ossio, Juan
1973   "Guaman Poma: Nueva crónica o carta al rey. Un intento de aproximación a las categorías del pensamiento del mundo andino." In *Ideología mesiánica del mundo andino*, edited by Juan Ossio, pp. 153-216. Lima: Prado Pastor.

1976-77 "Guaman Poma y la historiografía indianista de los siglos XVI y XVII." *Historia y Cultura* 10:181-206.

Paul, Lois
1974   "The Mastery of Work and the Mystery of Sex in a Guatemalan Village." In *Women, Culture, and Society*, edited by M. Rosaldo and L. Lamphere, pp. 281-300. Stanford, Calif.: Stanford University Press.

Quinn, Naomi
1977   "Anthropological Studies on Women's Status." In *Annual Review of Anthropology*, vol. 6, edited by B. Siegel. Palo Alto, Calif.: Annual Reviews Press.

Quispe, Ulpiano
1969   *La herranza en Choque Huarcaya y Huancasancos, Ayacucho*. Instituto Indigenista Peruano. Monograph Series, no. 20. Lima: Ministerio de Trabajo.

Rapp, Rayna
1977   "The Search for Origins: Unraveling the Threads of Gender Hierarchy." *Critique of Anthropology* 3:5-24.
1979   "Review Essay: Anthropology." *Signs* 4:497-513.

Reiter, Rayna Rapp (ed.)
1975 *Toward an Anthropology of Women.* New York: Monthly Review Press.
Roel, Virgilio
1970 *Historia social y económica de la colonia.* Lima: Editorial Gráfica Labor.
Rogers, Susan Carol
1978 "Women's Place: A Critical Review of Anthropological Theory." *Comparative Studies in Society and History* 20:123-67.
Rosaldo, Michele and Louise Lamphere (eds.)
1974 *Women, Culture, and Society.* Stanford, Calif.: Stanford University Press.
Rostworowski de Diez Canseco, María
1961 *Curacas y sucesiones, Costa Norte.* Lima: Minerva.
1962 "Nuevos datos sobre la tenencia de tierras en el incario." *Revista del Museo Nacional* 31:130-64.
1970 "El repartimiento de Doña Beatriz Coya en el valle de Yucay." *Revista de Historia y Cultura,* no. 4:153-267.
1977 *Etnía y sociedad: Ensayos sobre la costa central prehispánica.* Lima: Instituto de Estudios Peruanos.
1978 *Señores indígenas de Lima y Canta.* Lima: Instituto de Estudios Peruanos.
1983 *Estructuras andinas del poder.* Lima: Instituto de Estudios Peruanos.
Rowe, John H.
1948 "The Kingdom of Chimor." *Acta Americana* 15:26-59.
1957 "The Incas under Spanish Colonial Institutions." *Hispanic-American Historical Review* 37:155-99.
1963 "Inca Culture at the Time of the Spanish Conquest." In *The Handbook of South American Indians,* edited by J.H. Steward, vol. 2, pp. 183-330. New York: Cooper Square Publications.
1967 "Form and Meaning in Chavin Art." In *Peruvian Archeology: Selected Readings,* edited by J.H. Rowe and D. Menzel, pp. 72-103. Palo Alto, Calif.: Peek Publications.
1976 "El movimiento nacional Inca del siglo XVIII." In *Tupac Amaro II, 1780,* edited by A. Flores Galindo, pp. 11-66. Lima: Retablo de Papel.

Sahlins, Marshall
1981 *Historical Metaphors and Mythical Realities: Structure in the Early History of the Sandwich Islands Kingdom.* Association for the Study of Anthropology in Oceania, Special Publication no. 1. Ann Arbor: University of Michigan Press.
1985 *Islands of History.* Chicago: University of Chicago Press.
Salomon, Frank
1980 *Los señores étnicos de Quito en la época de los Incas.* Otavalo, Ecuador: Instituto Otavaleño de Antropología.
1982 "Chronicles of the Impossible: Notes on Three Peruvian Indigenous Historians." In *From Oral to Written Expression: Native Andean Chronicles of the Early Colonial Period*, edited by Rolena Adorno, pp. 9-39. Syracuse, N.Y.: Syracuse University, Maxwell School of Citizenship and Public Affairs, Foreign and Comparative Studies Program, Latin American Series, no. 4.
1983 "Shamanism and Politics in Late Colonial Ecuador." *American Ethnologist* 10:413-28.
Sanday, Peggy R.
1981 *Female Power and Male Dominance.* Cambridge: Cambridge University Press.
Schmitt, Jean-Claude
1978 *Mort d'une heresie.* Paris: Mouton.
Schwab, Federico
1943 "La fiesta de las cruces y su relación con antiguos ritos agrícolas." *Historia* 1:363-85.
Shapiro, Judith
1975 Review of M.K. Marten and Barbara Voorhies, *Female of the Species. Science* 190:874-75.
Silverblatt, Irene
1976 "Principios de organización femenina en el Tawantinsuyu." *Revista del Museo Nacional* 42:299-340.
1978 "Andean Women in Inca Society." *Feminist Studies* 4:37-61.
1980 " 'The Universe Has Turned Inside Out . . . There Is No Justice for Us Here': Andean Women under Spanish Rule," in *Women and Colonization: Anthropological Perspectives*, edited by Mona Etienne and Eleanor Lea-

cock, pp. 149-85. South Hadley, Mass.: Bergin & Garvey.

1981 "Moon, Sun, and Devil: Inca and Colonial Transformations of Andean Gender Relations." Ph.D. dissertation, University of Michigan, Ann Arbor.

1983 "The Evolution of Witchcraft and the Meaning of Healing in Colonial Andean Society." *Culture, Medicine, and Psychiatry* 7:413-27.

n.d. Field notes.

Silverblatt, Irene and John Earls

1977a "Apuntes sobre unas unidades político-económicas precolombinas de Victor Fajardo." *Revista del Archivo Histórico de Ayacucho*, no. 1:16-21.

1977b "Mito y renovación: El caso de Moros y los Aymaraes." *Allpanchis* 10:93-104.

Silverblatt, Irene and Helene Silverblatt

n.d. "Andean Folk Medicine: A Cultural and Historical Perspective." MS.

Solari, Gertrude

n.d. "Interpretación de los signos de una manta de la isla Taquile, Lago Titicaca." MS.

Spalding, Karen

1967 "Indian Rural Society in Colonial Peru: The Example of Huarochirí." Ph.D. dissertation, University of California, Berkeley.

1970 "Social Climbers: Changing Patterns of Mobility among the Indians of Colonial Peru," *Hispanic American Historical Review* 50:645-54.

1973 "Kurakas and Commerce: A Chapter in the Evolution of Andean Society," *Hispanic American Historical Review* 54:581-99.

1974 *De indio a campesino.* Lima: Instituto de Estudios Peruanos.

1984 *Huarochirí: An Andean Society under Inca and Spanish Rule.* Stanford, Calif.: Stanford University Press.

Stein, Stanley and Barbara Stein

1970 *The Colonial Heritage of Latin America: Essays on Economic Dependence in Perspective.* New York: Oxford University Press.

Stein, William W.
1961   *Hualcán: Life in the Highlands of Peru.* Ithaca, N.Y.: Cornell University Press.

Stern, Steve
1982   *Peru's Indian Peoples and the Challenge of Spanish Conquest: Huamanga to 1640.* Madison: University of Wisconsin Press.

Taussig, Michael
1977   "The Genesis of Capitalism amongst the South American Peasantry: Devil's Labor and the Baptism of Money." *Comparative Studies in Society and History* 19:130-55.
1980a *The Devil and Commodity Fetishism in South America.* Chapel Hill: University of North Carolina Press.
1980b "Folk Healing and the Structure of Conquest in the Southwest Colombian Andes." *Journal of Latin American Lore* 6:217-78.
n.d.   "The Devil and Commodity Fetishism in South America." MS.

Thomas, Keith
1958   "Women in the Civil War Sects." *Past and Present,* no. 13:42-62.
1971   *Religion and the Decline of Magic.* London: Weidenfeld & Nicolson.

Thompson, E.P.
1977   "Folklore, Anthropology, and Social History." *The Indian Historical Review* 3:247-66.
1978   *The Poverty of Theory and Other Essays.* New York: Monthly Review Press.

Todorov, Tzvetan
1984   *The Conquest of America: The Question of the Other.* New York: Harper & Row.

Trevor-Roper, H.R.
1972   "The European Witch-Craze." In *Witchcraft and Sorcery,* edited by Max Marwick. London: Penguin Books.

Urbano, Henrique-Osvaldo
1979a "Mythe et Utopie: La représentation du temps et de l'espace dans les Andes peruviennes." Ph.D. dissertation, Université Laval, Quebec.
1979b "Viracocha y Ayar: Ciclos míticos andinos y ideología de

las tres funciones en los Andes." Paper presented at the 43rd International Congress of Americanists, Vancouver.

1980   "Dios Yaya, Dios Churi, Dios Espíritu." *Journal of Latin American Lore* 6:111-28.

1981   *Wiracocha y Ayar: Héroes y funciones en las sociedades andinas.* Cuzco: Centro Las Casas.

1982   "Representaciones colectivas y arqueología mental en los Andes." *Allpanchis* 17:33-84.

Valcárcel, Carlos

1947   *La rebelión de Tupac Amaru.* Mexico, D.F.: Fondo de Cultura Económica.

Vargas Ugarte, S.J., Rubén

1951   *Concilios limenses*, vol. 1. Lima: A. Baiocco y Cia.

Wachtel, Nathan

1973   *Sociedad e ideología.* Lima: Instituto de Estudios Peruanos.

Warren, Kay Barbara

1978   *The Symbolism of Subordination: Indian Identity in a Guatemalan Town.* Austin: University of Texas Press.

Wolf, Eric R.

1982   *Europe and the People without History.* Berkeley: University of California Press.

Worsley, Peter.

1957   *The Trumpet Shall Sound: A Study of "Cargo" Cults in Melanesia.* London: MacGibbon & Key.

1984   *The Three Worlds of Culture and World Development.* Chicago: University of Chicago Press.

Zuidema, R.T.

1964   *The Ceque System of Cuzco: The Social Organization of the Empire of the Inca.* Leiden: E.J. Brill.

1967a   "Decendencia paralela en una familia indígena noble del Cuzco." *Fénix* 17:29-62.

1967b   "El juego de los ayllus y el amaru." *Journal de la Société des Américanistes* 56:41-51.

1972   "The Inca Kinship System: A New Theoretical View." Paper presented at the Symposium on Andean Kinship and Marriage, 71st Annual Meeting of the American Anthropological Association, Toronto.

1973   "Kinship and Ancestor Cult in Three Peruvian Communities. Hernández Príncipe's Account of 1622." *Bulletin de l'Institut Français d'Études Andines* 2:16-33.

1977a "Inca Kinship." In *Andean Kinship and Marriage*, edited by R. Bolton and E. Mayer, pp. 240-81. Washington, D.C.: American Anthropological Association, Special Publication no. 7.

1977b "Shaft Tombs and the Inca Empire." *Journal of the Steward Anthropological Society* 9:133-78.

1982 "Myth and History in Ancient Peru." In *The Logic of Culture*, edited by Ino Rossi. South Hadley, Mass.: Bergin & Garvey.

n.d. "What Are Asymmetric Alliance Systems?" Mimeo.

Zuidema, R.T. and Ulpiano Quispe

1968 "A Visit to God: A Religious Experience in the Peruvian Community of Choque Huarcaya." *Bijdragen* 124:22-39.

INDEX

Aca Guarmi, 52
Acas (town), 32, 33, 204
Achaguato, Madalena, 188
Achikee, 178
acllas, 80-108 passim; as *capaco-chas*, 94-100; and celibate women in colonial religious organizations, 203; and chastity, 82, 83, 84, 85, 101-103, 107; and conquest hierarchy, 87, 91, 107; description of, 82-84; distribution of by Incas, 82-84, 87-89, 92; holiness of, 105-106, 107; in Inca economy, 85; in Inca political structures, 85, 87-89, 91-92, 94-95, 107; in Inca religion, 103-105; as priestesses, 103, 104; as punishment for rebellion, 92; reverence for, 103-104; as subjects of Cuzco, 94, 103; as symbol of Inca dominance, 89-101 passim; as tribute, 93
acllawasi, 82, 84, 87, 92, 93, 101, 105, 106
Acomayo (province), 123
Acos, 123
Acosta, José de, xxiii; on *ayllu* sexual customs, 102
airiguasara, 26
Aixa, 97
Allauca, 71
Alvarado, María, 188
amaru, 192, 194
Anahuanca, 182
Anas. *See* Yupanqui Coya, Doña Angelina
Ancash (department), 68, 94, 180
Andahuaylillas (town), 156
Angaraes Indians, 17
Angulo, Domingo, 116

Antisuyo, 97
Apo Ingacha, 71
Apo Parato, 183, 184-87, 189
Apu (mountain god), 182; as Spaniard, 200
Apu Achache, 63
apupanaca, 83, 101
Apurima, 48-49
Apurimac River, 48
Ariguanapampa (plain), 199
Arriaga, Father José de, xxiii; on *ayllu* divisions, 68-70; on Saramamas, 26; on sexual customs, 102; on Thunder, 77, 80
Asquem (village), 78
Asto Mallao, 203
Atahualpa, 104, 106, 116, 178
Auquilibiac, 20, 37
Avendaño, Hernando de, 199, 200
Ávila, Francisco de: and Huarochirí, xxiii, xxiv, 74; on Inca secondary marriages, 90; and the persecution of native women, 209
Axomama, 25, 28
Ayacucho (department), xxiv
ayllus: breakdown of, 131-32; in colonial economy, 112, 117-18, 125-38 passim; in colonial government, 148-58; description of, 217; division of labor in, 9-14, 29; under Inca rule, 5, 7, 14-19, 40-41, 46-47, 52, 81-108, 223-25; as kin-based community, 3-5, 217-22; marriage in, 8, 15, 87, 90, 132, 221; premarital sex in, 102; subsistence rights in, 4-5, 218-21. *See also* conquest hierarchy; *curacas*; religion in *ayllus*
Azangaro, 123

257

INDEX

INDEX

gender: and class relations, xix, xxvii, xxviii, xxix, 3, 15, 19, 53, 66, 68, 81, 108, 212; hierarchies of, xxviii, 14-19, 66, 108, 212; identities of, 3, 4, 212; ideologies of, xix, xxvi, 8, 14, 19, 67, 212, 213, 217; relations of, 8. *See also* conquest hierarchy; Spanish colonization

gender parallelism: and Inca Empire, 40-66 passim, 220; and kinship and inheritance, xviii, 5, 19, 20, 31, 34, 53, 119, 120, 121, 132, 220; in ritual, 38; and social structure, 7, 20, 31, 218; and structure of cosmos, 20-31 passim, 35n-36n, 40-66 passim; and structure of religious organizations, 21, 23, 24, 29, 31-39, 48, 53-66 passim, 155-58; and transmission of religious office, 36-37; undermined by colonial policy, 132, 133, 155-58

goddesses; as ancestors, 34; in *ayllus*, 20-21, 52-53; in Inca religion, 7, 44-52, 64-65

gods, in *ayllus*, 20-21

Gomez, Don, 128

Gorgor (village), 203

Guaca. See *huaca(s)*

Guacaquillay, Francisca, 205, 206

Guacayllano, 37

Guacayllano, Catalina, 199-202

Gualparoca, 121

Guamancama, 204

Guaman Poma, Felipe, xxiii, xxiv; on Coya and lunar cult, 54, 55; on *coyas*, 59, 61; on destruction of native society, 142-43, 145-46; on exploitation of native women, 10, 129, 131, 134-46 passim, 153, 154-55; on hair-cutting ceremonies, 219; on *hapinuñu-*

duendes, 179; on Inca vs. colonial society, 137, 147; on mestization, 145; on midwives, 30; on native colonial authorities, 138, 154; on Spanish work ethic, 10; on Thunder's children, 78; on women as enemies of mankind, 180; on women's rejection of Spanish authority and Christianity, 207, 208; on women's rights to land in *ayllu*, 219

Guamgri (village), 199, 200

Guánuco (Huánuco; city), 93

Guarco, 63

Guari. *See* Huari

Guaripisco, Santiago, 201

Guarmi Paso, 65

Guaro, 88

Hacas Poma, Hernando: on festival to Saramama, 25-26; on Mamarayiguana, 28; on Moon, 51; and selection of women as religious leaders, 38-39, 204-205

haciendas, 139, 197

Haller de Gamboa, Melchor, 152

Hambato, 17

hapinuñu, 179-80

Hatun Jauja (village), 18

Hatun Lucanas (village), 135

headmen. See *curacas*

Hernández Príncipe, Rodrigo: on *acllas*, 94-99; on elderly woman's suicide, 208; on local religion, 71; on Thunder-Lightning, 23, 34, 73, 78-79

Hobsbawm, E., xxii

Holguin, D., 179

Hospital of Charity (Lima), 32, 33

huaca(s), 22, 25, 33, 44n, 54, 55, 94, 96, 98, 170, 181, 182, 185, 186, 194, 198, 201, 203, 204, 205, 208, 209; dangerous quali-

Titu Cusi Yupanqui, Diego de, xxiii-
  xxiv
Tocto Sicsa, Leona, 121
Toledo, Viceroy, 131, 132, 136
Topa Cusigualpa, Don Alonso, 121
Topa Inca (Yupanqui), 59n-60n, 63-
  64, 116, 118
Toulouse, 163
Trevor-Roper, H. R., 162, 163
Tupac Amaru (rebel), 123, 194
Tupac Amaru (last Inca), 194
Tupayache, Felipe, 152

Uchusquillo, 190
Urbano, H-O, 41n, 173
Urcon (*ayllu*), 94, 95, 98, 100

varayoq system, 36, 210
Vecochina, 38
Ventura, Don Pedro, 78
Venus of the Evening and of the
  Morning, 42, 43, 44-45
Viracocha, 41, 44, 49; as culture
  hero, 41n; in Pachacuti Yamqui's
  diagram, 41, 42, 43; as name for
  Spaniard, 186

Wari Empire, 72n-73n
witchcraft: and devil worship, 161-
  62, 165, 171-72, 180; forced labor as punishment for, 208; as
  heresy, 162; as Spanish invention,
  174; and women, xvii, xxix, 30,
  32-33, 158, 159-62, 165-69, 171-
  72, 184-96 passim, 213
witches: as challengers of colonial
  rule, xxx-xxxi, 187, 188, 190,
  194-96, 213; confessions of, 174-
  75, 176, 180, 181, 182-94 passim
witchhunt: in Europe, 159-69, 176-
  77; in Peru, 159, 176-77
"wives of the Sun," 80, 84, 85, 103.
  See also *acllas*

Wolf, Eric, xx
women: in Europe, 167-69; as exchange objects, 221; as "others,"
  xxvi, 214
women, elite: in colonial economy,
  xxix, 114-19; in *Coya raymi*, 66;
  erosion of power of, 150-53, 213;
  identification of with ancestral
  Inca noblewomen, 123; in Inca
  government, 62-63; as legal minors, 119-22; marriage of with
  Spaniards, 118-19; material conditions of, xxviii, 7, 19, 62; religious organizations of, 47-58 passim; in Tupac Amaru rebellion,
  123. See also *curacas*; gender parallelism
women, peasant: abuse of by colonial authorities, 138, 153-55; association of "conquered" with,
  68, 86; and child rearing, 10; in
  colonial economy, xxix, 115, 128-
  38; in colonial religious organizations, 198-206; in contemporary
  Andes, 209-10; and division of labor, 9-15, 82; effect of Inca tribute on, 5, 7, 223-25; erosion of
  power of, 213; as exchange objects, 221-23; material conditions
  of, xxviii, 5, 219, 223; as religious
  officiants, 32-39, 71, 76-80, 156-
  57, 198-206; religious organizations of, 31-39, 155-58; sexual
  abuse of, 138-47 passim, 213. *See
  also* cross-transmission; culture of
  resistance; Devil; gender parallelism; Incas; priestesses; prostitution; Thunder-Lightning; witchcraft

Yalpay, Isabel, 32
Yalpo Cocha, Inés, 200
yanaconas, 118, 121, 139, 197

265

INDEX

Yasali, 74, 75
Yauri, Don Pedro, 188
Yaurillancha, 74, 75
Yucay Valley, 115, 116, 117, 120, 121, 152
Yucyuc, 28
Yugachiguan, Don Januario, 122
Yuncas, 74, 75

Yupanqui Coya, Doña Angelina, 116

Zárate, Pedro de, 188
Zuidema, R. T., xxii n-xxiii n; on Andean social structure, 86; on conquest hierarchy, 67n; on Inca marriage, 87

Library of Congress Cataloging-in-Publication Data

Silverblatt, Irene Marsha.
Moon, sun, and witches.

Bibliography: p.
Includes index.
1. Incas—Social life and customs.   2. Indians of South America—Social life
and customs.   3. Social structure—Peru—History.   4. Incas—First contact
with Occidental civilization.   5. Indians of South America—First contact
with Occidental civilization.   6. Peru—History—To 1548.   I. Title.
F3429.3.S6S55 1987   985'.01'088042   86-22514
ISBN 0-691-07726-6 (alk. paper)
ISBN 0-691-02258-5 (pbk.)